Outside the Spotlights

Conversations with Unsung Creators
Behind the Screens in Hollywood

Elaine Spooner

Elaine Writes Media

Printed in the United States of America, First Printing, 2021

Elaine Writes Media

Sebastian, FL 32958

elainewrites3022@gmail.com

Outside The Spotlights / Elaine Spooner

ISBN: **978-1-7357911-2-8**

Library of Congress Control Number: 2020923918

Disclaimer: This book is a truthful recollection of events in the author's life. I in no way represent any company, corporation or brand mentioned herein. I have described events, locales and conversations from my memories of them. Participants in this book have done the same. Memory has its own story to tell, but I have done my best to make it tell a truthful story.

Contents

DEDICATION

This book is dedicated to the people outside the entertainment industry who insisted that I could do whatever I imagined for my life.

First, to my family, who were happy for me as long as I was happy. You can't buy that foundation for self-esteem. I am beyond grateful.

There are a few others without whom I wouldn't have enjoyed my life as much.

Carol O'Keefe, my best friend in L.A., supports me with endless patience and listens to my latest angst or success.

Monique Barnum, my best friend on the East Coast, considers me part of her family and gave me a break from Hollywood when I came home to visit.

Karen Siegmund, an unforgettable woman I met in high school, suffered from multiple sclerosis and died much too young. While she was here, she gave me unwavering support and confidence to pursue my dreams. In fact, she insisted that I do so.

I dedicate this book of life stories to them and to the people behind the scenes in entertainment who enabled my dreams and should not be forgotten.

"Art is telling your story from your perspective.

It's unique, and if you don't tell it, it will die in your brain."

– *LIN-MANUEL MIRANDA*, Creator of *Hamilton*

FOREWORD

I remember a *Vanity Fair* article about the actor Chris Pratt that quoted him as saying, "Everyone needs a story to make sense of their life." That's always seemed reasonable to me. I find people's stories fascinating.

Still, I conceived this project without knowing what it was. If you're reading it now, it's clear that I ended up writing a book. Wow. I never thought I would do that.

The stories of the fascinating people I met are told from my perspective, which by necessity is a narrow window onto the technical revolution that overtook the entertainment industry in the four decades when I played my part 'in the business.' The people I knew come from all walks of entertainment. Some have more traditional roles like actor, director, writer or producer. Others worked, like me, way behind the scenes as IT professionals, marketing gurus, studio executives, game developers, web designers, distribution experts or music managers. Some of us helped lead the way and define new business models, technologies and software. We were there when personal computers and digital video began their invasion of the studio's production, distribution and business management processes.

It's amazing how it all happens. How do all those pixels appear perfectly in everyone's living rooms at the same time? The technology also thrives today in theaters, video games and internet apps and works seamlessly most of the time.

I interviewed my subjects to document their careers in the evolution of entertainment, not just the parts that I know from personal experience, and to catch up on their lives today. Each is a behind-the-scenes contributor who inspired me with creativity, innovative ideas and dedication to excellence. For those no longer with us, I wrote their profiles from memory and research.

How did I know that I wanted to be part of the businesses that created entertainment? I just knew, and my commitment never wavered. It could have been crazy optimism or just plain craziness, but I felt I was supposed to be there.

I got married when I was 19 and still in college. My plan was to get a degree and figure out how to use it to join the TV world. My husband encouraged me to go for it.

While still in school, I got my first work experience in the John Hancock Life Insurance IT department. There for six years, I learned how to write COBOL and PL1 code and then how to build, motivate and lead a team after I was promoted to Project Leader. I graduated from college in 1977 with a Bachelor of Applied Science in Computer Science from Boston University. Learning programming turned out to be the best choice I could have made.

My husband and I split before I completed my degree. I married a good guy, but we were young and realized that we wanted different things from life. We weren't yet divorced when I moved to the West Coast in 1978.

I was lucky enough to get hired at four major studios. My timing and love for the work drove my career—I arrived in Hollywood at about the same time as the personal computer. From that moment, I lived and worked thousands of miles away from my family. Kudos to my parents for supporting what I know they didn't quite understand.

I was that rare-ish woman in technology, yes, but one who didn't expect that being female would be an impenetrable barrier to where I was headed. I would run head-on into people who wanted to slow me down. More on that later.

Influencers From My Personal Life

Fortunate to benefit from family and friends who provided an unbeatable support system over the decades, I am well aware that I couldn't have accomplished what I did in the way that I did without them.

My Family: She Works in Hollywood—Something to Do With Computers

Mom loved the glamour of the movies. It impressed her that she had a daughter at the studios who could experience all that up close. She was a cheerleader for my ambitions and a perfect audience for my stories in our frequent phone calls and always ready to hear the latest.

She was the heart of the family and admired by all of us. Her curiosity about everything exposed me to possibilities beyond where I grew up in rural New Hampshire. When her children were growing up, she nurtured in all of us a respect for the wider world and a curiosity about people in particular. She loved to people-watch. Widely read [she was a librarian], she showed us the wonder of books of all kinds.

As a professional writer, she emphasized the importance of grammar and story structure to me while I was in school. I still don't want to write a paragraph that uses the same descriptive word or phrase more than once. According to my mom, that's a lazy way to write.

Both my parents told me I could do and have whatever I wanted to work for. When I applied for colleges, I found that none of the schools I looked at offered computer degrees. I was about two years too early—that's how old I am! The high school principal encouraged them to push me to apply for a Math program at an Ivy League school. I rebelled. I'd found a junior college with a computer-programming track and wanted to move to Boston to attend. The principal was horrified. My parents said, "If that's what she wants, it's fine with us."

Not many parents would have had that strength. It worked out OK, of course. I applied for the new BAS program in Computer Science at BU a couple of years later and transferred there to get my degree.

Not intimidated at all because I didn't know I should be, I found my way: first as a college student interested in computers, and then into the entertainment business. I'll bet both my parents had a tough time watching my sister Linda and me drive out of their driveway on our way across the country to L.A. when I moved out there. Linda helped me get settled in when we arrived. Sue and Dave, my other siblings, came to visit later. I can't say enough how grateful I am that they are my family.

I do remember thinking to myself as I left New Hampshire, "What am I getting myself into?" But I never thought of turning around and not going.

Karen Siegmund: You Must Follow Your Dream

No two life stories are the same, and most are never documented. Karen Siegmund's life is a perfect example. While she didn't work in entertainment, her influence on my life was crucial. She helped me aim for the high ground and celebrated with me when I achieved any part of my vision.

I met Karen through my sister Sue, who went through school with her. Karen's family moved to New Hampshire from Brooklyn, N.Y., and that, all by itself, made her an object of curiosity for those of us growing up in a small town in a small state. She had been places and seen things we could only plan to perhaps see at some point in our lives.

I knew in my gut that my dreams of a life outside of Woodsville, New Hampshire—even the town name evokes 'the sticks'—could become a reality, and Karen encouraged me to make that happen.

Flash forward to our early twenties. Karen went off to college to study Russian, of all things. She had dreams of her own and wanted to be an interpreter at the UN. I didn't see much of her for some time, but I heard the news when Karen got engaged and then married while still in college. She was also a bridesmaid in my sister Sue's wedding.

Then she was diagnosed with MS. The disease came on suddenly when she wasn't even 25. She dropped out of college. Her husband decided he couldn't take what was coming and left. She moved back to New Hampshire, where her parents made sure she had the best care available.

Sue and I visited her as often as we could. Over the years, the MS symptoms came and went. Eventually, she was confined to a wheelchair. She became a spokesperson for the rights of the disabled, but in a quiet way. She spoke out when she saw a reason and didn't shy away from doing what she felt was the right thing.

All of that doesn't completely explain why I loved her and learned so much from her. Any visit to Karen was a time of laughter and incisive discussion. She read widely and could talk intelligently about diverse topics. Interested in what I was up to, she spoke with me about the entertainment business and my evolving place in it. When I told her I wanted to work more directly in TV, she told me to go for it. When I felt uncertain, she gave me courage.

Because of Karen, I came to see that if I wanted to meet and work with the best in entertainment, then I had to do that. She wouldn't allow me to limit my reach.

In 1999, at the age of 46, Karen died. I still feel her loss, but mostly I feel grateful to have known her. Sue and I set up a scholarship in her name at the high school we all attended. Each spring until the scholarship ended in 2016, we chose recipients who exemplified Karen's admiration for those who overcame hardships and planned to dedicate their college studies to learning how to help others. Quickly, we found that there are many more students in dire need than we could help. We chose our honorees well, I think.

Monique Barnum: Boston BFF

Monique Barnum became an important person in my life after I hired her to work on my team at John Hancock Life Insurance in Boston. That was in 1976, I believe.

We forged a friendship that's continued for more than forty years. She's married to a terrific guy and has two accomplished daughters. We've traveled together, and to this day have a comfortable, unmatched camaraderie.

Monique's father was a Dutch citizen of Chinese ancestry, her mother from The Netherlands. By the time she was born, they had moved to the US, so she received both Dutch and US citizenship. She went to high school in The Hague and has relatives all over the world. When I met her, she was the most traveled person I knew. I heard about adventures in Portugal and Argentina. She and her husband PT went to China twice to adopt their girls, where she also saw the Great Wall and Tiananmen Square.

I was flattered to be asked to write a recommendation for Monique and PT when they applied to become parents for children adopted in China. It was the easiest recommendation I ever wrote.

When I split from my husband, Monique supported me. I filed for a divorce in Massachusetts before I moved to L.A. At the time, the Massachusetts no-fault decree required more than a year of predetermined steps. I figured the process would eventually come to an end even if I left the state, so I moved and expected the paperwork would follow me. When it didn't, I decided to get a no-fault California divorce.

Monique saved my sanity. She contacted my ex, met with him and watched him sign the papers. To say I was grateful is an understatement.

As I followed my dream of working at the studios, she became my East Coast best friend. Whenever I flew home, I arrived in Boston and spent a few days with her on one end of my visit in New Hampshire or the other.

Her latest business, Serenity Designs, specializes in staging homes for sale in the hot Boston real estate market and allows her to exercise her artistic talent. She has a warehouse full of furnishings she moves in and out of homes around the city.

Carol O'Keefe: L.A. Family

One person from my first L.A. job at Union Bank [1977-1979] became a lifelong friend and major cheerleader for my work at the studios. Carol O'Keefe and I developed the kind of friendship everyone should have in life. We've stuck together through it all. There is no price on that.

We spent holidays together if I was unable to go back East. I could count on her if I needed anything. I've attended multiple Thanksgiving dinners at her place, where she cooked for a small group of close friends who were also holiday orphans. Popular with her peers and staff, she maintained close friendships among a group of people who admired her ability to find the fun in both work and personal endeavors. She has a welcoming laugh, which draws people to her and made working with her a joy.

Carol understood my ambitions in entertainment and acted as my sidekick at events. One night, after I'd started at Fox, we drove to the lot for a screening of all the *Star Wars* films released to date, a rare opportunity for studio employees and guests.

We were excited to see the movies together in a package, but, as we walked from the car to the theater, I heard her tumble to the ground. I turned to find her sitting on the pavement.

She tried to get up and said, "Uh, I don't think I can walk."

Instead of watching the movies, we went to the emergency room. She emerged with a cast for her broken ankle and was on crutches for weeks.

About a year before the 1984 L.A. Olympics, I would need similar services from her when we attended a gymnastics qualifying event at UCLA's Pauley Pavilion. As we walked to our seats, I slipped off a step and sat down, slightly twisting my ankle. We watched the whole show and had a great time. I got up to leave and immediately sat back down.

I looked up at her and said, "I don't think I can walk out of here."

We stared at my ankle, which was about twice its normal size. She found someone with a wheelchair and away we went to the emergency room ... again. I didn't break my ankle, though. It was severely sprained, enough to keep me on crutches for weeks!

Fans of the famous Queen Mary Sunday Brunch, we drove to Long Beach many times. Other weekends, we drove to Riverside, California, for the brunch served at a now-defunct restaurant located in an old Victorian mansion, surrounded by an orange grove. They served orange-focused dishes not available anywhere else. I loved them all, except for the orange pie, which just didn't work.

In 1991, environmental artist Christo created an exhibit called *The Umbrella Project* in the hills between L.A. and Bakersfield. This "whimsy along the interstate" consisted of over 3,000 randomly placed umbrellas stretched across the hills. A major event unlike any before or since, it's now a part of L.A.'s cultural history. I loved it and so did Carol.

After working at Union Bank for her entire career, Carol retired more than twenty years ago at the age of 55. I was nowhere near ready to be jealous of her free time. I couldn't yet fathom wanting to be out of the professional world I had worked so hard to join.

I may have made it sound like Carol and I are more alike than not, which is actually not at all true. We are opposites in many ways.

She found it satisfying to work for one company, a conservative bank no less, for her entire adult life. I want faster results and continuing variety, which drew me to TV over films, where the process moves much more slowly. In TV, air dates control everything, and they come every week without fail in traditional prime time television.

I admire that she has *so* much patience with people. Carol would tell me about the people on her team who would one day become good executives and how she thrived on their success. Satisfied with a ten-year plan for improvement and what seemed to me as glacially slow progress, she persevered.

It takes tremendous patience to nurture a dream across multiple decades. Carol helped me evolve as a manager in the same way she mentored her team at the bank. She was the perfect person to know while I took chances and became an entertainment technology pioneer with a growing network of peers and experts.

It's an invaluable gift on top of a friendship I treasure.

People I Met in Entertainment

I lived through a revolution in the entertainment industry and helped shape some of it. The people no one knows in Hollywood are some of the most talented, creative and intelligent professionals. They support the glamour and the fame and the wealth by working every day to keep the 'magic' lights on. And, they made me better throughout my career.

The people in this book are some of those instinctively innovative people. As a group, we love to tell stories that have an impact. We also seek to make each product better than the one before. We're not afraid of change, in fact we're agents that create, embrace and manage it. If it hasn't been done before, we have confidence that we can figure it out. We may interact with the famous, but are anonymous in public. And, we prefer it that way.

In part, writing these stories stems from a decades-long desire to be able to tell my family and my non-entertainment friends what I did for all those years in L.A. My second goal is to highlight the careers of the amazing people I've worked with and known. Most still work in the business in one capacity or another. They represent different time periods, different professions and different backgrounds. Particularly, different backgrounds. Rarely does anyone's trajectory go in a straight or predictable line.

I wanted to write about people no one knows in a business everyone knows. Most outside the industry understand that entertainment is multi-faceted: there are the performers, of course, and the major studios, production companies, networks, agents, managers, fan publications, and the glamour seen and assumed by a voracious public. I worked in a different world that was way behind the camera and felt privileged to be there. Many of the people I write about plotted entertainment careers from the beginning, like me. Others lucked into it without an exact plan, but then stayed because of the motivating environment. A few left to pursue other priorities.

I hope you enjoy meeting the people I met.

PART I: Before I Arrived in Hollywood

By the time I noticed television in the mid-1950s, the industry was on its way into more American living rooms. "Watching TV" became a popular activity in our house and particularly for me.

I consumed favorite shows with my parents and siblings since we owned just one TV. In those days, our small-town New Hampshire house received only two channels: ABC and CBS. I was a devoted fan of shows like The Ed Sullivan Show, Voyage to the Bottom of the Sea, Burke's Law, That Girl and The Red Skelton Show, but managed to grow up without ever seeing some of the most watched programs, like Star Trek or Bonanza, because we didn't have an NBC channel in Woodsville.

I received good grades in school, so my parents allowed me to watch TV and study at the same time. When I realized there were people who made a living in the TV business, I knew where I was headed. It just seemed obvious to me. I paid more and more attention to shows and how they were created, particularly since Hollywood is in winter-free California. I hate winter.

Before I could move to the other side of the country, I was sidetracked into learning computer programming. Coding was a new profession then, and it fascinated me. I observed that all companies [including TV studios!] needed people who knew how to write code. It seemed to be the pass to fulfilling my dream. And so it was.

Years later, when I worked briefly in Manhattan during the .com boom, I met someone who fueled my passion for all things TV because he actually participated in the early years of television. From James Sheldon I would learn how it was to work in live TV, how live TV became mass entertainment and how he moved from the birth of the industry in New York to the heyday of Hollywood's assumption of TV production.

James was still directing TV when digital technology first made its appearance and began to revolutionize the process. He was open to the changes, which put him in the minority of working professionals at the time.

I viewed the beginnings of television from afar as an avid fan. James was the real deal. He helped pave the way for all of us who eventually migrated to L.A. and contributed our skills to the business of entertainment.

CHAPTER 1

JAMES SHELDON: We Made It Up As We Went Along

James Sheldon began directing television in 1948 and continued working for the next forty years. He directed many shows that I watched and others that were before my time: *That Girl, MacMillan and Wife, Dukes of Hazzard, Julia, Quincy, The Equalizer, The Virginian, Wagon Train, Cagney & Lacey, M*A*S*H, My Three Sons, The Twilight Zone, The Fugitive, Mr. Peepers, The Bing Crosby Show, Death Valley Days*, and on and on.

He spent hours reviewing his memorabilia collection with me. He seemed to know everyone: Bing Crosby, Wally Cox, James Dean, Clint Eastwood, Barbara Stanwyck, Rock Hudson, Paul Newman, Carroll O'Connor, Lee Remick, Tony Randall, and so many more. He introduced me to his behind-the-scenes friends: Joy Schary, the daughter of influential former MGM studio head Dory Schary, and Judy Lewis, the initially-hidden child of Loretta Young and Clark Gable. He took me places I never would have otherwise been invited. I even let him take me to a performance of opera in Central Park one summer evening. He was a major opera fan—hence his apartment in Lincoln Center—but opera is just not my thing. Even so, I had a wonderful time that evening.

I am very glad that I got to meet, work with and know one of the original creators of mass-market entertainment. I never expected that, but, like many things in life, the best often happens when you aren't expecting it. Over the time we knew each other, I learned more about television from him than from anyone else.

3

The history of the medium was written by people like James. As it morphs into digital storytelling on multiple devices in multiple formats, television as I knew it for most of my life is evolving. The changes are invigorating to me and would likely be welcomed by James, too.

Once James and I got to know each other, he became a mentor for my sometimes-ignored interest in writing, in television history and in the people who made that history. He encouraged my writing style and wanted me to work on a book he thought he might publish one day. He told me I had it in me to give form to his vision and make his stories interesting to complete strangers. That's quite a responsibility, but I felt I could do it because he was sure that I could.

He thought that side of my talent was wasted in IT, and I did agree with him about that. While I never wanted to be in front of the camera or to be a fiction writer, I was and am fascinated by the process of production, the mechanics of completing a show and the stories of those who work in the industry. When I worked at Universal that was the best part of the job: supporting the writers, production managers and producers who were aiming to create their best work week after week.

One of the stories James shared with me was about the time he got his first job in TV. He was working as a page at NBC, seating audiences for the live shows at Rockefeller Center. There was a job opening on a crew and he wanted to apply. He went to the office of the man doing the hiring and started talking to his attractive assistant. As he tells it: "I went home that night with her, and the next day I had the job."

Even then, jobs in television were highly sought after, and it was important to impress the right people! It took more than that, though, to continue to succeed. He never gave less than his best when he was hired to direct.

I didn't meet him until I was in New York working for the eDrive [Entertainment Drive] website in the mid-90s. By then, he was in his seventies. A friend of the eDrive CEO, he came on board to write TV history pieces for the site. We met one day at lunch and began a conversation that basically never ended until it had to. After I left New York City and went back to Portland full-time, I invited James to speak at the Portland Creative Conference, where he was adored by the audience.

As a first-hand source of information about Hollywood, he spoke to our audience about directing live television in 1948 and staying in the industry as an accomplished director into the late 80s. Along the way, he gave Clint Eastwood and Tony Randall their first TV roles, mentored James Dean and directed episodes of more shows than he remembered. He spoke about solving the issues of the new medium of live television that included talent like Billie Holiday, Bing Crosby and Kitty Carlisle.

He was so nervous about speaking at the conference. I had the honor of introducing him to the audience, which made me nervous! But once he began, it was clear that the audience loved him. His unassuming, but not matter-of-fact, way of telling what happened to him was captivating. He obviously loved what he did, and could communicate what it was like in the early days. His unexpected wealth of information about television and how to make it good was just what the Creative Conference was about.

That year, we also invited Steve Buscemi [*Fargo, Pulp Fiction, Boardwalk Empire*] as a speaker, and the two of them hit it off. I was thrilled to spend an evening with them. They fed off each other seamlessly.

In my career, I have occasionally been held back by men who didn't think I could handle, or that I deserved, a promotion. More than once I went over the obstructionist's head to make it clear that I wouldn't be denied for the wrong reasons.

I think anyone with a long, successful career runs into this in one way or another. How you handle it is very important. Both James and I tried not to burn a bridge—almost never a good idea. But sometimes it can't be avoided. If you do that, though, be absolutely sure you can deliver for those who support you. I believe in aiming for excellence, and so did James.

He was there at the beginning of television and helped shape it. He told me, and his other audiences, "It was all live, and no one knew how to do it. We made it up as we went along."

For him, the joy was in working with actors and interpreting the scripts on different types of shows. He began at NBC in N.Y. and later moved to L.A. with his family. It sounded like a life I could only dream about, but he hated L.A. Eventually, he moved back to his condo in Lincoln Center.

The Creative Conference audience loved James, as I said. Soon after that, he accepted a gig as a guest lecturer on a Panama Canal cruise ship. Of course, he was a hit there, too.

James kept telling me that he was certain "no one would want to read my stories. They're just not that interesting."

That was absurd, of course, which I told him often! He lived through the launch and the mass-marketing of the television industry. More than that, he created his share of it. We eventually worked through most of his career during meetings in his apartment, on the phone and when he made a few of his rare visits to L.A.

For me, knowing James and helping him catalog his life story was always a pleasure. I could sit on the sofa in his apartment across from Lincoln Center and listen to his stories forever. Those were some of the best afternoons of my life. Eventually I worked with a friend of mine to write the book proposal for his memoir. Unfortunately, as time went on, he became less convinced that he could create an interesting story that anyone would want to read.

As it happened, we saw less of each other after I moved back to Los Angeles and began working in IT at Fox. As I said, he hated L.A. and I wasn't able to make it to New York often. I kept encouraging him to write the book, and eventually he did. He partnered with a different writer in New York and Before I Forget was published in 2011.

When the memoir came out, he seemed pleased— maybe just that it was finished! I'm very glad he did it. The richness of his memories should not be lost. I'm mentioned in the foreword and have an autographed copy.

I wish I could package how nice he was and how much good feeling he gave me.

I proposed to the TV Academy that they include an interview with James in their TV Archive, which they eventually did. You can go online and view six short conversations with him, so it's possible to hear him talk about his career himself. That's the best way to hear his stories.

I wish we'd had more time. I last saw him in 2015 when I visited New York briefly with my sister, brother-in-law and niece. James invited us to dinner, and we had a remarkable time hearing him tell more stories. By the end of the evening, my family was as in awe of him as I am.

In his last years, we exchanged Facebook messages and emails. We compared notes about new TV shows and movies. My final message from him was a holiday email a few weeks before he died, in response to my recent birthday message. It simply said, "Thank you very much for the birthday greeting and wish you were in New York to help celebrate! I hope 95 is a very good year. I'm feeling fine and look forward to hearing more about your Florida retirement. Thanks for remembering. Love, Jim."

I found out later that he knew then that he had cancer, but he never told me. He often seemed amazed that he was still going at over 90 years old. I hope I'll be able to do the same.

Here's the review of his book that he sent me. His note said, "THIS FROM THE DGA QUARTERLY MAGAZINE: THOUGHT YOU WOULD ENJOY IT."

Summer 2011 Classic Bookshelf. Continuing our celebration of the Guild's 75th anniversary for 1945-1965, we've collected some of the most interesting books about directors and the era.

Before I Forget: Directing Television 1948-1988 By James Sheldon. If there's an emblematic career that showcases the entire history of television from its postwar inception to the late '80s, it must be James Sheldon's. Literally in at the creation, he started out as an NBC page during the war, but by 1948 was the director of the radio show We the People the night it became the first CBS national television broadcast. His four-decade career witnessed every technical upgrade, every format change, and the switch from ad agency-based to network-controlled production. He was part of the geographic upheaval in the mid-'50s that saw the industry move west from New York to Los Angeles. Along the way he directed sitcoms, talk shows, Westerns, and dramas for nearly every network and studio, and in every format imaginable: multi-camera and single-camera; location shooting and live simulcasts; and with and without live studio audiences. The range of his credits is dizzying: Studio One, Naked City, Route 66, The Twilight Zone, Gunsmoke, The Love Boat, and M*A*S*H. And at 90 years young, Sheldon feels no need to pull punches in assessing the people he worked with. His recollections are filled with turf wars, moody stars, difficult writers, mad producers, and even the occasional moment of blissful harmony, offering an entertaining roller coaster ride through television's early decades. Review written by John Patterson.

PART II: Wow! My Name's on a Parking Space at 20th Century Fox

I finally moved to L.A. in 1977. My detour to learn computer programming in college turned out to be the best choice I could have made. Computers were taking over all businesses—including the major studios, where managers were looking for knowledgeable people who could help them leverage new technology.

After interviewing at several studios that had no openings [darn!], I accepted a position at the downtown L.A. offices of Union Bank. I was quite happy there, mostly because the people were great, I wasn't prepared when, about fifteen months later, my boss came into my office and sat across from me.

"I don't want you to get excited, but I have news," she began. "Dan just accepted a job to run the Data Processing Department at Warner Bros. I know you're going with him, but I would like it if you proceed calmly."

She smiled broadly as I tried unsuccessfully to keep my cool. I had never kept my goal of working for a studio from her, so she knew what this meant to me.

Dan, an MIS [Management Information Systems] department head at the Bank, did, in fact, take me with him. Within a few weeks, I was walking on air as I entered the Burbank Studios lot [a joint venture of Warner Bros. and Columbia, TBS for short] for my first day—perhaps the luckiest day of my life so far. I was assigned to work on the HR/Payroll systems, which required me to learn everything about time cards, union rules,

9

IRS requirements and above-the-line [actors, producers, writers, directors] contracts.

At last, I was among my people. I felt immediately at home. It was my pleasure to learn everything I could as fast as I could.

The job at TBS lasted about eighteen months. Dan reported to a long-time occupant of the VP Data Processing role who was not as open to change as some would have liked. Soon, he and Dan clashed. In my corner of the group, I was having a blast, but Dan was not so lucky. About a year after he took the job, he left.

I was devastated. The man who'd given me the opportunity of my life was moving on. Dan seemed OK with it, but I would miss him more than I knew.

Shortly after he left, there was an opening for a team manager. Having been a project leader twice in my previous life, for Union Bank and John Hancock in Boston, I decided to apply.

Part of the process was an interview with the VP. I went to his office and heard the following [paraphrased since so much time has passed], "Thank you for applying, but I don't think you have the experience to be a manager. You should spend more time in the analyst role before taking on a bigger job."

I politely pointed out my previous manager experience and quickly realized that this guy had no idea about my background. He'd never read my résumé and wasn't ready to give me a promotion.

I asked him how much more time he thought I would need and got a vague "a few years, I imagine." I learned later that other women may have run into this same roadblock with him.

Realizing he would never see me as an equal, I began looking for another job. This time, it was a different market. Studio positions were available, and I saw opportunity. Unable to sit still in a place I no longer fit, I reached out to people I knew who could help and began reviewing the job listings in industry newspapers. Within a few weeks, I was accepted as a team manager at 20th Century Fox!

For a woman from small-town New Hampshire, it was heady stuff to work at such a famous place. My enthusiasm for the business grew. I wanted to understand how the company worked, so I signed up for a UCLA Extension Certificate Program in Film Production and Distribution, which I completed a few years later.

It was 1980. My boss's boss, the Fox MIS VP, lived today's inclusion goals long before they were recognized. Omer Simeon, a rare African-American executive, admired and respected everyone from staff to peers and bosses. He played no favorites that I could see.

Omer gave me unwavering support even when I no longer reported to his department. Not long into my time with Fox, the MIS department was decentralized. It would be a theme in my career. Organizations would either centralize IT or decentralize IT in an effort to figure out the best way to manage technology. When Fox decentralized IT, my team was taken out of Corporate MIS and moved to report directly to the group we supported, Studio Facilities, which was responsible for all the production support departments on the lot. My new boss was a man named Bernie Barron, who would turn out to be an amazing mentor. I was the first woman who ever reported to him, and we learned how to navigate that together.

As a manager, I was given a parking space with my name on it. That never happened again. Today, reserved spaces have numbers for the most part and who parks where is tracked on a computer somewhere. I smiled every day when I pulled into that spot.

During the next few years, as the first woman Facilities Department MIS manager, I learned how the studio ran from the inside. We provided computer support for departments like Special Effects, Props, Music, Locations, Production Accounting and Stage Rentals.

The atmosphere at Fox at the time felt like a small-town family to me. Dennis Stanfill was in charge. It was the era when Sherry Lansing became the first woman to take over as Theatrical Production Head. I recently read her biography and found myself thinking that we had very similar experiences in some ways. We never met, but she writes about the push back she got from male executives, some of it direct and some subtle. We experienced similar reactions from the staff around us and became pioneers in our own corridors.

One of the best and most welcoming Facilities staff members for me was the post production supervisor. He gave me an opportunity to hold my first Oscar. I found it heavier than expected and beautiful.

One day, the phone rang in my office and he said, "The L.A. Philharmonic is here scoring the latest Dudley Moore film, *Unfaithfully Yours*. Want to come down and listen?" Of course, I went. Who would want to miss that?

I met and became friends with Henry Kopecky, who ran Special Effects. Knowing him will always be one of my warmest memories. He and Bernie passed away early in the 21st century, but both showed me respect and gave me insight into the kind of smarts and innovative thinking required to support ongoing production.

I love the Fox lot to this day. It's small enough that you can walk it during a lunch break. In the sixties, before my time, the physical studio took up more space. Then they sold the land that became Century City. The remaining lot I wandered was full of creative activity. Those were the days of *M*A*S*H* in Stage 9, and shows like *The Fall Guy, Trapper John, M.D.* and *9 to 5*.

History was everywhere. The huge outdoor murals honoring films like The Sound of Music are still there. The commissary's multi-wall mural of famous Hollywood stars, including Janet Gaynor, Will Rogers and Shirley Temple, is iconic. Some of the structures, like the Old Writer's Building and the bungalows that housed stars like Marilyn Monroe and Shirley Temple are still working offices and now in the National Register of Historic Places.

The atmosphere on the lot changed when Marvin Davis acquired the company. He brought more corporate thinking to management, and the family-style feeling was tempered with an emphasis on budgets and profits. Managers began to leave.

After three years at Fox, I decided to move on. Partly because I felt less motivated in the Davis era, but also because I wanted to stop being known as 'the IT person.' I identified more with the TV business than IT and wanted my title and responsibilities to reflect that.

CHAPTER 2

OMER SIMEON: For a Time, It Was the Best Place on Earth

Omer Simeon's ability to select the best people to work on his teams is what gave him a crucial management advantage. He chose candidates who complemented his skill sets and applied them better than he did. I was privileged to be on his team at Fox from 1980 to 1983.

He was my boss's boss and an admired Fox Corporate MIS VP. Oblivious to race or status, Omer managed a dynamic, inclusive group. As comfortable at a Board Meeting as he was talking ideas with a group of programmers over a beer, Omer valued people and built possibly the most race-blind studio department of its time.

Before your first meeting with Omer in a restaurant or in front of a building, you would likely be told something like, "He's a handsome dude. He'll be in a double-breasted suit, a silk tie and handkerchief." That's what stood out. People would totally forget to say that he was black.

I didn't know it then, but Omer would be a part of my life until the present day. After our time at Fox, we met again when he and his partner, Cynthia [now his wife], worked as consultants for my team at Universal in the 1980's. They built and supported our successful domestic syndication system, and designed applications for other departments, including TV Business Affairs and Universal Studios Florida. The Business Affairs project was especially challenging because it was 'known' that the contracts for above-the-line talent couldn't be automated. They were too individually customized. Omer and Cynthia helped prove that wrong.

Omer is part of the extended family known to everyone involved as 'the Simeons.' I am pleased to say that I continue to
be a card-holding member. The Simeon family is large,
friendly and always willing to help anyone in the group. Because my own family was so far away in New England, I was
adopted by them and attended many warm, happy events at
their homes in L.A.

Everyone in his immediate family was encouraged to attend
college, and all became successful in different fields. Parts of
the clan relocated to Portland over the years. I moved up there
in 1990 for a change from L.A. and arrived with a built-in family as a result.

For a time, an invitation to Omer's home meant going to a
stately old Hollywood house on Franklin Avenue that was
known for being one of the trysting sites for Katherine Hepburn and Spencer Tracy. It has a huge front porch with majes-
tic two-story white columns. At the holidays, the living room
sported the biggest Christmas tree I'd ever seen.

I house-sat for Omer and Cynthia on multiple occasions, attended birthday parties, weddings, Thanksgiving dinners, and
never missed the famous annual gumbo event. The family is
the proud owner of Omer's mom's secret gumbo recipe, and,
once a year, the coveted invite went out to hungry gumbo lov-
ers. I confirm that this gumbo is the absolute best I've ever
eaten.

Omer's combination of love and inclusion that was ageless,
colorless, and sexless attracted more and more people every
year. The event grew to be so well-known and large, they reluctantly decided to call an end to it. There are still smaller
events where gumbo makes an appearance. I'm sure the recipe
will live on through the younger generations of the family.

Because Omer treats everyone as a valued friend, he maintains
close relationships both in and out of Hollywood, people
who've been friends for decades. He is perhaps the most calm-
ing influence in any gathering. His wife, Cynthia, his sister
Lola and his sister-in-law Pam are close friends of mine. He
adopted two kids and you can't tell them apart from his biolog-
ical children.

I feel completely welcomed in the Simeon family, supported and included in a remarkable group of people. Thank you, Omer, for aiding my professional success and welcoming me into your family's orbit.

Omer's Story
Omer Simeon's intelligence enabled him to be accepted into Loyola University after excelling at the SAT's with only one day to prepare. Also athletic, he played basketball—well. After college, he chose to go into engineering, which was a fortuitous decision.

He graduated in 1958, with a degree in electrical engineering. His first job was in aerospace at General Dynamics in Pomona, where he learned the Fortran computer programming language.

"I was given responsibility for a missile digital simulation. This was still in the keypunch and IBM punch card days. The simulation produced monstrous printouts where you could review numbers for proposed trajectories for upcoming missions."

After three years, he led the digital computing side of the department, an expected replacement for the then-current analog computers. It was his first manager job, but he didn't give much thought to his long-term direction at that time.

"It was a reasonable thing to do and I did it," he muses.

Soon, he was promoted to manager of the entire section, a young success story in charge of both digital and analog computers as Director of Engineering. He was later promoted to Director of all computing, including for business and manufacturing. Next came the job of Director of West Coast Operations.

He was recruited to interview at Fox, which he joined in 1975. Shortly thereafter, *Star Wars* came out and changed everything for the good.

"For a time, it was the best place on earth to be. Fox had Jane Fonda producing films; Mel Brooks was making *Young Frankenstein, M*A*S*H* was shooting there. It was a good time to be at Fox."

One night in 1976, Omer was invited to attend the Fox Board screening of the new movie Star Wars. It was a heady experience, especially when he realized he was seated next to Grace Kelly.

"She was just like she was portrayed in the press, a lady and a gentle person.

"After Star Wars was released, our challenge became figuring out how to handle the sheer size of the revenue pouring in. Our systems couldn't handle the big numbers required and crashed more than once. That was an unusual problem!"

In the ensuing years, Omer managed MIS through a decentralization. That meant that while he was responsible for everything computing, several of his teams became direct reports to various other departments, such as Studio Facilities.

"I had excellent managers, and the transition generally went very well.

"20th Century Fox was sold to Marvin Davis in 1981 ... and he took it private. Alan Ladd Jr. left to form his own company. Alan Hirschfield and the Davis cronies came in and the company changed. The new people were primarily bankers who did not know much about the movie business. They tried to influence things toward banking and away from entertainment.

"I was responsible for Worldwide IT, and managed to stay until 1984. The best part of working there was a chance to oversee international projects, including visits to our distribution offices in Paris, Australia and London. I spent time in our offices and learned a different side of the business. There was always an opportunity to learn more.

"The differences between me and my boss became so great that I knew it was time to get out. I went to work for DMR, a consulting company focused on the banking industry. That's where I met my partner, Cynthia. When I joined DMR, they were just opening the office in L.A. because of the Olympics that year. I got a chance to go to many events at the Games. It was a magnificent time to be in L.A.

"When I left DMR, First Interstate Bank offered me a job to take over Operations, which I turned down. That was the part of the business that I really didn't like.

"Instead, I continued consulting for the next twenty-five years. Cynthia and I formed our company, HTM Co, and supported clients of many different types. Lots of movie clients, banking clients, software clients."

One of HTM's contracts was for Universal Studios Florida, working with then division head Bernie Fisher.

"I was proud of our contributions there. We were in Florida quite a bit. The job was to select all the IT resources for the location, including computers and software, and hire the first IT Director. I was at the grand opening, which was a grand event for sure.

"One of our clients was a company called dBase. The job was strictly management consulting, and we turned things around for them. Our best recommendation was for them to buy the software called FoxPro. They wouldn't do it. They could have closed the deal for $4 million. That mistake ultimately put dBase out of business. FoxPro was a much more effective database and won business."

The advantage for Omer and HTM was that they became familiar with both dBase and FoxPro. "We used that knowledge to build the international distribution system for Universal, for example, and worked with the TV Information Services group, led by a manager who worked for me at Fox years before [Elaine]: a great example of using your connections to get contracts. We also consulted on distribution systems with MGM, Warners and Columbia.

"One task we undertook at Universal gave us the opportunity to do something the internal tech people said was not possible. The Department Director worked with a form that showed everything happening in post-production. We gathered the schedules and came up with a system to automate them and portray the schedule in a consolidated package. They loved it.

"Everyone in the automation industry remembers the feared Y2K computer collapse in the year 2000. At the time, we were consulting at Kaiser Permanente, frantically programming changes. I was at the data center in Corona at the stroke of midnight on 12/31/99. Nothing went wrong. We were in good shape preparation-wise. It seemed like a lot of hype for nothing, but it could have been disastrous without the effort and money thrown at it at the end of the twentieth century."

Omer never actually retired, even though HTM was disbanded in 2010. "I accepted consulting work after that. The last job I accepted was at Home Savings. I worked for friends from First Interstate who were now also at Great Western. When the banking merger frenzy happened, I changed to consulting for small independent companies. One day, a prior banking friend called me and asked if I wanted a job for his upstart mortgage company. I worked in International IT at Countrywide until 2011 or so until the company closed down."

Omer liked management consulting in both old and new companies, but confirms that his best clients were entertainment companies. "I didn't want a full-time job at a studio, though. I did take some interviews. One at Disney, but we could never reach terms. I met with the IT head at Warner Bros. That didn't work out either."

Glad that he valued people over code, he still connects with friends from all over Hollywood. From his time at Fox, he vividly remembers former Chairman Dennis Stanfill, a man he admired for his ability to motivate talented people. "He ran the corporation when I worked there and was one of those who left after Marvin Davis took over. He landed at MGM after that. He's in his mid-80s and we still talk on occasion."

Based in L.A., Omer never left the city where he grew up. "My interests include traveling, often to jazz concerts and festivals. Italy was the best trip on a client's dime for Fox and my favorite spot."

The way he's lived his life is now a model for high school kids at the Verbum Dei school in the Watts neighborhood of Los Angeles, where he donates his energy to mentoring students. His passion for education and professional accomplishment is being passed on in an under-served area of the city. He's cementing a legacy for a new generation of kids who want to make their lives better through education. ---

--- Interview 5/2019

CHAPTER 3

I've Never Had a Woman Report to Me ·Before

When I worked at Fox the first time from 1980 to 1983, the company's decision to decentralize IT resulted in an assignment as a direct report to Bernie Barron, the head of the Fox Studio. I'd never met Bernie, but he was a big deal, so anxiety ensued. However, it turned out to be one of the best experiences of my studio years.

Partly because of my Bernie experience, I prefer a decentralized reporting structure for this reason: it puts me closer to the day-to-day business functions my teams are expected to know. I feel strongly that superb technical skills must be there in each team member, but our loyalty should be to the business first, and to IT second.

I set out for my first meeting with Bernie on a typical California sunny morning. His office was in what is now called the Old Executive Office Building and it was the biggest office I'd ever seen. Bernie sat at the far end behind an absolutely huge desk. He wasn't a tall man, but he was football-player built and sported a full salt-and-pepper beard. The office layout served to enhance his presence. As I sat down, he smiled at me and began our relationship as follows:

"I want to be totally honest with you. I don't really know what you do and I don't think that's necessarily important. I hear you do it well, so just keep that up. Secondly, I never had a woman reporting to me. Not a problem for me, but it will be a challenge for some of the department heads. We'll have to learn how it works together."

Shortly after that, the meeting ended. I liked him for his honesty, and following that initial face-to-face, we got along very well. I respect and appreciate smart, caring, talented people, and he was all three.

Bernie moved my team to its own trailer on the back lot and, as requested, we continued to do what we did. Our responsibilities encompassed all the facilities departments on the lot. Bernie was in charge of logistics, stage rentals, below-the-line service departments and maintenance of the studio lot itself.

As the first and only woman in the Studio Facilities weekly staff meetings, I received a warm reception from some of the 29 male department heads and a total chill from others. That warmth made up for those who refused to even talk to me. They just didn't know what to make of my presence in their lives. This was in the early '80s, but I admit to being surprised that a woman manager was such an anomaly. I sent my male team members when we dealt with those who couldn't figure out how to talk to me. I hope I changed the minds of some.

Bernie sat at the head of the table each week and coordinated the conversation. I knew I was noticed because every time he or one of the attendees said a 'bad' word, they looked at me and apologized. I tried to tell them it was OK—I'd heard much worse—but some of them never got over their discomfort that I was even in the room. Occasionally there was another woman—the HR rep—which didn't help much since she wasn't running a studio work group.

I worked for Bernie for a couple of years and, as I said, loved it. My team learned quickly, creating and maintaining technology used to track locations, production budgets, prop inventories and other facilities business. Bernie became more comfortable with me, and together we managed my budget and priorities. I came to respect his ability to corral a large group of direct reports. His style was informal and he treated the job as "work is fun." I don't recall ever hearing him angry with me.

Bernie passed away a few years ago. He'd left the studio many years earlier, and we never spoke again that I recall, but I will always remember him fondly. I was his first female manager, and we both learned how to navigate that with our professional friendship intact. I'm grateful for what he taught me and for the support he gave me when individuals in the Facilities group refused to even acknowledge my existence.

Bernie used my surprise assignment to him as an opportunity to learn about how technology could help him do his job and what it meant to have a woman on his staff. We both benefited from our time together.

Since writing this profile, I used the great facilities at the Dartmouth College Library to find Bernie's obituary. It's excerpted here because it taught me things about his life that I didn't see from my narrow perspective. I do remember that, at that time, Fox included multiple divisions beyond the studio, but I was unaware, for example, that Bernie ran Western Costume and Marineland. For me, he was a supportive and fascinating manager. Apparently, he applied that success across multiple businesses during his lifetime.

Daily Variety. 314.42 (Feb. 29, 2012): p16.

Copyright: COPYRIGHT 2012 Penske Business Media, LLC

Partial Text follows:

Barron helped to pioneer TV broadcasting at WLH television in Cincinnati. After relocating to Los Angeles, he joined Pathe Laboratories, where he ultimately rose to head of sales.

His shift to work in studio operations began with a stint managing the newly acquired Chaplin Studios for American Intl. Pictures.

Barron then spent eight years as general manager of Columbia Studios and 14 years at Twentieth Century Fox Corp., where he held positions as senior VP of studio operations, co-chairman of CBS/ Fox Studios, chairman of Western Costume Co., president of Twentieth Century Fox Licensing Corp. and president of Twentieth Century Fox Marineland.

CHAPTER 4

A 16,000 Gallon Tank of Lemon Jell-O

When Henry Kopecky answered his phone at the studio, he never knew what he'd hear.

"Listen, Henry, we need a 16,000 gallon tank of lemon Jell-O for a scene that shoots at 8 am tomorrow ... OK?"

"Henry, we have this idea for a dog washer. You know, like an automatic car wash."

He was paid to translate fantasies like these into reality literally overnight. As Director of Fabricating Services, it was his job to give form and substance to the dreams and imaginings of writers, directors and producers. His expertise was special effects, although eventually he would lead fourteen Fox studio departments as Director of Operations.

Henry wasn't the only smart, innovative, curious and talented Department Head I worked with while I led the Facilities IT group, but he was my favorite. I interviewed him at one point when drafting an article about his story that unfortunately was never published. What follows combines material from that article with my recollections of the time we knew each other.

Henry summed up his work like this: "To be successful requires an enormous storehouse of useless information. We have created everything from the homemade still that *M*A*S*H* characters Hawkeye and BJ couldn't live without to a first-of-its-kind replica of a fetus in a test tube that hiccupped on cue."

He learned the skills of prop making from do-it-yourselfers in his native Czechoslovakia. His trade was metalwork, but his hobby was skin diving.

Unable to acquire the necessary equipment, he and other members of his skindiving club built their own. One of the few men in the world at that time to have lived under water for three days, he corresponded with his hero, Jacques Cousteau.

In 1968, while Henry was vacationing in Yugoslavia, the Russians invaded his homeland. Certain that there was only one way to live the life he craved, Henry made an irrevocable choice. He left his family, his girlfriend and his possessions to escape, first to Italy and then to the United States. He arrived in New York City during a December snowstorm, in the middle of a garbage strike. He spoke no English.

As soon as he could, Henry brought his girlfriend to California where they were married in a small church in Pasadena. A friend asked him to accept a five-day assignment in the Blacksmith Shop at 20th Century Fox just before Christmas in 1976. The extra money was most welcome. When his friend quit after the holidays, Henry was offered the job that would become his work home.

Home turned out to be a little-heralded department called the Prop Shop. The fact that they were asked to do things never done before fascinated Henry. His first job was to assist a crew of twenty in creating three replicas of the Love Boat with matchsticks. The work took several days, since each replica contained over 40,000 sticks. They were used in a party scene and then accidentally destroyed as part of the script.

Henry and his family worked hard to make it in the US and became proud citizens. By the time I met him, he already had a long history of working on films and television productions. His accent was still thick, and the twinkle in his eyes and his glorious laugh I will never forget.

I spent hours hearing his stories and marveling at how he could invent something on the spur of the moment that saved a scene. I guess I could call him the MacGyver of Fox Studios, but that does him an injustice, since he was an expert in several pertinent sciences, as well as the owner of an unusual amount of commonsense genius.

He would reminisce about the unknowns that he so loved about his job. "A director needed a section of the Colorado River heated to 72 degrees so that his 200 actors wouldn't freeze while standing in it. A few calculations told me and my crew that there was not enough electric power in California, Arizona, Colorado and Utah combined to run submersible heaters to do the job. On the other hand, simple is often better. The next morning, each actor wore a wet suit under his robe and the film, John the Baptist, continued in production."

He loved to surprise me with a tour that included his latest un-expected solution to a problem on whatever show we were discussing. In my time at Fox, he was often contributing to stunts for shows like *M*A*S*H, Dynasty* and *Hart to Hart*. Budgets were small and the director's visions bigger.

I didn't see Henry much after I left Fox for the first time in 1983 to move to Universal. I learned later that he eventually became one of the experts at Disney Imagineering, contrib-uting to Disneyland, Disney World and the international Dis-ney parks.

I regret that we didn't cross paths again. Imagineering is a wonderful place where the best animators and theme park cre-atives get to play. I believe Henry fit right in. I toured their of-fices one day while I worked for Disney.com, not realizing that he'd been at yet another company before me.

Beyond the fact that Henry was crazy good at many things, his sense of fun about his work was contagious. Of course, he worked in a glamorous business, but, as is sometimes said, it's all just work when you do it every day.

Henry made it more fun for me, that's for sure. I loved visiting the effects building on the Fox lot. No longer there, it's been replaced by new office buildings. In Henry's time, it was a sin-gle-story workshop noisy with activity. He was always there, except when he'd be called to one set or another to provide the 'Henry' solution to a show's latest problem.

The Lee Majors series *The Fall Guy* was the source of one of the two requests to Henry I mentioned at the start of his story. One evening he got a call from the director of the current shooting episode. In the morning, they were set to film a scene that included two people Jell-O wrestling. The director wanted to know, "Would you set up the ring and fill it with Jell-O in time for the scene?"

Henry, of course, said, "Yes." He soon regretted that because he found that it would take too long to find, buy, cook and cool enough Jell-O to fill the space.

His eventual recipe for 16,000 gallons of lemon gelatin: Call the Purchasing Department and instruct them to locate 400 pounds of un-boxed, powdered gelatin. Assemble several vats of boiling water, 20,000 pounds of ice, 70 gallons of lemon food coloring, one tank twelve feet square and one sound stage, well chilled to 55 degrees. Mix all ingredients thoroughly during one night of alternating heat stroke and chills for you and your crew.

Task completed, Henry staggered home at 4 am. At 8 am, another call came. "Henry, we have a problem. The shoot will be postponed for three days," the producers told him.

Rather than tempt pneumonia twice, they decided to simply keep the stage at 55 degrees for three days.

Problem solved—almost. When shooting finally got underway, the actresses who were to Jell-O wrestle in the scene climbed into the ring. At the first punch, one wrestler fell, only to bounce right back to her feet! The well-chilled gelatin was stronger than rubber. The effects team cut and softened the Jell-O and shooting continued.

I've included a portion of Henry's obituary from 2001 below because it provides an outline of his accomplishments. Much of it I didn't know until I read this tribute.

Thank you, Henry, for encouraging my fascination with how movies and TV shows get made. I was privileged to know and work with you.

Publication info: Daily Breeze; Torrance, Calif. 13 Sep 2001: A4.

Partial text follows:

A true Renaissance man has died. [Henry Kopecky] was born in Plzen, Czechoslovakia. As a blacksmith, he helped to restore some of the best decorative gilded ironwork in the Cathedrals of Czechoslovakia. He immigrated to the USA in 1968, and became a proud American citizen. Henry owned two wrought-iron businesses, Redondo Blacksmith and Anpro, Inc. His love of the ocean led him to become a commercial deep-sea diver. From diving, he moved to 20th Century Fox, where he started out in the blacksmith shop and worked his way up to Director of Operations in charge of 14 departments. He was involved with such shows as *Love Boat*, *The Fall Guy*, *M*A*S*H*, *Hart to Hart*, and many others. Henry continued his career at Walt Disney Imagineering's Special Effects Department for the next 12 years, contributing to Euro Disneyland, Walt Disney World, Disneyland, Tokyo Disney Seas, and Disney's California Adventure. He was a highly respected visionary man, understanding what had to be done to create the "wow" in his projects, as well as in his life.

PART III: PCs Arrive at the Studios

After looking around for a studio job that would allow me to apply my technology expertise outside formal IT, in 1983 I accepted a position at Universal Studios in a department called Internal Management Consulting.

IMC was a new group at the studio staffed with internal consultants assigned to groups all over the company for a variety of projects, with a focus on more than just IT. At first, I collaborated with Studio Facilities as they reviewed options for updating their automated services, perfect for me after my Facilities contributions at Fox. As part of our research mission, we evaluated new digital technologies for what would become laser discs and eventually DVDs.

Soon another decentralization happened in my world. IMC was broken up into separate groups, each supporting one division. I became the Director of Television Information Services, or TVIS. My new team was responsible for making recommendations for how UTV [Universal's Television Group] could navigate the personal computer revolution that was enveloping the studio. Timing was once again in my favor.

TV writers began asking for individual PCs they could use to write scripts. The studio didn't know enough about how to respond or whether to approve the new expense. TVIS was charged with recommending how PCs were purchased, introduced, and integrated around the lot for TV departments and productions.

If asked, I might say that these years were the best of my career. I was in the right place at the right time to launch the introduction of computers in every office and on every production location.

James Korris, a creative executive for UTV, was the TVIS boss. He was as excited about the potential for PCs as we were.

James and I recruited a small team of enthusiastic computer nuts who happened to really love television. It was my conviction that I could teach the computer stuff to bright people with an interest in it, but I couldn't buy a passion for the business. Hilton Smith, Geoff Fairbanks, Peter Siegel and Karla Aber each contributed mightily to the mission.

Under James' leadership, we recommended software and hardware that shows could implement for functions like business affairs, location accounting, casting and production budgeting. The first critical task for TVS was to define how scripts would be typed into a PC using new formatting software designed specifically to generate text on a screen based on traditional script rules.

We evaluated newly available tools, recommended the standard for the studio and trained the writers and their assistants on how to use it.

Training the entire writing population was a daunting challenge. At that time, Universal was producing lots of TV—shows like *Knight Rider, Airwolf, Quantum Leap, Whiz Kids, Simon & Simon, Magnum P.I.* and *Murder, She Wrote.* TVIS consultants were invited into production offices around the lot. Joset Cook from *Miami Vice* was an enthusiastic early adopter who sometimes assisted us in training other writers' assistants.

One day, James called me and said, "I'm transferring Jim Michaels to your team. He's an expert at creating on-screen computer graphics for our shows, and I want TVIS to be the home for his work."

Before long, I was responsible for working with Jim on the creation of the next round of designs and onscreen graphics for the series *Airwolf*.

The best assignment ever came when the studio sent me to Hawaii to set up computers in the production office of one of my favorite shows, *Magnum, P.I.*

I loved Hawaii from a previous visit, and now I loved the people I met on the show. Producer Charles Floyd Johnson was responsible for the transition to personal computer services. He set a marvelous tone and welcomed the improvements we could bring to his complex coordination of a series on distant location.

Because of the time difference between L.A. and Honolulu, I would get up early for sightseeing, then head to the production office by 9. I visited Waikiki to see the mesmerizing beaches and Pali Lookout to take in the glorious views of the island of Oahu, drove to the North Shore, walked in the Punchbowl Cemetery memorial park and touched the iconic King Kamehameha statue at City Hall.

The days were long—it was always dark when I left the production office. But I absolutely loved the immersion in a major Hollywood production. It was my first experience with a production on location and, without a doubt, the most fun I had at work to that point.

Back then the studio was really nice to us when we traveled. I flew first class, and a driver picked me up at the airport. There was a car at my disposal and my hotel room overlooked the ocean. When I showed up for the first day in the production office, the location accountant gave me my per diem for the whole stay—in cash.

During my final years at Universal, I was recruited to participate in a pivotal experience in my life. One of my employees and his partner wrote and mounted an original rock musical based on the book *Shades of Gray* by Oscar Wilde. Most of the staff in my department volunteered in one capacity or another. We were lucky. The reputation of TVIS was stellar, so we were left alone and continued to do our job in the middle of putting on a show. Everyone made sure that our customers never wanted for service during the preparation and staging of the production.

At various times, I was assistant casting director, financial manager, production stage manager and lighting director during performances. I learned a lot and loved every minute of it. I thought the music was wonderful. I still have the tapes. [Yes, the tapes. This was happening in the late '80s.] I also have a DVD of one of the performances.

Auditions for the cast were astonishing reminders of how many talented people compete for jobs in Hollywood. A wonderful actress from Chicago named Sharon Mahoney got the diva role. She never became a household name but her career flourished in commercials, series guest roles and regional theater. She's still a friend today.

Shades of Grey would not be a hit. The show opened in a waiver theater on Melrose in Hollywood and ran for a few weeks. Our reviews were mixed. While the music and some of the performers were complimented, the story and book were evaluated as overly dramatic. My recollection is that the writer-producer began taking input from others. He tweaked and tinkered with the dialog and scene structure and ended up with something different than the wonderful first draft I fell in love with.

I stayed at Universal for a total of six years. My TVIS team was highly successful because I recruited people who loved the entertainment business, in addition to knowing computers. Many of them are friends to this day, as are some of the business pros we supported.

For example, Business Affairs executive Cheryl Birch worked with us to automate above-the-line contracts and speed up reports from ratings systems.

With Universal funding, entrepreneur Jeff Lane initiated, designed and launched a new automated package called The Studio System, the first ever TV credits database and pre-production service.

As leaders in the automation of TV production, TVIS team members also participated in new industry groups that sprang up. I helped launch the Association of Entertainment Computer Professionals and co-taught a UCLA Extension Course in New Media. I still support the business through membership in the Producers Guild of America and the Television Academy of Arts and Sciences. It was a glorious time to be alive and working in TV in Hollywood.

CHAPTER 5

JAMES KORRIS: What Can We Do to Use Technology Better?

To understand how unique our situation at Universal Television was, it's important to know that when we created the TVIS department there were literally zero PCs used by production at Universal.

The executive in charge of TVIS, James Korris, embraced technology and was always asking me, "What can you recommend that we could do to improve our use of computers? Find me fun, innovative stuff that will help our business."

I loved that. Since the team was like-minded people, when he gave our recommendations his blessing, our enthusiasm grew.

When we met, he was Senior Vice President of the MCA Television Group, which included Universal Television. His role as a creative affairs executive meant he was responsible for the content of shows rather than for budgeting or physical production.

I'd never worked for a creative affairs executive before—most IT groups reported to either financial or corporate functions in those days. I enthusiastically supported the TVIS assignment to Television because I wanted to be a part of the production of shows and report directly to those in charge. James and I shared the challenge of defining the role for the new department, staffing the team, creating the first budget and starting the projects we prioritized.

Leading TVIS enabled me to make my dream of working in TV production a reality. It was a pleasure. James gave me the opportunity to establish whole new ways of doing business in

Universal Television. My team worked with producers and crews on every show currently shooting at the studio. The job required us to leave our offices and visit production companies all over the lot and all over the country. It was complex, all-consuming work, and we loved it.

James's Story
James Korris initially wanted to work in film; television was a thing he came to later.

"TV and film were things I always wanted to do, but I wasn't sure how to make it happen. I began at Horace Mann High School in New York, which had a guy named George Baumann who had a little film program that was actually pretty good. They taught me critical thinking about film, how to shoot film and how to complete a movie.

"At Yale, there were no film courses when I arrived, but I made films anyway. At Harvard, where I received my MBA, there were a couple of electives, but that was it.

"My sister worked as a film editor in N.Y. after earning an MFA in film from Columbia. She let me help her out during summers when she worked for legendary editor Dede Allen [*Bonnie and Clyde, Dog Day Afternoon, Reds*]. She also worked for Cannon Films, which made its money on *Joe.* I worked as Music Editor on *Silent Night, Bloody Night.*

"We sometimes put new material into movies, which led to my first time creating movie sounds as a Foley artist. Today, there are software tools to create all the sounds we meticulously added to the scenes. I wore my shoes with creaky leather to walk on boards and make creepy shoe sounds.

"I learned directing from reading a magazine article. It didn't seem hard, but I had more gumption than brains. 'Sure, I can direct,' I told anyone who asked."

When he got out of school, James accepted film and video work in N.Y., but not in entertainment.

"The work there was limited—mainly documentaries and commercials. A couple of people produced film in N.Y., like Woody Allen and Mike Nichols, but it was small volume compared to L.A."

He decided he would figure out a way West. The first work he got in California was from an ad-campaign pitch he made to a clothing manufacturer, including copy and strategy. They liked it, so they hired James and his sister to shoot commercials for them.

His sister wanted more consistent work, so she soon returned to New York. While he was hanging out in California, James got in touch with Harvard classmates with jobs in L.A. He networked his way into some interviews and landed something at Universal TV.

"They were an organization that was a decade beyond their heyday, but they had a strong organizational will to succeed again in TV, to invest and expand. UTV President Robert Harris hired me. I worked directly for TV VP Dick Lindheim, and that became a very important professional relationship.

"What made me an unusual executive at UTV was that most of my peers didn't have a serious technical grounding in film. I could see the technique, but they couldn't. They tended to come from an agency or without actual film credits. Other people were readers and submitted script coverage as free-lancers or transitioned from below-the-line positions. I brought a new perspective in my role.

"My first job was Programming Executive, responsible for two shows: *Magnum P.I.* and *Simon and Simon. Simon* was considered a moribund project after the network ordered thirteen episodes that didn't do that well. My job was to finish the order. *Magnum* was a bona fide hit.

"Dick Lindheim, who had a background in audience measurement and research, had an idea. He looked at *Simon and Simon* and saw that it attracted the same audience as *Magnum*, so he told the network to move the show after *Magnum.* Simon became an instant hit. We got a reprieve."

The TV business as it was defined at the time used a simple equation. "On paper, suppliers like UTV operated series at a deficit at the beginning because network licenses didn't pay for a show. Rerun licenses paid for the residuals owed to talent and major crew members when episodes aired more than once during the season. Money was made by the studio when they sold product overseas. UTV shows were typically action shows and they sold well."

Beyond international sales, shows with a sufficient number of episodes were sold into domestic syndication. "After the show ran for three years in prime time, it would make lots of money in syndication—around $1 million per episode. It became important to keep a show on the air until there were enough episodes for a syndication sale.

"Some success was luck, some was shrewd scheduling and some was marketing," James elaborates. "Dick Lindheim implemented another inspired idea to spend money to promote shows ourselves. He realized we could get radio ads to supplement free network promotion, so we purchased ads over a three-to-four day period leading up to the air date. It pumped the ratings back when a survival viewing was a 30 share. We increased renewals, which increased profitability."

A share is the percentage of the total viewing audience at a specific time who are watching a show. Today a hit share is much, much lower because there are many more choices of shows to watch at any given time. It's different from the rating, which is a percentage of the total possible audience that is watching the show.

James next developed new shows. "Our success enabled us to shape shows in such a way that they succeeded with little adjustment over time. *Miami Vice* became a big hit, even though it was initially heading on a bad trajectory. We worked with the NBC promo people to promote it as a stylized, violent show. They had been trying to sell friendly and nice. They also didn't like the title because it was too dark. We convinced them to keep it and run promos that were better targeted. In 24 hours the intent to view increased from 20 to 70 percent.

"I introduced Maurice Hurley, a producer I hired for Simon and recommended as a producer for the series *Equalizer*, to Rick Berman, producer of *Star Trek* in syndication. In a few months, they called to tell me that, as a thank you, they'd created Captain Korris for a future episode!"

Because of James' interest in technology, Robert Harris asked him to take on the launch of Television Information Services. "My theory was that, since the axiom at Universal was 'nothing interferes with production,' TVIS would succeed if they could be the Maytag repair man for PCs. I told the staff, 'No matter when someone calls, you make sure there is one of our team members to deal with it immediately.' Impeccable service would be our calling card.

"IT work for our shows spanned a spectrum that included desktop computing, script processing, spreadsheets, script development, business affairs and a bit of on-screen CGI. I sent TVIS experts to our distant locations: Hawaii, New York, Miami, Orlando. Team members were bright, enthusiastic and just plain good at figuring out how to embed new entertainment software into existing production operations.

"Phil DeGuere, creator *of Simon and Simon*, was a technophile. TVIS helped him expand technology in support of his shows. He next produced *Whiz Kids*, which was about tech. A pioneer and the first producer to set up a LAN [local area network] that he made on his own, he ran ethernet cable around the office so everyone could collaborate."

James left UTV in 1987 and moved with Robert Harris to start a TV group at Imagine Films, Ron Howard's company. He stayed for a year and a half. "It was not an especially good fit. I didn't have much to do.

"While at Universal, we'd worked with Scholastic Publications, which had great successes in children's titles like *Babysitters Club*. They developed a UTV show with us called *Charles In Charge*, which did quite well. Scholastic approached Robert about starting an independent company, which became Harris and Company, and gave us funding with a deal for us to develop screenplays and TV shows for them. We also made movies for USA and Showtime and Starz It was a nice run."

Robert got a new UTV deal in 1993 to produce cable long form [the equivalent of a TV series on broadcast] and a couple of theatrical features, and James returned with him.

"I discovered by accident that I possessed a capacity as a writer when we developed a property called Random Access. Robert's idea was to do a movie about an IT terrorist who manipulated data and upended lives. The response to the script by the first writer was 'a good idea but not a great screenplay.' The writer wrote thrillers and went on to do quite well. He was briefly in the public eye during the OJ Simpson trial because he lived in the condo where the crimes occurred and heard the events in the courtyard.

"We couldn't sell the script, so I offered to rework it with my ideas on how to change the story. Words to launch a thousand failures. My feeling was: How hard could this be?

"After a month, I finished a screenplay with a new name, *Twilight Man*, and Robert liked it! I was so convinced it would be a public humiliation that I put a pen name on it, a combination of the middle names of my mother, father and me: C. Lawrence Henry. To my total surprise, the script got a good response. We found it a home with the Universal Longform group, which wanted to make it as a Starz! movie and financed it at $5 million. We made it with Tim Matheson and Dean Stockwell as leads.

"Because I was naive, I thought I could write again, but I learned it's not especially easy. I did get additional assignments, including an episode of *La Femme Nikita*. I still get residual checks from that one. For a while, I thought I was a made man.

"After a few years, Harris and Company was winding down. We'd done moderately well, made a few movies, but had no giant hit. Robert *decided to work creating content at AOL. Our last film The* Killing Yard was for Showtime in 2001, with Alan Alda as attorney Ernie Goodman, who represented one of the defendants in the Attica Prison uprising. It won the Silver Gavel from the American Bar Association.

"The closing of Harris and Company teed up the next chapter in my professional life. I received a call from Dick Lindheim, who was now at Paramount and working as studio liaison on a Paramount-sponsored research unit at USC called ETC, the Entertainment Technology Center. The intent was to facilitate the development of content and distribution technologies in the entertainment space. Pac Bell, SBC and Apple were involved, along with distributors Fox, Paramount, Warner and Universal. Disney had not yet joined.

"Dick said, 'The Executive Director is leaving and we need a new Director.'

"I thought maybe it could be a fit for me. I assumed it was a volunteer job, but he said it was paid and the offer was attractive. I accepted. When I started, I quickly saw it as an incredible piece of luck and understood that we needed to do something to get people to pay attention to what we could accomplish.

"What I knew from the production business was that there is a huge amount of paper on the creative side. Shows use a ton of colored paper to track script revisions, for example. Colored paper is not easy to recycle, and I felt strongly that the industry needed to be more environmentally sound. In 1998, I got an eBook company to demonstrate how we could create digital scripts with a system for distributing screenplays and tracking the revisions. That got us some ink in the L.A. Times."

Dick Stumpf, Chief Engineer at Universal, gave ETC its next step forward. "At the time, video projection for TV was CRT quality. It did not look filmic when shown in the 525-line interlaced NTSC [National Television System Committee] standard used then and the forerunner to progressive scanned, which is used on current TV displays. The more Dick talked about a new digital technology he'd seen, the more I thought it sounded great. To test it for the industry, we recruited the donation of a Pacific Theater that was damaged in the 1994 Northridge earthquake as our evaluation site. Originally built for *The Jazz Singer* in 1929, it had become the Warner Theater in Hollywood."

James defined ETC's mission as ground zero for digital cinema, and the theater became its lab. Anyone who wanted to show technology to the industry could show it there and have it evaluated. The ratings group from the AMPAS [Association of Motion Picture Arts and Sciences] also conducted research there.

"After I'd been on the job about six weeks, Lloyd Armstrong, the USC Provost, called to say, 'We have a chance to get a government contract and we'd really like to win it. Their choice is between us and UCLA.'"

James knew it would be a great opportunity and immediately got to work on a presentation.

"I represented ETC at the final presentation for the government reps. Before my turn, there was a very long presentation from the USC engineering school on their technology. When I stood up to speak, I looked around and saw that it looked literally like something from the set of a crime movie—all *Godfather* lighting and guys in 3-piece suits and military uniforms.

"I began, 'Hi. I'm from ETC. Our members are movie and television studios and technology companies.' I see they are all smiling and nodding, so I wrapped up and sat down. I knew better than to sell past the sale.

"A week later, the Provost called. 'Good news. The Army will be funding this with us.'"

Their one condition was that James be on the project. "Suddenly, I had two jobs and the new Institute for Creative Technologies [ICT] became a university-affiliated research center with $44.5 million in initial funding.

"We attended a meeting early on in DC. I asked around and heard that the Army was embarking on something big—the Future Combat System—a pet initiative for General Eric Shinsecki. He was concerned that the platforms in the Army were going to be antiquated. They were 35 to 40 years old and very heavy—a tank weighed 72 tons. There were no aircraft that could carry them anywhere."

The Future Combat Systems initiative would build a lighter platform. "We planned for less armor but unbeatable situational awareness. Through our complex network of relevant operational-picture information, the Army wouldn't have to worry about how to handle threats because they would simulate them in advance.

"One day, I answered a call from DARPA [Defense Advanced Research Planning Administration] about the Objective Force Warrior initiative. They wanted to set up a research center called Solider Systems that demonstrated technology for ground-based infantry combat. I proposed visualizing their ideas by making a movie that ended up being five minutes long. Before we started, I made sure they realized that I was uncomfortable with the idea that warfare is fun or easy. I was opposed to contractor videos that made it look like fun to use weapons. For me, warfare is the greatest possible human tragedy.

"My movie featured a lot of technology, but it was ultimately a human story about people who end up, by courage and resourcefulness, overcoming a problem by using technology.

"The video was shown to Congress in conjunction with a presentation about soldiers of the future. They awarded the Army $160 million on the spot. My phone started to ring. Next, we were asked for a visualization showing how the entire future combat system would work.

"On the strength of that, we started making 'serious games' on small unit command for the Maneuver Center of Excellence in the Army, including a first-person experience as a squad leader in an Xbox game called *Full Spectrum Warrior*. Microsoft required us to have a commercial release in order to get the right to publish on their platform. So ... we built an entertainment version and added a special key that unlocked the Army version.

"Most entertainment software simulations of tactical combat were meaningless, because they emphasized marksmanship, not decision-making. You didn't have a weapon in our game. The squad leader could only give instructions to a fire team and a more limited number of orders to individual soldiers. Success was about decision-making under pressure.

"The game was published by THQ and won five awards at the 2003 Games Developers Conference.

"In 2004, we started a major adventure. General Kevin Byrnes, a 4-star general, once told me that 'when it comes to teaching the physics of artillery, we're great. But in terms of cognitive decision-making, we're like a third-world country.' They needed a training system to focus on that.

"The head of the Fort Sill Battle Lab, George Durham, was a visionary who added one important requirement to the list: the ability to train Close Air Support [CAS]. CAS turned out to be extremely important for fighting an insurgency in Iraq and especially in Afghanistan.

"Our Close Air Support Module was built as a cylinder. We couldn't project the virtual environment image on a curved surface above the player, so we used a flat roof, which cemented its 'beer can' nickname. The game was, of course, one hundred percent virtual and quickly embraced for qualifying CAS operators. It runs for 2,000 hours a year, booked full time. The Army has saved between $17 and $20 million a year.

"While all this was happening, the Army scheduled a program review for the Future Combat Systems project, which completed the concept development phase at a cost of $4.7 billion in 2004. The next portion would cost $14.7 billion.

"I remember that the guy who came to evaluate the next phase presentation was General Schumaker, who had returned as the new Chief of Staff of the Army. After seeing my presentation, Schumaker told Secretary of Defense Donald Rumsfeld, 'This was the best presentation the Army ever had. We have to do it.'

"Rumsfeld replied, 'OK, but you have to come out of retirement.' He did, and the project proceeded."

Around this time, James began getting calls from industry. "Boeing called. They wanted a visualization. After pointing out to USC that this wasn't research any longer, I asked how they would feel if I did this in my spare time. It worked out and I made films for Boeing through my own new company, called Creative Technologies, Inc. I left USC officially in October 2006.

"CTI did one of the first mixed reality Pentagon projects, and we're working on a project that applies machine learning to one of the Navy's sonar systems.

"Oddly enough, I maintain my membership at the Writers Guild by virtue of the interactive applications [serious games] that we've produced over time. One was a program that ran for five years for IARPA, the Intelligence Advance Research Projects Activity, which invests in high-risk, high-payoff research to tackle intelligence challenges. Our product trains students to recognize and mitigate cognitive bias. We sell licenses to governments, universities and enterprises.

"I'm very grateful for what is almost completely serendipitous. I've got to be the poster boy for being in the right place at the right time.

"What I'm hoping is that, sometime in the next decade, there will be an exit strategy for me. My father was a great guy—he owned a dental practice, and then retired and became a professor at N.Y.U. school of dentistry until he was 94. It would be perfect if I can volunteer or teach wherever I might be needed."

--- Interview 2/2019

CHAPTER 6

HILTON SMITH: On Day One, I Went to Robert Zemeckis' Office

Hilton Smith's enthusiasm for production was the reason I wanted him on the TVIS team at Universal.

To this day, I believe that technical skills, while important, are not as important as an affinity for the business IT supports. I could train people in the specific computer skills I needed, but I couldn't give them that unique something that meant they'd work extra hard because they loved what they were doing for television.

Recently graduated from the UCLA Film School when we hired him, Hilton came to the job with a thorough understanding of how a studio works and on-site knowledge about Universal from his recent internship with the Internal Management Consulting Department. He also demonstrated the technical skills to implement the team's mission to automate Universal Television productions.

He more than met my expectations. After his time with TVIS, he became a production accountant, then a production manager and then producer for multiple series, receiving more influential credits with each season of each show.

He was also a key reason I joined a memorable project. Executive Producer for the original musical *Shades of Grey*, Hilton offered me the opportunity of a lifetime—to participate in a production from the inside. He was still with TVIS at the time; and most of the department contributed in one way or another. We managed to continue doing excellent work at the studio while working nights and weekends on *Shades*. None of us minded. I am immensely grateful for the experience.

Shades of Grey opened in an equity waiver theater in Hollywood and ran for several weeks. The show wasn't the success
we'd all hoped for, but the ups and downs of the project and
its aftermath demonstrate why Hilton was destined to succeed. In all his endeavors, he built an excellent reputation, a
requirement in a business where there are more people looking for work than available jobs. Staying employed is just not
that easy.

Hilton and I get together every so often and talk about the
business we both love. After our most recent lunches, I've felt
energized. I may not miss the regular day-to-day time-consum-
ing work schedule I had before retirement, but I do miss being
a part of the business. Knowing Hilton and keeping track of his
accomplishments helps me stay involved.

Hilton's Story
Hilton Smith was five when cast in his first Christmas pageant.
He laughs as he says, "By third grade, I was writing plays and
producing them in the classroom. For one, I turned my friend
Patrick's hair green to make him Frankenstein!"

He continued to find reinforcement for his showbiz ambitions
through acting in class plays. "I was the second male lead in
Taming of the Shrew—the guy who got the pretty sister. I was
also Daniel in a *Daniel and the Lion's Den* production. My singing wasn't as good as I wanted it to be, though. I peaked early,
getting all the leads in the school plays until tenth grade."

At the time Hilton grew up in Winston-Salem, NC, the town
implemented a desegregation plan that meant students
changed schools every two years. When he started senior
high, he met different people, and he moved behind the scenes
to build sets, hang lights, and pull ropes. He worked on occasion at Wake Forest University, where his father taught, sometimes helping grad students with their plays, as well as getting
involved in community theater.

"My high school was named after RJ Reynolds, the tobacco
mogul whose business was the lifeblood of the town at the
time. There was a designated smoking area for high school students."

One of his theater tech mentors was Howell Binkley, a lighting designer who had just graduated from North Carolina School of the Arts.

"He's still in the business—last year he won a Tony for his work on *Hamilton* on Broadway. Because of people like him, this community theater was really like no other. I worked there to get the behind-the-scenes experience I sought and because I was still trying to act for a while.

"We mounted a *Jesus Christ Superstar* production in which I played a role. The city recently built a new band shell on the grounds of the Graylyn Estate [another tobacco heir], and *Superstar* was the first show to perform there. A very talented, 33-year-old New York actor who'd been Judas on Broadway came down to play Jesus. The local opera teacher was also in it. I was in the chorus, which made me available to be designated lifter. That was my entire dance career. I couldn't dance, but I could pick people up and carry them around the stage. A friend and I were the chorus members with the job of whipping Jesus. Then we carried the body around."

Because he'd been a math whiz in high school, Hilton planned to start college as a math major and theater minor. He found it difficult to find the joy in differential equations when he'd been up all night focusing lights for the big musical, and his college life shifted focus to theater.

"I knew the teachers and became a teacher's assistant in the scene shop. I taught set building halfway through my freshman year. By the time I was a senior, I was a full-time staff member on salary and a scholarship. I was in charge of running the new music hall at Wake Forest Chapel, a 2,000-seat church that converted into a concert auditorium. It was the road house for the campus where the rock bands played and also the church where I directed the Christmas pageant so long ago.

"The summer I graduated from college, I was the production manager for *Vision and Dreams, the Wake Forest Sound and Light Spectacular.* It celebrated the 150th anniversary of the University and told its history. To mount the show, we put in a seating section from the Coliseum on the quad. We lit up all the buildings and the church spire. There were speakers under the seats to shake everybody. We used manual light and sound cues because it was just before computers were able to do it.

James Dodding, one of our best theater directors, directed the show. I was in charge of the money. Howell Binkley designed the lights. My best friend Robert was the stage manager. Calling the show took both of us. It was my first time being the boss and I learned a lot. I was young and strong and tried to do too much myself."

It seemed inevitable that once he graduated, Hilton would become a full-time staff member. He could now hire students to run events so he didn't have to be there unless he wanted to be. He found time for a tour with the North Carolina Shakespeare Festival as a master electrician. Soon, he calculated that he was probably the highest paid theater techie in the state. It was clear that it was time for a bigger challenge, so after the year off, he went back to graduate school.

"I found I hated all the theater management degrees I could find. They wanted to teach me to write grants and beg for money. I wanted to do something that paid for itself. The only theater program that called itself a Producer's Program was at UCLA. One of the professors there, John Cauble, was actually from North Carolina, and proved to be a marvelous mentor.

"I realized that I could be the executive director of a small regional theater upon graduation, with a tiny salary, or I could be entry level in the film and TV world, and make four times as much—with unlimited growth potential. I thought I could go back to theater on the side if I wanted to, which did happen with my first independent musical a few years later.

"My future as a professional film and TV person officially began when UCLA placed me as an intern in a group at Universal called Internal Management Consulting. I would work forty hours a week for three months, for a small stipend. On day one, I went to Robert Zemeckis' office [director of *Back to the Future*] and I was hooked. At the same time, I worked as a teacher's assistant at UCLA, manning the box office at the Melnitz Movie Theater. That's how I made enough money to live on. After a month, the Director of Management Consulting said she'd hire me to help out so I could stop the theater job. Every week after the forty-hour internship, I did an additional twenty hours at a better hourly rate than UCLA was paying.

"Because of the extra hours, I was often the last person in the office each day. I taught myself the DOS operating system for the new personal computers that were invading the studio. It seemed natural that I would write my master's thesis about the formation of the TVIS department I was asked to join as soon as I graduated."

The TVIS team was ten people when it began in 1987. The department's business goal was to automate tasks that generated savings equivalent to two percent more TV sales income. That job met its money goal and gave Hilton the world's best opportunity to learn about everything, especially during the year he worked with *Quantum Leap*.

TVIS was in a position to ask any questions about how production worked and its staff could go everywhere on the lot.

"One change we championed was to treat in-town shows like location shows—organizing the crews by production instead of by department. That's standard practice at Universal now, but it took an amazingly long time for things to change. Warner Bros. TV just got around to it about two years ago."

His computer skills quickly gave Hilton a long list of Hollywood insiders he'd met. "It's fascinating to people I meet today that I set up computers for the original *Law & Order*. Creator Dick Wolf is an industry giant now, but then he was getting started. We knew everyone in his office, trained his script assistant staff and taught his writers how to write screenplays using new software called *Scriptor*.

"In the late '80s, I produced my first production, an original musical called *Shades of Grey*. We successfully financed and mounted the show."

Hilton now sees that our biggest mistake with *Shades of Grey* was "not prioritizing publicity. The second biggest was giving the creator, a friend of mine, too much leeway to tinker with the show. The other lesson we learned is only do the show you can afford to do. Go small in a small theater."

Shades led to *Jacks Are Better*, a film Hilton produced with his own money after he'd worked on other people's shows for a while. He finally had enough money to be the ultimate boss.

"The buck stopped with me, superb training for what I do now. My house was the production office. My Yukon truck did everything. We shot down the hill from the Greek Theater. I showed up in the morning, re-positioned the generator and gave the keys to my truck to a crew member, who shuttled the crew to the set. I dropped off the film at the lab every night and the trash at a convenient dumpster. Each morning started with me planning shots with Robert [my friend from North Carolina and the director]. It was hard work, but one of the most rewarding things I've done.

"After TVIS, I moved on to location accounting in the early 90s. During a break between assignments, one of my first tasks was to inventory the *Jaws* sharks. I found myself in a ware-house helping set up an accounting system to track shark parts after *Jaws 4* finished shooting. Who knew fake sharks would be so valuable!"

Hilton's career as a TV producer began when he accepted a position as an assistant on *Silhouette*, an MCA USA movie. From there, he moved from show to show, building his reputation and earning more responsibility and larger titles on each production. He's an example of how many professionals in Hollywood manage and perpetuate their careers. Even though the shows he worked weren't all hits, each one gave him knowledge and the opportunity to meet people who hired him for their next show.

His experiences on shows that were good, bad and mediocre make up what the lucky ones in Hollywood call a typical career. As a pro, you must be ready to go where the show goes, work with new teams and meld quickly with highly dynamic environments. When you're working on a show, it's your life. If you're good and in demand as a result of building a wide network, when an assignment ends you move on to the next job.

The detail credits for his career can be found on the Internet Movie Database at www.imdb.com, but just seeing the credits doesn't tell the story of how it feels or what it takes. Day to day problems can seem overwhelming. Mostly they arrive with the speed of a runaway train and demand solutions even faster.

On one of his first assignments, his computer skills literally saved the day. "Their accountant formatted her hard drive three times, wiping out the show's files each time. I was hired to protect the computer from her. I also did data entry and was very good at it. I learned about the politics on a set and filed the lessons away for later.

"On another show, called *Taggart*, the plan was to shoot in L.A. for $2 million. We were based in tiny offices across from the CBS Radford lot and found local locations to substitute for sites all over the world. I went to set more often than other accountants because I wanted to be there.

"I met Producer Drew Mirisch at Universal when I taught him about computers for TVIS. My friend Robert and I created the onscreen graphics for one of his future shows, since computer effects were a new thing at the time. Robert also got cast. I was in charge of script revisions. Unfortunately, Robert got appendicitis, so I ended up running the graphics on set for him.

"I sometimes worked on feature productions. On a film shot in Portland, Oregon, I was hired as Assistant Accountant. It was a mess for reasons I still don't quite understand. The UPM [Unit Production Manager] was a Pearl Harbor survivor about to retire. He saw his opportunity and took the show for everything he could to help him move to Portugal. Disney didn't stop it because they employed a lot of junior execs who didn't know what they were doing. One day, we stopped filming because the noise from execs yelling at each other in the street could be heard during a scene. The stress led to abuse for my boss, the show accountant. She was so beaten that she wasn't really fighting back anymore when an exec told her, 'Things are out of control, and someone will get fired. It won't be the UPM because he has a 'pay-or-play deal.' [That means he gets paid whether he works or not.] I left with her after assisting with the transition to a new guy, who was really good and able to move things through, which helped me learn how that's done.

"After the fiasco, I found myself in NJ as a first-time show accountant, for less than scale pay. At the time, IA [the tech union IATSE] and NABET [National Association of Broadcast Employees and Technicians] in New York were in merger talks. As a result, we got a cheap union crew and cheap deals elsewhere, too. I stayed in a hotel next to the office. My office didn't have a door and the hotel was full of hookers. That was my first show-accountant gig. Amazing that I ever wanted to do it again!

"When I came back to L.A., I got an assignment as accountant on a TV series called *Cutters* for six episodes. It was a lovely experience because the execs were big deals and great to work for. Robert Hayes starred. I knew him because he'd been on the show in Portland. He sang happy birthday to me on my 30th birthday—not bad!"

Hilton then joined a deeply troubled show at Sony called *Good Advice*, a sister show to *Mad About You* starring Shelley Long and Treat Williams.

"The two shows shared a crew. Producer Danny Jacobson tried to showrunner both, but he couldn't do it. They hired new writers for *Good Advice*, but it was so far behind it never achieved a consistent result. The network burned off the episodes by airing them all quickly and, surprisingly, got ratings. So, the show got picked up rather than canceled."

Hilton returned to the production. "We came back and they replaced the writing staff again. Soon, Shelley developed a health problem. We were shut down off and on for a long period. Then the 1994 Northridge earthquake happened. There were also periodic script problems. We managed a total of only eighteen episodes over two years.

"Since my schedule was a bit haphazard, I booked pilots for Sony on the side. Then I moved into single camera shows like *Party of Five*.

"I got offered the chance to production-supervise *Johnny Tsunami* in Hawaii, which turned out to be one of the most successful Disney Channel movies ever. We filmed skiing and snowboarding scenes in Utah, along with surfing scenes in Hawaii. I learned how to ski on that show. At one point, I went out with the second unit. My job was to make lunch plans because I couldn't keep up with the stunt and camera ski experts."

His next job for Sony was as accountant, but this time they offered a Co-Producer title. He worked on *Family Law* for three years and then moved to a gig as Production Supervisor on season 1 of *Deadwood*.

"That led to my entire career as a producer. As a result, HBO got me into the union and I got my UPM card, which is the first step on the producer title ladder. Then on season 2 they made me a Co-Producer."

He continued to log credits around Hollywood—a year of *John from Cincinnati* with David Milch; the *Sarah Connor Chronicles* TV series; multiple pilots. He was benched like everyone else during the last major writers strike.

"After the strike, you took all jobs. I did a pilot for HBO that finished with a week of night shoots. While that was going on, the second season of *Sarah Connor Chronicles* was prepping during the day. For that one week, I slept in a hotel near Warner Bros. for about two hours a night. It almost knocked me out."

Hilton doesn't regret a minute of the past decades. "I still love what I'm doing. I'd like to move into more of a creative role, and managed some of that on my recent assignment on the comedy *Survivor's Remorse.*

"One year, I took a job as an executive for Endemol for about nine months. I liked the people, but when you're a producer, everyone reports to you and everything is going in one direction. Nobody works directly for the studio executive. You need to convince everyone to do their job—legal, publicity, casting and so on. It felt like my job was all about nagging."

He next worked on the series *Lucifer.* Fox canceled the show after three seasons, but Netflix signed on to produce season 4. Hilton stayed with the show because he liked and respected the people, plus at this point he prefers to work in L.A. if he can. It's not easy anymore [if it ever was], but for now he'll be doing what he loves in his hometown because he's accepted a position as Co-Executive Producer with the successful series *SEAL Team.*

--- Interview 7/2018

CHAPTER 7

GEOFF FAIRBANKS: I
Never Thought I'd Be
Interested in Reality

While the rest of the founding members of the TVIS team [with one exception] left Universal a long time ago, Geoff Fairbanks is still employed by Universal, mixing his duties at the studio with an active writing career. He survived multiple reorganizations and is currently part of a customer service and automation support group for Feature Productions.

We met when I offered him a position with my team at Universal in 1988. As a TVIS rep, he traveled around the lot to sets and production offices to install and monitor personal computers for TV productions. Geoff was sent to distant locations, including to Orlando, where Universal shot several of its sitcoms at the time—shows like *Charles in Charge* and an updated version of *Leave It to Beaver*.

In addition to successfully navigating his day job, Geoff built a diverse second career as a screenwriter and producer.

He happens to be one of the nicest, most loyal and upbeat people I know. I can't imagine where he finds the time to pursue his myriad interests. I've never known him to do it differently, however. He makes it happen because he sees the fun in his work, brightens the day for the people he works with and even loves the writer's daily grind. While I admit I don't understand how he can continue to do basically the same job at the studio after all this time, I'm sure it's at least partly because it gives him a financial foundation and time left over to pursue his passion for storytelling. He completed a Master's Degree in Screenwriting at USC and an MBA at Pepperdine, which serve as the basis for him to excel in both creative and business roles. As a result, whenever I catch up with him, he's eager to talk about the development of one or more new projects.

Geoff's Story
Geoff Fairbanks originally came to L.A. to act. Blessed with a sought-after SAG card from a Tucson-based role in *Little House on the Prairie*, he thought he would take the world by storm and land an amazing series shortly after his arrival in Hollywood.

From his Arizona beginnings, he knew what his priority was and possessed the intelligence and work ethic to juggle more than one thing at a time. "I finished my business degree at the University of Arizona, taking classes while working as an actor. One day, I was running late from set and went to an econ final in full costume. I grabbed the exam, answered all the questions quickly and left twenty minutes later. People were amazed, but I was due back on set! I passed the exam."

Geoff arrived in California with his acting credits and knowledge about how to program a computer. "The easiest job to get was at Hughes Aircraft, for which I acquired a top security clearance. They let me off to take my acting classes, and soon I wanted out of the job. I met with the woman running the temp staffing group at Universal and jumped."

The temp agency trained Geoff on weekends in how to use a 5520, one of the original mainframe word processing machines. At the time, companies used it for all sorts of documents. His new skill served as the clincher for his initial assignments.

"My first job at a studio was in Purchasing, where they installed a computer system no one knew how to use. I told them, 'Of course I can do that.'

"I read the books and got up to speed. The job was originally set for three months, but they wanted to hire me. I loved the job because it gave me the time to travel around the lot and learn where everything was."

He declined the full-time offer, however, and his next assignment was in TV and Film Legal, as substitute assistant for different lawyers and attorneys. "They asked if I could red-line. I said, 'Sure.' It just meant marking differences in documents, so no problem."

He met colorful lawyers in this office. One, a 60-year-old, came in one morning and sheer ladies stockings fell out of his briefcase. "OK," Geoff thought. "He likes to wear women's underwear. Turns out, that was generally known among the staff.

"There was a man in International Piracy who was the son of one of the stars of a UTV series. When I worked there, I learned that he sometimes drank and was medicated for anxiety. He always answered any question in about three seconds and moved on before you could absorb what he said. He went all over the world dealing with piracy, and lost either his passport or his wallet on each trip. We replaced them each time. Once, when he was gone for three months, I happened to be in his office when the famous father himself walked in with three months of receipts and asked me to do his son's expense reports. To comply, I pieced together his trips—it seemed his time in Paris resulted in only hotel charges. There were no food bills because he'd suffered a nervous breakdown and never left his room. Later, when he returned, we began a comedy routine of sorts to get his business done. He'd come out of his office and ask me to connect him with so and so. I'd start to do that, but almost immediately his office buzzer went off. I answered, only to hear, 'Please get me so and so.' 'OK,' I replied. I tried to get so and so as quickly as possible, hopefully before he could buzz me, and we'd go around the circle yet again.

"After surviving that, I was moved to assist an executive producer. My new boss had fifteen filing cabinets full of scripts. I was expected to know all of them, so I started reading and soon realized, 'I can do this.' That's when I started taking writing classes to learn the formal rules and began to write my own stuff."

Before long, Geoff came to understand that, in addition to lots of required reading, there were potential issues of sexual harassment in his latest office. "Apparently, the powers put me there to prevent harassment that could occur if the assistant was female, which was just a bit naive, partially because we were in a private building off the lot. Back in that day, actors paid to come in and read for producers. Before long, the people sending me actors to see my boss paid me to make sure no one went home with him."

Meanwhile, Geoff made the most of the opportunity to learn about script and project development. He accompanied his boss to places like London for production meetings, which added to his experience.

"At the end of his deal, my boss left when the studio declined to renew. I then shuffled to a temp job with a Corporate film casting director. She liked me because I knew how to work the computer and process contracts. I knew I could always find her on sets, not in the office, because she was star-struck. One day, because of the fiasco that was *Howard the Duck*, the assistant for the studio's overall Head of Casting quit. My boss moved to fill the vacuum and was soon Head of Casting, with her own assistant—me."

On Friday evenings, they would get a list of scripts for weekend reading. Geoff read the scripts for his boss so that she could go into Monday's meetings and talk intelligently about them. He created a way for her to compile casting lists for each project on the computer.

"She would throw staplers, tape dispensers and other heavy objects while she was on the phone. I made sure I didn't go into her office until the throwing stopped. After six months, HR told me I must take the job permanently or leave. I knew this could get me in the union, so I decided to do it—especially when the Head of Feature Production approved a special rate for me because of my training.

"When I met with HR to set everything up, they grilled me about my background in computers and then proposed two other jobs I could apply for—one in a new department called Television Information Services, or TVIS, and the other with a sister team for the Motion Picture Group, to be called MPIS. When she found out, my boss called the Head of Feature Production and he agreed that I would not be allowed to interview for the other jobs. But, the meetings were scheduled, so I went. I was interested because I knew and liked the people who would be directors in the new groups. I decided to join the TV group because I realized I could learn more from them."

Geoff does not regret his decision to leave Casting. "I've been in this job now for thirty years and worked with other departments, like Animation, along the way. I asked for and received approval to do the work after hours and got paid to write scripts for the Animation Group. I honed my writing skills when I wrote for the company newspaper, interviewing celebrities, including Craig T. Nelson. I found out later that when the newsletters came out, people loved the no-holds-barred conversations I documented."

He often met or interacted with the famous and more famous. "My hero is Steve Martin. One day I was called to his office on the lot. He was experiencing problems with the computer the studio provided, so I was sent to his trailer. The weather was ugly—105 degrees. When I arrived, I was told, 'He's here so you can't do anything right now.' Lovely. Shortly, he invited me to come in rather than wait outside in the heat. He then proved he was a real gentleman. When he was called on set, I met another roadblock—they told me to leave when he wasn't in the office! Mr. Martin came back, heard about the conundrum and made an exception just for me so that he could get his computer fixed. I must have been somewhat memorable, because when I saw him later, he knew me.

"Another day, I was waiting to see the developer for one of my British projects when Bette Midler came in. I told her I loved her recent HBO special. She asked for specifics and we had a wonderful conversation. I saw her a month or so later and she, too, remembered me and gave me a hug. One of the benefits of working in Hollywood!"

Of course, 30 years is a long time. Universal morphed, and then morphed again, while Geoff continued to excel at his job. When the studio was bought by Panasonic in 1990, Geoff wondered if he'd even have a job. Turns out, he did. "I stayed during the transition and continued with writing classes, pitching stuff for TV companies outside of Universal. I was hired as a ghostwriter for books and got paid for that, careful to avoid any conflicts of interest from this work. Then we were bought by Seagram's, then Vivendi, which was a French company that was wonderfully people-oriented and pro-education. MBAs were preferred, but they agreed to finance my MFA in Screenwriting at USC. I met some incredible writers and directors and sold some little things, along with a few options. That meant I sold the right to develop my idea or treatment for a period of time when it can't be offered to others. Options are also not a guarantee that the project will ever be made, which is what happened to me.

"Alas, the company next became part of GE, which tried to run production like an assembly line. They also owned NBC, which was given the task of managing Universal to model the GE search for excellence through conformity. It didn't work—the cultures were completely different. It became us vs. them, and no one won.

"GE insisted that we use only their systems and that everything be justified via at least one form. They shut down our computer systems and took two months to get their system up and running. We got so far behind with vendors, we almost never caught up.

"Today, we deal with Comcast. They are people who favor the bottom line. For a recent movie called *The Purge*, they decreed that it must be made for only $5 million. To keep within the budget, we stopped all filming while Producer Jason Blum made ten other movies, including *Get Out*. He is a penurious producer and the powers were convinced that his method should be the new model. They learned that it worked only for some things.

"None of this craziness required me to give up writing. While we were still owned by GE, the company proposed a new education initiative, and I was finally convinced to get that MBA. It made sense because, even though I was collaborating with producers to put together a slate of projects with pitches written by me and number crunching prepared by me, the deal would sometimes die because I didn't have an MBA and couldn't be trusted with the business side of things.

"Near the beginning of my time at Pepperdine's MBA program, my class took the ubiquitous Briggs-Meyer personality test. The teacher spread a map on the floor and we all stood in our designated corner based on the results. Most of my classmates were in the analytical area. I was in the creative corner all by myself. The teacher asked me to stay after class and said, 'Perhaps you should rethink this.' But I was determined. I stayed and was successful. Halfway through, you have to pick a major. I chose entrepreneurship, which is perfect for understanding entertainment companies."

Currently, because of his connections at Universal, Geoff is developing two reality TV projects. "I never thought I'd be interested in reality. One project is built around my niece, who is a world-renowned psychic. Several places are interested in our pitch for her. The other project is about a couple who uses tattoos to help people through past trauma. Both excite me because they're wonderfully uplifting.

"I'm writing a biopic for a man falsely accused by the Feds in the 1970s. Think *Shawshank Redemption*. And two of my kids book series were just grabbed by a producer."

If that's not enough, Geoff has two features out for options right now. Two other feature scripts are semi-finalists for the Nichols Fellowship, the Motion Picture Academy's international competition for new screenwriters. There are other scripts in competition at Slam Dance. His next TV projects are being developed with connections from USC.

All of this sounds impossible as efforts from just one individual. "I would probably be a good show runner because I understand the creative, budget, directing and business silos of TV. I know how to think of the overall arc for a show. I'd try it if I could still write and develop at the same time. I don't want to focus on only the business end of my projects. When I get the chance, I'd like to produce features as well."

His day job keeps getting more complex as the technology morphs. Geoff's group is responsible for setting up elaborate systems that manage the intellectual property. "Marketing wants to allow consumers to re-edit raw footage, for example. Consumers want materials from old films, and we have to design storage and retrieval mechanisms for that. We've become traffic cops, data wranglers and security police.

"I know I have to understand more about digital effects. The vocabulary changes every couple of months. There's also the fact that the business is evolving at light speed—from theater to home viewing, which muddles delivery windows and requires re-imagining of business models.

"My joy is to concentrate on writing. It uses both the left and right brain. The right comes up with the ideas and the left brain structures the production.

"I'm in my early fifties and the job at Universal is the only full-time job on my resume. I'm lucky to have lots of time left to do many more things. But, I'm realistic. I know I'll need to sell more projects before considering leaving the security of my job for the uncertainty of production. On the other hand, I've saved money my entire career, so I could retire soon if I want. My pensions will kick in at sixty. The potential is intriguing."

To keep even more options open, Geoff is always preparing for the next thing. It follows that he would propose, "I'd love to teach. I've taught acting and directing before at SAG/AFTRA."

He remembers to add, "Speaking of teaching, L.A. Valley College is interested in setting up a teaching gig for me."

--- Interview 5/2019

CHAPTER 8

PETER SIEGEL: No Staircase Is Complete Without a Tyrannosaurus Skeleton

Peter Siegel is that rare someone in your life who comes and goes but never truly leaves—and that's a good thing. An enthusiastic traveler, he gravitated toward the international distribution portion of the TVIS mission soon after I hired him in 1987. As a result, I budgeted for multiple overseas trips where he installed and trained local Universal office personnel in new computer systems.

During our time at Universal, the studio experienced significant upheaval in the business because of technology, and physical security issues began to surface that were not notable before. One day a member of my staff came running into the office to tell us that a guard at the main gate had been shot! She'd just missed the action on her way back from an appointment. Apparently, the shooter was angry because the guard wouldn't give him access to Michael Landon's shooting location. We were blessed to be inside and safe that afternoon.

At one point, I approved a round-the-world ticket for Peter to embark on a single multi-month trip because it was cheaper than sending him first to Europe and then the Far East. He added a few personal stops along the way in places like India and the South Pacific.

Peter stayed at the studio while I moved to Portland, Oregon. Eventually, he left to move to New York and manage the implementation of a website for the eDrive startup, which was the online version of the CompuServe Entertainment Drive site. The founding partners met Peter during one of their L.A. trips and asked him to join them in New York for the launch. He called me one day and said, "Hi. You're moving to New York." I, of course, said "No way." At first. He wore me down and I accepted a contract to act as Project Manager for the launch. He got me a great deal that included room, board and a promise to fly me home to Oregon every six weeks at a minimum.

The launch was stressful because the partners knew very little about building and designing a website. They attracted money to throw at the project but had unrealistic ideas about how much could be accomplished in a set period of time. Peter and I held our ground and gave them a portion of the site on schedule. The launch party, featuring Cindy Crawford, was a success [just barely, but no one knew what was really going on behind the scenes!] and they were thrilled. eDrive became one of the first online entertainment magazines and one of the first to 'broadcast' events like the Oscars over the Internet.

Again, I left first, and Peter stayed in New York. The next time we worked together, I hired him to work on my team for the startup Cenquest in Portland. Another stressful situation. If we've learned nothing else, we know that the success of a startup is totally dependent on the strength, background, and wisdom of the founder and the core management team.

The .com companies we helped were based on good ideas, but in our opinion beset by political and internal agendas that ultimately doomed them. We were lucky to work on innovative projects while they lasted. Each was, in its own way, a good time for a while. I will always be grateful that Peter was there for all of it. It wouldn't have been as much fun without him.

After Portland, Peter moved back to L.A.—this time before me. He got a great job at Warner Bros., where he remained until he retired and moved to a gorgeous house he just acquired in Puerto Vallarta. I can't wait to visit!

Peter's Story
Peter Siegel's early years were completely devoted to classical piano. "When I went to Boston University in 1969, I worked hard, but saw that I was not going to have a career in piano, either performing or composing. I withdrew in the middle of my second semester and got a job."

It was January 1970, and the Boston production of *Hair* was underway. Peter worked wardrobe for the run of the show, and then moved to San Francisco.

He found no real direction for about two years after that. One day, "I woke up and realized I didn't have a lot in common with the people around me, who were mostly smoking pot and not doing anything else. I wanted to go back to school, and Berkeley was my choice."

He set up an interview and learned that after one and a half semesters at BU, he would need to take courses at Berkeley Extension and San Francisco State to meet admission requirements. He signed up for seemingly random courses. One, taught by a researcher at Stanford, studied electrical activity in the brains of monkeys; another was called Magic, Witchcraft and the Supernatural.

"The courses were great fun. Over a two-year period, I got the credits needed to achieve junior-year standing at Berkeley. My intention was to get back to serious school as a psychology major. I graduated in 1975, rented a truck and moved to L.A., my goal since an earlier three-month stay." Once in California, Peter decided to continue school and get an MBA.

"But I was stupid and naive and didn't do the prep I needed to get into a decent school."

He scored horribly on the ATSGB test required for admission, and that changed his mind. He shifted direction to work in retail for a number of years at department stores like Robinson's and Bullock's Wilshire, but continued to want more. Recognizing a desire to work in entertainment, Peter felt the MBA goal was still the ticket to his dream job.

"I didn't know how or when or even why entertainment exactly, but this was the '70s, and I was in L.A., and entertainment was THE industry. Plus, my musical background could be useful."

His path was hardly direct, though. He moved to Laguna Beach and left from there to go to Switzerland for about eighteen months with friends to help them with their businesses.

"When I returned to L.A., I didn't know what I would do next. I ended up in Boston, then New York, then San Diego, and then back to L.A., back to San Diego and back to Switzerland again."

Finally, he went back to San Diego one more time to take a consulting gig with Mark Services, working in the banking industry. CEO Pam Rosenfeld started the company as a business to solicit proxies for savings and loans in the process of changing from mutual to capital stock.

"It was the start of the savings and loan debacle and an eye-opener that served as an accelerated course in transferable financial skills. I did many projects as project manager at Western Federal in L.A., and with other banks across the country. In 1983, Pam decided she was going to give management bonuses to all staff. When a project started, she put a team together, flew them to the required city for three months and then home. As a bonus, she gave everyone round trip tickets to wherever they wanted. West Coasters chose the Caribbean, and East Coasters chose Hawaii. I didn't want to do the obvious, of course. Pam sent me to Europe on a comparable ticket. I flew to Munich, took a train to Switzerland and then Milan. A friend who was a model let me hang out for a bunch of designer shows."

When he came back, Peter realized he'd learned a business language that he could use to market himself. That finally got him into business school. When he graduated from UCLA with his MBA at last, he was determined to land something with the studios. In due time, Universal hired him.

"I knew that I would receive an offer from TVIS after the interview with the Director of the group [Elaine]. It was a phenomenal environment with very cool people. I started there in 1987 and stayed until 1995."

Along the way, TVIS team members, enthusiastic entertainment types, took on an outside project to produce the equity waiver musical *Shades of Grey*, written by one of the department's staff members. Peter contributed to the wardrobe and sets for the production and enjoyed a throwback to his time in theater in Boston.

"It was a great time to be in the entertainment industry. Even though it was really hard work, it was also fabulous fun. It wasn't until the early '90s that Universal started being passed around among major corporations and the atmosphere changed.

"One day, as I went about my business, I ran into Tina Turner. On another day, I saw Kevin Costner. And once it was Dorothy Lamour outside the commissary. She was saying to her companion, 'Just call me Dotty.'

"Two people from the team took the department's golf cart, assigned to us because our job took us to production offices all over Universal City, and went through the *Battlestar Galactica* sets. When they pulled up to the gate at the set, the cart triggered the door to open. That was a surprise, but they figured 'what the hell' and drove the cart in. Next thing they knew, actors were running onto the stage and starting a scene. The cast expected to see a tram of tourists arrive and instead there was the cart. Its occupants floored the cart's accelerator and left as quickly as they'd come!"

The change Peter saw coming began to happen ever faster. "Eventually, they set up black concrete barriers around the entrances to the lot. It was a reaction to many things, one of which was the day an angry guy shot up the main administration building. At another point, there were thousands of protesters for the release of the movie *Passion of the Christ*. There was also a crazed fan of *Little House on the Prairie* actor Michael Landon who killed a guard at the Main Gate because they wouldn't let him on to the lot to visit the *Highway to Heaven* set. Soon, we all had security IDs to carry. All the studios did that. Suddenly, you couldn't visit the sets around the lot.

"Even so, I managed to get onto the set for *Jurassic Park* to see the administration building on Isla Nublar with a tyrannosaurus rex skeleton in the middle of the staircase. We decided to go back with a Santa hat to shoot a Christmas card, but the set had been ripped apart after the dino-rampage shoot. We shot a few photos anyway, but none came out—they were too dark."

Peter's job in TVIS entailed going around the world on "absolutely great trips." His role became the installer for new software in Universal's International offices. He visited Brazil, Europe and the Far East. Not a bad job if you like to travel.

Elaine Spooner

"When I left that job, I was burned out. In hindsight, I wish I could have stuck it out a bit longer. Digital technology was just emerging, and I could have done some very cool stuff. My mother had recently died, and I needed to sell her condo in La Jolla, so I left my job to have time to remodel it and put it on the market. Then I moved to New York and the condo sold a year later. I traveled around the world for two years on the inheritance.

"My work in TVIS included creating content for a new site called Compuserve. I also delivered marketing materials for AOL. The Compuserve people put me in touch with the founders of a new company called Entertainment Drive, who offered me a job. I jumped at it and returned to New York. I was there for just one year while we launched the web version of the Compuserve site as the new eDrive. I was miserable. It was the wrong place and the wrong company. I completed good work for about three months and stuck it out for a year, but it wasn't fun."

Peter moved back to San Diego and continued traveling—to Greece, Egypt, Morocco and Southeast Asia. "When I visited Greece the money was finally almost gone. Then I got an email from my TVIS boss asking me to come work for an Internet startup called Cenquest in Portland, Oregon. I accepted and began working on MBA course materials for online university degrees.

"I was there for two challenging years, in a company with management issues, but trying to build a business on a promising disruptive business model. I landed in a great apartment, among good friends, and close to the wine country and Oregon salmon. However, I was an L.A. boy very much out of his element in Oregon. The company went through multiple rounds of layoffs as they struggled to adapt to reality. One day, the COO called me into his office to tell me about another layoff, which was to include me. I initially felt devastated, but by 6 pm I was partying because I was free and could go back to L.A."

In August 2002, Peter took a job at Warner Bros. in technology for Domestic Television. "I tried to keep everyone happy. Initially, my role was to implement program license tracking and customer information systems for Domestic Syndication. Then I picked up responsibility for the Cable group. Three or four

64

years ago, I also took on International TV Distribution. We installed the SAP accounting system across Worldwide Television Distribution, and consolidated contract management and rights management systems as well. The project is the second biggest deployment ever at Warner Bros. The biggest was the SAP financials rollout to the entire company."

In July 2018 he was pulled from the Worldwide Television Distribution group into Warner Bros. Technology.

Peter waited until the AT&T purchase of Time Warner was finalized and then retired. "The process took months, with successive rounds of litigation as the government tried to block the purchase, which stalled AT&T's plans for the combined company, and left the Time Warner companies in a state of limbo. Rumors were rampant—will there be layoffs? [probably]; will there be staff buyouts? [HBO had initiated theirs]; has the wait eliminated the advantage the company had in pursuing a timely purchase in an industry that is now racing to compete with Netflix, Amazon and Apple? [unknown]."

After a career that spanned continents, entertainment platforms, technologies, and companies large and small, Peter is downsizing his life. As a leader in the business side of entertainment, he understood how to help drag the traditions of production and distribution into the future. Like all companies, studios are resistant to change. But, change they do, and he will tell you it was mostly a blast to be a change agent during the upheaval.

"I will enjoy my house in Puerto Vallarta, Mexico. But, of course, I will also travel on occasion in retirement! Let the next phase begin."

--- Interview 4/2019

CHAPTER 9

JIM MICHAELS: Film vs. Digital Drags Production Into the 20th Century

When your producing credits include long-running series like *Lois and Clark: The New Adventures of Superman,* *Everybody Hates Chris* and *Supernatural,* you can be considered a television lottery winner in my opinion. To have one multi-year job is not the usual experience of industry producers, much less more than one.

It takes many things going right to achieve a hit show. That's why it's rare—and life-changing—like a lottery jackpot.

Jim Michaels is not just lucky, of course. He's good at what he does, positive and supportive, and a great guy to know. When the opportunities came, he made sure he was ready.

To break into the business, Jim used his computer to program the display of on-camera computer graphics for multiple series. He gained a foothold by working as an effects producer and achieved success because he knew how to create graphics in the early days, when no one knew how it should work.

He joined the TVIS team at Universal and became a crucial part of our mission to define how computers would be used in series production. His credits included creating and managing onscreen graphics for early technically-savvy shows like *Air-wolf* and *Whiz Kids.* The images he designed played well when photographed and broadcast as part of the story.

I coordinated his assignments while he was part of the team and found him a pleasure to work with. He came to the lot to do a job he relished and made it easy for me to trust that his interactions would be positive and productive.

Before long, he accepted jobs on other shows as a technical associate producer, as a line producer [manager of the logistics of the production] and in due course as a creative co-executive producer. I'm not surprised at his continued success in a very tough business. His current series *Supernatural* shoots in Vancouver, but he continues to maintain a residence in L.A., which he calls home whenever he can. Home for his early years in the business was The Strand facing the beach in Manhattan Beach. Now he owns a home in the Hollywood Hills.

Over the years, we've stayed in touch and met for the occasional lunch. I look forward to hearing his stories. We're Facebook friends, which means I also know that he travels a lot to Europe and around the US. He's often checking in from one airport or another. It's a good life, and it's the one he chose.

Jim's Story
Jim Michaels planned to become a doctor and was pre-med for a year and a half. "I decided in my sophomore year of college that I liked biology and the idea of being a doctor, but I didn't love it. Besides, it would take too long to get to do what I loved. I talked to my biology professor/counselor and told him I didn't want to be a doctor.

"He thanked me for saying that straight forwardly and asked what I would do instead. My reply was: Get a degree in business.

"I thought maybe I could use a business degree to work with the NFL since I'd already abandoned my dreams of playing professional football. As good as I was, the gap between my skill and an NFL player's ability was big enough for a truck to drive through, as they say. I didn't come from money, so I couldn't own a team. I had no interest in coaching or being an official.

"My roommate, who was an accounting major, warned me that accounting was the hardest business degree to achieve. I read one of the program's books and didn't get turned off. It

67

seemed easy compared to nuclear magnetic spectrograms in medicine."

Once he graduated, and because he knew that Leigh Steinberg made news as the first high profile sports agent, Jim planned to find out more about being an agent. He thought it looked like something he might be able to do. Most sports agencies were based in L.A. in the mid '80s, which was fine with him.

"I decided a long time ago that I wanted to live there based on all the Beach Boys songs! I guess it's OK that I started a career that would actually restrict me to L.A. for a long time.

"My Beach Boys vision placed me in a house at the beach and driving a convertible before starting my MBA or law degree, one of which I felt was required to be an agent. In the spring of my senior year in college I joked with a friend from Chicago who worked at Universal Studios that I would soon need a job in L.A. and would be happy to take over his job should he not want to continue in his position with the studio. In short order, I got a letter from that same friend, who'd just started work at Universal Television as a technical adviser on a new TV series titled Whiz Kids. The show was starting production soon and, unknown to him before, the studio had budgeted a position for his assistant. I told him I would take that job if it was available and was hired. After six months, I realized I'd found my direction. My friend left before the first season ended, and I was promoted to his job.

"I sent a proposal to Universal Studio Head Dan Slusser recommending that we purchase a few minicomputers, hire a staff of artists, and write our own software to deliver better on-screen visuals faster and less expensively. I didn't think they'd go for it, but Dan and Post-Production VP Jim Watters saw the future. On *Whiz Kids* we proved that the technology we installed to set up more displays did reduce costs. People from the original staff that I hired back then, in 1984, have since won four Oscars for visual effects.

"We serviced other shows at Universal, including the *Airwolf* pilot, creating the graphics working inside the titular helicopter. At the time, the charge from outside vendors was $10,000 per second of on-screen visual, which meant thirty seconds for $300,000. No one thought we could loop the same ten seconds 3 times!

"After series like *Knight Rider* and other shows got pickups and moved production to Canada to save money, they shuttered our group, since we didn't have enough business from outside the studio. I transferred to general Post Production, working for Jim Watters.

"Electronic editing was the new thing at that time. Most shows still cut on film. People were either video or film and passionate on their chosen side. I knew both systems and processes very well, which was rare. I worked as a post supervisor, which meant I managed effects on set on eight shows a week. My commitments were detailed on four or five call sheets per day at times."

Jim soon observed a truism: "I became curious about producers. They owned nicer cars, which meant that job sounded most interesting!"

Then came the writer's strike in 1987. "James Korris, a tech-savvy creative executive at the studio, was a friend, and he put me in TVIS so that I could continue my graphics work for our shows. The TVIS team included some of the only other people on the lot who knew personal computers, and I fit right in.

"We got a lot of resistance at first. People were afraid that if computers took over, jobs would be eliminated, especially when software could upload shots directly to a mainframe from the camera.

"One of the initial processes we put in place sent scripts back and forth to Vancouver or Seattle over digital connections. Productions could script edit up there if they had to, which was unheard of at the time. It was fast on a 5600 baud modem. It took forty minutes to send a script!

"Over time, TVIS dragged people into the 20th century. We taught people how to use the technology, but they often simply asked us to do it for them because we were faster. Some were hoping they could retire before it was necessary to learn the new stuff. Some wanted it, notably the studio's Engineering VP, Dick Stumpf.

"For a long time, editors wanted to keep Moviolas and edit on film. The challenge was that electronic editing made financial sense, but fear of a new system often intimidated people not familiar with computers at all. Eventually, you had to learn it, with free training from the studio, or get left behind.

"Soon, owning a laptop meant you could take things on the road. James loved the possibilities and encouraged TVIS to break new ground once again. We trained local and remote production office staff in *Scriptor*, the first real script-formatting tool, and in budgeting. More people began to like it when they realized how much time could be saved."

After his time with TVIS, Jim moved to Lorimar as a Post Production Supervisor. It paid more and was what he wanted to do more than being an implementer of technology for the business side. He transferred to the Video Playback team for *Back to the Future Part II*. Then he became Post Supervisor, then Associate Producer on a series called *Midnight Caller*. It was on that job that he first worked with Bob Singer. They've now done nine shows together.

"It was a real career changer. I now knew Jim Watters in Post Production, James Korris in the studio executive suite and Bob Singer, who produced shows. I was the right fit for what they needed. I can confirm that it's critical to become familiar with everyone on the lots around town. The more prepared you are and the better your reputation, the more work you'll get."

His connections helped Jim keep working during the next phase of his career as he moved from show to show, often working on pilots that didn't sell. Bob Singer went to work on *Lois and Clark* and brought him in for his first multi-year run on a single show. Series after that included *Charlie Grace* with Mark Harmon and a short-lived Showtime series called *Odyssey 5*.

"By then, Bob had moved to Universal with yet another pilot that didn't go. James Korris [once again] and his boss Robert Harris hired me for a show that shot in Hawaii. After that, and because I kept my relationship with Bob, I started on another series with him. We did the pilot in the spring and it got picked up. It finished well in the ratings, but the landscape began to change. Shows were seemingly only picked up if the network owned some portion of them, like today's *Blue Bloods*. Our show, *Turks*, went away.

"Then Bob Minkoff at Universal called me about Cover Me for the USA network. Shaun Cassidy starred, and he and I got along really well. Next was a pilot at Sony called *The Guardian*, with Simon Baker, that was great. It sold, but the series producer brought in his own team and I was out. I stayed in town anyway because Sony kept me working for a time after that on little things."

Next, he was able to re-establish himself at Warner Bros. when he got a call to work on a pilot called Dr. Vegas.

"Out of the blue, I got a call from Paramount, where I'd never worked. They pitched a Chris Rock project, which became *Everybody Hates Chris*. I met the co-creator and got a job for the next four years. We shot the show unusually far in advance, which helped during the next writer's strike. Season 4 was completed ahead of schedule. Then, suddenly, Chris wasn't renewed for a 5th season.

"While this was going on, Bob Singer moved to the first season of *Supernatural*. I knew about the show, but couldn't do it because I was on Chris. Once that ended, I joined the CW's Supernatural in the fifth year and moved to Vancouver. I thought it would go for at least two more years, maybe three, after I started with it.

"Our show became a giant hit the year after the network's new head Mark Pedowitz featured us in a key part in the successful Upfronts presentation. Upfronts is an annual New York City event where each of the major networks shows off their series for the upcoming season. During a panel, someone asked Mark a question: 'What's your favorite show currently on your network?' His answer was what we all wanted: *Supernatural!* That one event was a real game changer for our show. We're now working on the fifteenth and final season.

"I've been promoted from Post Supervisor to Line Producer to Co-Executive Producer. These days, I'm more of a creative producer than many in my role. I'm not near the writers, but the current show is massive, and I'm involved in a growing list of activities.

"Our crew is one of the largest in television. We're on the road a lot. We've also recreated everything but Florida or Hawaii in Vancouver at one time or another. There's a large Art

Department of nine to ten people. Our construction crew is huge by itself. We set up our own post people in-house. For the 100th episode, the crew sheet was so big that our Warner Bros. Television liaison wasn't sure it was an accurate count when it came time for invites to the celebration. We're almost double the size of most crews. It works so well because we're only three hours from L.A. and there's no time change.

"Our show uses lots of CGI to change Vancouver to other cities, as well as a high number of visual effects for blood, fire or creatures that help to tell our story. There's even a CGI version of the car. It's very competitive to find people who can do this work, especially ones who like creating for just one show. Now all of them are Warner Bros. employees because Canadian tax incentives are highest for employees."

The nature of what Jim calls his "right place, right time" career, which paralleled production changes amid the transition from film to digital and digital cameras, reminds him to be grateful.

"We shot *Everybody Hates Chris* on digital. Supernatural switched from film to digital during its run. I understood the pressures a producer faces with a pilot, trying to get it right and make the best picture they can. But, cost and time are crucial in TV. One producer, whose argument was that there was quality improvement with film, asked me to review several scenes and challenged me to say which was on film and which was digital. I got them all right. His team couldn't believe it.

"Offline editing tools are very sophisticated today. Everything can be built in the edit bay. Sound and color timing are almost there. It's crippling the video houses that used to assemble shows. Steps in the process have been eliminated for outside companies, which frees up money to improve what's on the screen.

"I once did a pilot re-shoot with a director who wanted to shoot more film for his show. I knew that processing all that film would give him only a little time to finish editing the dailies. There would be NO time to finish the cut. Directors didn't always understand the time involved in film; they just knew they wanted to use it. I educated DP's [Directors of Photography] about using digital even though it meant they couldn't do what they were used to. Some today still use lighting for film but shoot digital.

In 1984, Jim did an interview in which he said, "This new CGI technology is just another tool. It won't replace anything else."

He feels the same way today, but with a caveat. "By that I meant that the originals will never go away. Eventually, we're going to live in a world where you'll be able to go on your computer and put other actors in the familiar roles in old movies. Imagine seeing Chris Rock as Luke Skywalker in a fully rendered, new, personalized version of *Star Wars*. It will happen."

With the rare decade-long run on such a successful show, Jim has the time to pursue his own passion projects. "You are always out there pitching your own shows. It's a rough game. We posted a documentary on Kickstarter and raised the funds to make a film about the largest maritime disaster in US history. Over 1,600 soldiers were killed when their ferry sank on the Mississippi just days after the Civil War ended. It was overloaded with 2,500 passengers. The boiler exploded about eight miles north of Memphis, and over 1,800 in total died, including mostly newly-freed Union prisoners of war from the Andersonville and Cahaba prisons.

"In my job, it's about showing up on time and being nice. In production, the long hours mean you spend more time with the people on the show than you will with your family. You have to work things out and stay ahead of potential conflicts. Many of our *Supernatural* crew have been on the show for fourteen years. I wouldn't be here if the people weren't the best."

--- Interview 1/2019

CHAPTER 10

KARLA ABER: Along With the HBO Execs, There Sat Jane Fonda and Ted Turner

Karla Aber, a singer and actress with a background that included touring with the Disney Showtime Singers, joined my TVIS IT team at Universal and helped us provide technology support to TV productions and business departments. For the *Shades of Grey* musical that TVIS staff helped mount, she accepted the task of being an understudy for all but one female role in the play and assisted with pre-production tasks, like casting.

At the crucial audition for the male lead, Karla's contribution was to register the actors and send them in to the producers [and me] for their performance. We had just released one actor when Karla put her head around the door and mouthed, "Wow." We soon learned what that meant when the next actor came in to sing his song.

"Wow" was absolutely the right word. He was perfect for the show's lead, which the writers defined as "the most charismatic performer in the world." We'd been afraid that maybe we wouldn't find someone with the stage presence and performing talent for our musical, but there he was. We were thrilled when he accepted the role. Turned out, he was perfect. And it was wonderful to work with him.

Karla is warm, friendly and giving. She laughs a lot and makes sure that, when you're a guest in her home, you are well taken care of. We became friends and remain part of the *Shades Of*

Grey family, which stayed close and often got together for dinner or events years after the show closed.

Her talents encompass traditional performance [singing and acting], finance [tax preparation, bookkeeping] and family management [mother, chef and volunteer]. She's a fascinating blend of her earlier performing experience and the person she became after moving to the largest city in the US and settling down in the suburbs.

I moved on from Universal in 1990, left L.A. and re-located to Portland, Oregon, for more than a decade. Karla and her husband Jeff had relocated to New York City by the time I was briefly working there at eDrive. Their home was my weekend oasis on several occasions. They lived a short train ride out of the city and, thus, easily accessible when I needed a Manhattan break. They still live in the area today.

When I made the drive from my summer home in New Hampshire to my new Florida home in the Fall of 2016, one of the people I wanted to see most was Karla. My sister made the drive with me, and we stopped for an overnight with Karla and Jeff.

As with the best of friends, it was as though we'd just seen each other, although it had been almost twenty years!

About to be an empty-nester, Karla is the kind of person who can do anything she wants. I'm curious to see where she goes from here.

Karla's Story
When Karla Aber left her small Alabama hometown to start college, she began in pre-med because she thought she wanted to be a doctor.

"I assumed I'd be a doctor or a lawyer one day because those were the folks in my hometown who were considered 'successful.' And my parents wanted me to have financial success and not struggle as they did.

"I found the idea of being a doctor more engaging, so I followed the path. Chemistry soon kicked my butt, and I thought, 'Maybe this isn't what I want to do.' While wrestling with what I did want, I discovered a show choir that I joined for something totally different. I was shocked and thrilled to be accepted since I was told I couldn't sing that well when I was younger.

"We performed locally and were lucky to travel to what was then the Soviet Union, Poland, Guatemala and Venezuela as musical ambassadors. That was when my passion for travel, exploring other cultures and ways of living began.

"Soon the choir got me interested in theater and I started auditioning. I took acting classes, voice lessons and stage combat lessons and got some nice roles in the college productions, including *Anything Goes, You're a Good Man, Charlie Brown* and *South Pacific.*"

"When I decided to end pre-med, I changed my major to psychology so I wouldn't lose all my credits and have to start over. I thought I would be able get a job sooner with my new degree."

As fate would have it, when it came time to graduate, Karla found that getting a job in psychology wasn't happening all that fast after all. Friends of hers from the show choir were about to go to Birmingham to audition for Opryland and she went along with them.

"That was it. I got the gig and worked at Opryland for two seasons—back when Opryland was a theme park filled with music and not just a mall. Then I landed a season or so with Disney World and traveled all over the world with the Showtime Singers, further fueling my travel bug!"

The tours had business objectives that exposed Karla to then-current management practices for marketing to international travel entities that would attract more tourism to Disney World and soliciting countries to open Pavilions at Disney's new venue, Epcot Center.

"The Showtime Singers were the live entertainment at each event. Once I even swapped roles with one of the character performers and got to dress up like Snow White. I can vouch for the fact that it's great to be paid to travel. I really liked that!"

When the Disney job ended, Karla joined a friend who was working with a bus and truck tour in Dallas. She traveled all over the US performing two tours of a retro show called *The Nineteen Forties Radio Hour*. In between the tours, Karla and her boyfriend at the time, also an actor who is now a Hollywood writer. moved to Los Angeles to try their luck in the big time.

"I was an actor moving to L.A. to pursue acting. Such a cliché, right? I did odd jobs to pay the bills: receptionist, retail clerk, waitress. I performed in dinner theater and was a disaster as a waitress. I would pay other waiters to carry my stuff to the customers! And I took classes and auditioned. But I was not having great success.

"In the meantime, my boyfriend went to UCLA and earned a business degree in entertainment management. I saw what that could do, the doors it opened for him."

At just about the same time that she finally got the call to be in a movie, Karla decided she wanted to work behind the scenes. "I was tired of being a performer and feeling like a puppet at the end of everyone else's string. I needed more control."

Her next job came through someone she knew at UCLA, and she became an assistant to the Director of Development at a television production company called Phoenix Entertainment.

"It was fun and I learned a lot. My boss was generous and really taught me so much, but I felt that I needed a Masters degree to jump ahead. I applied and got into UCLA so I could be near the center of the TV business. I geared all my class projects toward entertainment, which got me in to see professionals and allowed me to learn from the best. When I finished, I applied for and got an Internal Consultant position at Universal Studios. The offer came via a pay phone [remember those?] attached to a post outside our cabin in Yosemite while I was on a post-graduation trip.

"At first, I worked with a group providing tech support to the studio, and then for a most congenial group that did the same thing for TV. Our offices were in the basement of the commissary, which meant food was never far away. No one bothered us. We had substantial flexibility as long as our customers were happy."

Karla did OK in IT, but it wasn't really who she was. "I knew I was doing something wrong when a person in the video division in Home Entertainment called me 'the computer lady.' It was definitely time for a change! I needed to get my résumé out and make it happen."

Make it happen she did. She moved through creative executive jobs for production companies, including Qintex, Von Zerneck-Sertner Films and then Davis Entertainment.

"Qintex, an Australian company focused on long-form TV, was my first real executive job. As Director of Development I acquired and developed material for not only telefilms and miniseries, but also first-run syndication and low-budget features. My boss was great and taught me many lessons, including that when you submit your first expense account, make sure it's a really big one. The accountants will never question your expenses after that! We were successful and produced several Emmy winning telefilms, including *The Josephine Baker Story* starring Lynn Whitfield for HBO, the miniseries *Separate But Equal* starring Sidney Poitier, and *The Incident* starring Walter Matthau. Unfortunately, the company imploded [not unusual in that business]."

Luckily, her old boss from Phoenix, now at Von Zerneck-Sertner, was looking for a Director of Development. "I was hired again by the woman who really got me started in the business. She was instrumental in getting my TV career off the ground.

"One of my favorite projects was a series of American Indian films for Turner Productions and HBO. The partners and my boss put me in charge of the research to determine the most compelling stories that might make the best films. I read a lot of books and met with American Indian writers and actors to put together the package of shows. When the day came to pitch the films to HBO, I was included in the meeting. It was so exciting!

"I walked into the room and, along with the HBO execs, there sat Jane Fonda and Ted Turner! I have to admit, I was a bit star-struck. After initial pleasantries, one of the partners started to pitch the first story. Suddenly, he turned to me and said, 'Karla, why don't you tell them this story?' Now, I had never pitched a story to anyone, much less Jane Fonda and Ted Turner. Having no other choice, I jumped right in, told them a couple of the stories I recommended. And I guess I did OK because they bought the whole series of films. We produced Golden Globe-nominated *Lakota Woman*, Emmy-nominated *Crazy Horse* and Emmy-winning *Geronimo*.

"Then they fired me. I'd done a good job, but as often happens in entertainment, the company confronted challenges that had nothing to do with me, and they let me go. It was traumatic, but my boss helped me find my next job."

Karla moved to John Davis' company, Davis Entertainment, which was owned by his father, Marvin, one-time owner of 20th Century Fox. As VP of Television Development, Karla was responsible for the development of television movies, miniseries and episodic series. "That was one of the best jobs I ever had. My boss was just lovely and really smart. We got a lot of things on the air, including *The Last Outlaw* starring Mickey Rourke for HBO and *Voyage aka Cruise of Fear* starring Eric Roberts, Rutger Hauer and Karen Allen for USA Network."

As Karla moved up, she hired wonderful people. "I am most grateful. It's not always the case in any industry that you work with supportive people. I was really lucky. I was also eager to grow, to learn more, to do more. Unfortunately, there was no room to move up any further because my boss was happy where he was. I asked him to teach me about line producing, but despite his good intentions, it never happened. He really needed me to stay in the office and take care of things so that he could be on set and not worry. I tried to expand by bringing movie projects to the Feature Film division, but that never took root. So, even though I loved working at Davis, it became time for me to take on more responsibility, and to do that, I needed to make a move.

"When I heard that Reeves Entertainment needed a VP of Development in their TV Department, I went for it. They offered me the job, and John Davis finally agreed to let me out of my contract for a buyout fee, which Reeves paid.

"Now I had a whole division to run. It was wonderful and scary at the same time, and it toughened me up. We pitched multiple projects, and I managed shows from some of their in-house producers. Some won Emmys and Golden Globes.

"One I'm especially proud of is *A Mother's Prayer*, the true story of a single mom, Rosemary, who contracted AIDS in the early days of the disease in the US. In those days, there were no programs in place to assist in the placement of AIDS orphans. She became her own adoption agency for her eight-year-old son, advertising, interviewing and searching until she found a loving home for him. Rosemary passed away just hours before we found out the film was greenlit [going to be produced]. *A Mother's Prayer* went on to win a Cable Ace award and was nominated for a Golden Globe, but more importantly it helped shine a light on the plight of AIDS orphans in our country."

Once again, the company imploded. Karla was starting to wonder if she was jinxed.

"This time, my job didn't end immediately. Instead, I dismantled everything I'd worked to build. Again, traumatic.

"From there, I went to Saban Entertainment, which turned out to be a nightmare. My TV Division was sort of an afterthought to the Power Rangers main event, which was where the company really made their money. One of the producers basically told me he didn't have time to produce a telefilm that CBS bought! I wasn't sure why I was there after a time. When they consolidated offices and brought in someone from N.Y. who did the same thing I did, they let me go. I was so relieved!"

Karla has Hollywood name stories to tell as a result of her work in production. "At one of my jobs, the elevator in our building was locked down after a certain hour and needed to be activated in order for anyone to come up in it. Once, William Shatner, of *Star Trek* fame, came to the office late in the day to pitch a project. When the receptionist called me and asked, 'Should I beam him up?' we all died laughing. That was what we always called it. The receptionist didn't even think of how funny that was until after she said it in front of Mr. Shatner. Luckily, he thought it was charming and hilarious!

"While still at Saban, I got engaged, so once they let me go, I had time to plan a wedding. We married and decided to move to New York in 1995. I didn't immediately look for work, but tried to acclimate to my colder, snowier environment. I joined the Newcomers Club in my neighborhood, became an officer and began to get to know people and understand the area.

"I worked briefly at a photo lab hoping to learn digital photography. Then we got pregnant. I wanted to be home with my children, a luxury my own mom did not have. I loved being a stay-at-home mom and met lots of other parents through my kids' schools and volunteering in various capacities with the nursery school and then with the district PTA. The volunteer work helped me keep my business and creative skills somewhat active."

Karla stayed on this path until 2014, when she decided to work with her father-in-law. "He owned a home health care business and wanted someone to take it over. I thought it was time for me to get back out there in the business world, as my kids were getting older. I could see the day coming when they'd be off to college and I'd need something to do. I signed on for a perfect storm that eventually tanked the company. We started our new venture by setting up a different company with new contracts. Then two of my largest vendors decided to stop paying me, one being the VA. They said their systems were screwed up and they couldn't pay for the time being. It took two years to get the money. Some medical insurance companies never did pay. I tried so hard to keep it afloat, but eventually it became apparent that I had to close the company.

"It was terribly stressful. I would have closed shop sooner, but a family member was involved. From a financial and business perspective, leaving earlier would have been smarter. I just kept trying to make it work.

"I was not in a good emotional place after that, so I took time to get myself back on track. My mom came to live with us and I had kids at home, so I took care of all that. Mom broke her ankle and needed a lot of support. My kids were getting closer to leaving home and I wanted to spend time with them. Eventually, I decided to pick up a couple of days of work. Something flexible that left me open to be there for Mom and my kids when needed."

As can be the case, Karla found something from an unexpected source. "Cindy G. and I had mutual friends, but I didn't really know her. At one point, one of our mutual acquaintances said to me, 'I have this friend who is a CPA and tax attorney with her own fast-growing business and she needs assistance.' I knew I could do that. It wouldn't tax [tee hee!] my brain, and she lived just five minutes from me.

"When she heard about my background, Cindy thought there was no way I would want to do the job. But, in fact, it was exactly the low-key, low-stress work I needed to do. It was perfect.

"I started working two days a week for her and we had a ball. She's so smart, completely irreverent, and we even like the same music. It's been several years now. Recently, one of her clients, who managed a small business and a complicated household, became ill. Suddenly, she needed bookkeeping and more for the household and her business. She hired me for two more days a week in November 2017. I now had two part-time jobs, both in the financial arena, both flexible and both minutes down the road from home."

Karla took on a third job at an architectural firm helping to put their financial billing system together. She's ending that because she needs more time to help her mom and her son, who will graduate high school next year.

"I'm doing business-type work and not entertainment stuff. I do yearn for showbiz, especially now that my youngest son is interested in the entertainment business. I go to the New York theater as often as I can, see him in his high school productions and teach him a little bit about how the business works. It makes me remember how much I loved it. Even though I miss it, I don't know what I would do now, especially since my current situation is perfectly flexible.

"I continue to think about what I want to do after my kids are on their own. The experiences, accomplishments, and reinventions of my life have been challenging and exciting. It's so interesting to look back on it from this perspective and observe how the journey has unfolded so far. I met great people with a strong, mostly positive impact on me. I learned so much, had a ton of fun, enjoyed my fair share of success, found my way through sorrows and disappointments, and remain optimistic. Most of the time! I don't know what my next chapter is, but I'm looking forward to the adventure."

--- Interview 6/2019

CHAPTER 11

CHERYL BIRCH: People Who Work in TV Don't Have Time to Watch

Cheryl Birch was a Business Affairs Executive at Universal in the '80s when she consulted with TVIS for one of our most challenging system builds: the design and launch of an automated process to generate and track Television talent deals. It's true that no two Hollywood deals are alike, and many "in the biz" were certain the job could not be computerized.

Smart and caring, Cheryl is definitely the busiest woman I know, with more energy than two normal people. She thinks and talks fast because there's lots to communicate. I assigned one of my best analysts to work with her on the design of the new system, a woman who also spoke quickly. Watching the two of them work together was hilarious. They talked over each other and said more words in less time than I'd ever heard.

Many legal or contract systems work by incorporating boiler-plate for the detailed agreement terms. In the case of TV Business Affairs, anyone who's anyone negotiates exceptions based on his or her perceived clout and status in the industry. Computer systems don't like custom provisions, but, with Cheryl's insights, the TVIS team figured out how to make unique language fit into the system we built. Amazingly, the logic worked and the program was a success!

Cheryl and I have been friends for more than thirty years now. She began working for the Business Affairs Department at Universal Television after graduating from the UCLA MBA program. She loved the work and quickly earned a stellar reputation. Her accounting degree and business education helped her learn to negotiate, prepare and manage contracts with the above-the-line talent in UTV productions.

She stayed at Universal longer than I did, but eventually left television to work as CFO for a research unit at USC that produces training and simulation software for the US military. Her TV experience remained relevant, since the software utilized leading-edge digital video technologies like VR and AR before they became mainstream.

One day, she invited me to go along on one of the tours her department provides to interested parties. It was the most fascinating two hours I'd spent in a long time. Clearly, the military remains at the forefront of using software tools to support its goals.

One of the best things about Cheryl is that she brings loads of enthusiasm to all things: her job, her friendships and her life in general, which she views as amazing and fascinating.

Cheryl's Story
When asked to summarize her life so far, Cheryl Birch says without hesitation, "I'm living an extraordinary life that amazes me most of the time." She worked in Hollywood for years and relished the opportunity to go to parties and events like the Emmys, which totally satisfied the star-struck aspect of her childhood dreams. After all, many of her idols were in the same room.

Her accounting degree came from Cal Poly in San Luis Obispo, California. She started accounting classes in her second quarter of college, then took the intermediate classes during her second year and did very well.

"At the end of that year, one of my professors [a great mentor] asked me if I would join the accounting club. I went to the next meeting, which was the last one before the current seniors graduated. Most of them joined the club because it was something good for the résumé. There would be only two of us left, and the other person didn't want a leadership job. That's how I became President!

"We decided to have a career day and invite accountants from multiple industries to come talk with the students, which gave us positive outreach chops. The club went from those twenty graduating seniors at my first meeting to sixty-five students from different classes when I graduated. Now membership is over three hundred people, with sub-clubs and great networking to help members get jobs. It's humbling knowing you helped build an organization that is not just surviving, but thriving years later. I go to the annual spring banquet that celebrates the students and present the alumni-funded scholarship. It's a tradition now."

Cheryl's path to a job in entertainment actually began much earlier. "I was such a huge *Star Wars* fan that I consumed everything about how shows and movies were made before I ever entered a studio lot. I achieved initial access through the fan club. Their newsletters focused on the model makers and tech artists. I read the George Lucas bio as soon as it came out."

She emphasizes that her progress is proof that success starts with honing the proper skill set. "I compete against myself to be the best I can be. I went back to school at UCLA for my MBA because I wanted to understand more about PCs. I knew that would be critical to succeeding in the world of accounting and business in the future.

"A Universal executive came to the school to interview MBA students. You were required to bid to be allowed to interview. I put all my energy and points into that. I grew up in Sacramento and this was the chance of a lifetime for a small-town accountant."

She was hired at Universal after graduation because her new boss was looking for an accountant who understood computers. "Opportunity met preparation. I knew exactly the right skills for the job. Shortly after I arrived, one of the execs needed statistical software to do a requested analysis of audience survey data on a hot new show, *Miami Vice*. The goal was to figure out what elements of the show were most important to fans. Was it the alligator owned by the lead detective, or the star? I learned why something so seemingly superficial could lead to important business decisions.

"My previous work for the head of the business school computer center at UCLA came into play in solving this challenge because he had the right software needed to do the analysis. We couldn't officially engage him, but we traded carpet and paint for his computer center in exchange for his agreement to run the analysis on their statistical software. I attended the results meeting and met the man who would influence the rest of my career, Richard Lindheim.

"Richard provided my next project when he needed to estimate national TV viewing habits based on overnight ratings in a few cities. At the time, national numbers were not available until the afternoon of the day following air. I created an excel spreadsheet that allowed them to do what he required.

"I was lucky to meet Universal executives who mentored me in the same way my professor mentors did while I was in school. We developed genuine friendships. I was impressed that I knew someone like Richard, for example. Someone who did what he did as the man responsible for managing the creative execs who managed TV productions. I was thrilled to know him and thrilled to help him. I met and helped several high-level execs that I never would have encountered if I'd taken a boring accounting job with less ambitious possibilities. You have to be willing to exercise your creativity to do a little above and beyond.

"We also built a system to handle accounting analyses to determine productivity for writers and producers under contract with the studio. To do that, I worked to totally understand the business need and translate it to IT. We succeeded, and the system we developed was still used many years later.

"It was a joy to meet many of the creative people who successfully launched and maintained the studio's TV shows. I met the creative talent on *Quantum Leap* and played on the softball team with the cast and crew. This was particularly thrilling because when I read the *Quantum* pilot script prior to deal negotiations, I loved it. I made sure that I was assigned as the Business Affairs Executive for the show, working with creator Don Bellisario to see a pilot through to a successful series.

"During a major writers strike, I was able to spend time with producers and learn their challenges and priorities, which was fascinating. I came to know icons in the TV business—not just Don, but producers like partners Richard Link and William Levinson.

"Some of my colleagues had held their jobs since the days of *The Jack Benny Show*. I wasn't an attorney, but one of Universal's best and longest-employed business affairs experts, Paul Miller, trained me in negotiating contracts. Even more important than learning about the mechanics of negotiating, I learned about maintaining integrity—to honor the deal you made even if there's nothing written on paper. When you don't act honorably, colleagues will know it and you'll never be trusted again."

Cheryl is still connected to the people she worked with at Universal because she moved on with some of them to an organization that used her skills to make a difference in real-world scenarios.

"In the wake of 9/11, I met the people who work in counter terrorism and saw what they were up against. It was such an extraordinary thing. I could hardly believe I was in the room listening to them. It was a bit scary, but also a place I fit.

"Richard Lindheim in particular led me to many opportunities. After Universal, he brought me to Paramount, where I continued to negotiate deals with the talent who worked on TV shows.

"The shows I worked on there were even more aligned with my interests. They included *Star Trek Voyager* and *JAG*, the *NCIS* spinoff created by Don Bellisario, who also joined us at Paramount. I saw the birth of a new show from within a current successful show on that project.

"I spoke with David James Elliott, the star of *JAG*, who was waiting for the series pickup and was clearly not expecting the change in his life that was about to happen. I advised him to consider that he would be on a hit show in all likelihood and what that would mean.

"Eventually, Richard also brought me to USC and showed confidence in my ability to learn a job I didn't know much about. The position involved management of Federal contracting, Hollywood deals and university accounting. My motivation was, and is, to learn by doing. I rolled up my sleeves and learned whatever was called for. It was not easy, but I didn't give up. I also learned lessons about how to engage others to help you on projects.

"I'm glad I was immersed in the business of television for all those years; but it's far from a perfect environment in some ways. It sounds weird, but people who work in TV don't have time to watch it. They put in long days and do extremely hard, detailed work under serious time pressures. It's an exciting business that is also very competitive, which can cause folks to be very challenging to those around them. People in television know there's a world outside entertainment but can't imagine what it is or why anyone would want to be in it.

"I moved on from TV and started my job at USC in 2000. My title today is Director of Finance, Operations and Human Resources. I have a staff of about nineteen. They're really good at what they do, and they're good people.

"My department was new when I started here, and we took on staff who were let go from other USC departments. Unfortunately, they began with a chip on their shoulders that didn't serve us well. Today, I fully appreciate that I have a bright and talented staff inspired to do good work."

When Richard Lindheim decided to retire from USC, he was replaced by someone Cheryl went to high school with, a transition she welcomed. She's come full circle from Sacramento in that way. "In my hometown, friendships and activities with friends were everything. Whether we were supporting each other in a softball league or playing in the marching band, it was always fun."

Cheryl's experience reinforced what she believed when she started her career. "The best jobs you will be offered are ones where you didn't even know there was an opening. Someone recommends you.

"For example, a high level job opened up at USC, and somebody gave the president of the university my name for consideration. It would mean leaving my company and officially moving to the school. I'm not sure it's the right thing for me at this point in my life because my current work/life balance is really good, but I was flattered. At the same time, USC is seriously considering offering an early retirement program, for which I would be qualified.

"My boss's boss sent me a note saying he hoped I wouldn't accept the promotion. I'm currently thinking that it may be that staying in the job I have is the best decision. It's a great job with a wonderful boss, but knowing that people at high levels of my organization think well of my work is a huge compliment!"

Whatever her choice, Cheryl will continue to thrive, I'm sure. She's not worried either. Challenges are to be welcomed, not avoided. I expect she'll keep smiling no matter what.

--- Interview 11/2018

CHAPTER 12

JEFF LANE: Twelve VCRs in My Dining Room Recorded Primetime TV Credits

I admire Jeff Lane's entrepreneurial spirit. He made a deal with my department at Universal in the mid-1980s that gave him the right to license his vision for a new automated service called *The Studio System* to other studios once it was successfully launched at UTV. For the company, his leading-edge creation was a wise investment. For him, it became the basis for a career.

To this day, he prefers to lead his own business. His latest venture is a suite of software tools that video content production companies might not even realize they need. The package is called *Concept to Camera*. It includes apps that automate and streamline the front-end processes of film, TV and web content creation: script development, budgeting, scheduling, location scouting, casting, business affairs, pre-production.

Jeff gave me an invaluable gift by helping me realize I probably wasn't cut out to run my own company. I responded to his infectious approach and loved working with him to build a first-of-its-kind business tool when we collaborated. But I'm not cut out to be a salesperson and acting as the evangelist for the vision is not my talent.

I work best and experience less negative stress when I let others handle the big-picture business stuff like sales, marketing and contracts, while I do the fun stuff: actually making the vision a reality.

I didn't know it then, but my experience with Jeff was not my last as a partner to industry visionaries looking for someone who could contribute the practical to their "what if?"

Jeff's Story

At the age of 22, Jeff Lane found himself in the soap opera world. He'd graduated from Syracuse University with degrees in film, TV and business, majors perfect for the career he wanted. His decision to take computer classes in the pre-PC era now seems eerily on target for what came later.

After moving to L.A. in 1984, he mined his network and contacted a Syracuse alum he knew who was the office manager on a new, not-yet-aired soap called *Santa Barbara*.

"He was someone I knew in L.A., so I wrote to him and others. I was thrilled when he wrote back to ask, 'What are you doing right now? Can you be here in half an hour and help?' I went and kept coming back. At last, he hired me."

It was definitely a gofer job, but Jeff was 'in' the TV business. On the first day, he installed TV sets in the producers' offices. He thought: "Wow—my parents will be so proud."

He admits loving the soap job because of its proximity to the beautiful actresses he saw every day. He now also says, "It was the best job I ever had. As one of the youngest people there, and someone who knew the basics of a PC, I could help with the one computer in the office. Word didn't even exist then. They needed help and I could provide it." He was assigned to prepare the shooting schedule, which coordinates the filming of all scenes, in this case taking into account special requirements for star Dame Judith Anderson, and school and working hours for the children in the cast. He did it all on the computer, cementing his value and knowledge about how to leverage a computer in showbiz.

After Jeff worked diligently for a month or two, the producers realized that a production assistant was creating the crucial shooting schedule, and they took it away from him and gave it to someone more important.

His next job was at Disney, a position he scored from someone he met during his brief soap opera career. "I worked as an assistant to a couple of writers. They were soliciting scripts as vehicles to produce or rewrite. Their agents at William Morris and Triad sent scripts and I would do the coverage."

Coverage documents present a summary of the story with pros and cons for possible production. Writing coverage is often an entry-level position in Hollywood.

Jeff leveraged the opportunity. "I was one of the first to document coverage on a computer—in 1985. And the first I know of to propose a computer system designed to make coverage easy and efficient."

To build on his idea, he pitched a computer developer acquaintance who knew the basics of what became *The Studio System*. He decided to build applications not just for script coverage, but also for tracking industry phone numbers, development projects, talent and production resources. Everyone wanted this information, but it wasn't generally available in a single, organized place.

His ideas were further defined when he met a developer for the company Ashton Tate—one of the creators of Dbase, in its day a world-changing database tool. He remembers that "he connected with me through a guy on my hockey team. Don't let anyone tell you the path for any career is predictable!"

Jeff and his new friend became partners and designed four basic *Studio System* modules in less than a year. He was the front man who went out and sold the end result.

By 1987, he was pitching to studios while still working at Disney. "First, I went to a Disney division, Hollywood Pictures. I gave them a demo of the feature film data module and they said: 'It's great, but we don't want to do the work to collect all the detailed data and set it up.' They needed a service that would do the prep work."

Jeff and his partner mulled it over and decided: "OK, so be it." They chose to build both program and database, focusing on the Talent Book/Credits module first.

"I began entering the data myself between 9 pm and 3 am, using the industry trade papers Variety and The Hollywood Reporter. They printed items that announced that 'So and so is writing this film and here's his agent.' I lifted what we needed from their excellent reporting."

When he was finished, Jeff's company now owned a unique industry-wide database of feature film talent, their credits and their contact info.

After he launched the first version of *The Studio System* at Hollywood Pictures, and then at other production companies, Jeff left Disney to run his business full time.

"I supported it for two to three years before taking the idea to Universal in 1988. They liked the whole concept, but needed *The Studio System* to track credits for television, not just films, which is all we had so far. We made a deal for me to update TV data on Universal computers once a week. We didn't realize it yet, but TV data would really make our reputation, because there is such a huge volume of detail that no one wanted to do it themselves."

While TV execs thought he was crazy to spend all the time needed to collect the data, they loved him for it!

Once he secured the Universal deal, he wrestled with how best to collect such voluminous data for every prime time show on TV every night of the week. Ever the self-starter, Jeff bought twelve VCRs and recorded all the credits sequences for all the major network prime time shows. He and his staff entered the data from the video. "The VCRs were all in a cabinet in my dining room," he elaborates.

Of course, there were only four networks by then—nothing compared to what needs to be tracked today.

"In 1990, I licensed the system to Paramount. To ace the demo, I bought a color screen for $6,000 because I felt I needed to show it in living color to major TV executives. Somehow, I got a meeting with Kerry McCluggage, a former Universal executive who was then President of Paramount TV.

"Almost as soon as I started demoing, he took the laptop from me and walked down the hall to show the other execs on the floor. When the company President does the demo, you're in. After we signed Paramount TV, we added CBS."

Jeff sold *The Studio System* in Oct 1999, after he'd run it for thirteen years.

He recently ran into one of the guys that took over after he sold the business, who told him, "The way that you used to do it is not far from how we do it now. We use DVRs, but it's basically the same. We still play the credits back and type them in."

Jeff's original process was by necessity people-heavy. "I remember I did it with one guy at first. Then I hired 3, then 10, then close to 25. I sold it when we employed around 30 people. In the era of Peak TV, it's likely the current 80 people won't be enough for long.

"I sold my company because it was the time when venture investors were crazy for Hollywood technology. But, of course, there was too much money chasing too many people, all thinking they could do the same thing. I had to convince somebody to bankroll me, or sell while I could."

Jeff's timing for the sale couldn't have been better. Many businesses crashed and burned when the tech bubble burst two years later. "The limitations of tech for the web, including bandwidth issues, made it impossible to create the complete package I wanted to build at that time. Unfortunately, even to this day Hollywood can be a backward industry when it comes to using technology to run the business side."

As often happens, timing makes a whopping difference. Today's studio margins are shrinking. Jeff is there again to help them finally look at technology as a cost saver. Amazingly [or maybe not], Jeff is making money by pitching the grander vision of *Concept to Camera*.

"The pricing model that I used back then is close to how it works today. The price point was slightly below what the studio would spend to do it themselves. A win-win for everyone."

Support for the new vision didn't arrive without numerous twists in the story of the original *Studio System* applications. "I consulted with the new management for a year after they bought it, but I didn't like the way they were doing things, so I moved on. Unfortunately, they went belly up in 2001 or 2002, after making the same mistakes other startups made. They

amassed $100 million of venture capital money, staffed up
from my 35 to 350 people and rented offices on pricey Wilshire Boulevard. Investors included Michael Fuchs, Frank
Biondi, even Steven Spielberg, all substantial names in the industry. To salvage something, they eventually sold the company in pieces and offered *The Studio System* to Baseline,
which bought it.

"The *Baseline Studio System* application existed for two years
before being sold to the N.Y. Times. The Times was searching
for a survival strategy in the rapidly evolving digital world and
thought if they installed a Hollywood app on their news site,
they'd have a stable income stream from entertainment. It was
not to be.

"After 3-4 years, they sold it back to Baseline for $6 million,
under ten cents on the dollar. Baseline updated it and sold it to
Tribune Broadcasting for $50 million, a crazy price except for
the fact that venture money was still chasing Hollywood tech
companies. Tribune added TV network affiliate data for local
shows, at a steep cost. The combined business was eventually
sold to Nielsen in 2015 for $500+ million, after a likely Trib-
une investment of maybe $250 million. The core is still the
thing I created on my dining room table thirty years ago."

After their expensive purchase, Nielsen set up a one-year contract with Jeff.

"They wanted to figure out how to bridge the gap from their
new system to the web. At that time, Nielsen was owned by a
Dutch company called VNU, which also owned Billboard, The
Hollywood Reporter and Entertainment Data—all great source
reference properties. They saw an opportunity to create a
dashboard for the entertainment industry that combined all
that data. It was right up my alley, so I agreed to build it. We
designed it, but they never pulled the trigger.

"The genesis for *Concept to Camera* originates before that from
a contract I started with Sony in 2007. My task there was to
launch a new script-tracking system to replace the one that
may have been mine from the 90s. It was not web-based and
not exactly working anymore.

"When it was ready, I pitched our efforts under the *Concept to
Camera* umbrella and they thought it was a great idea. The

project was to be funded for five years, based on a model where they took a fee from active productions to develop it. The idea was again to take the application to other industry companies once it was running at Sony."

As everyone knows, Sony suffered some very public problems in the past few years that resulted in reduced head count at the studio, among other things. As a result of the infamous hack of their systems, it was suddenly difficult to fund a project of this size. It took over two years to get the deal done. Jeff's team couldn't talk to Sony attorneys for months or access documents while existing systems were unavailable.

Eventually, he told them, "Sell this thing to me and I'll take it out into the world and maintain it for you. You will pay me a license fee and a royalty."

"They'd spent $5 million in development by then, so payback was attractive."

Because his contract at Sony was through UST Global, a large outsource IT company, he convinced the UST Chairman to sponsor the system officially in order to get it back on track after all the delays. The deal finally closed in April 2016. Since then, Jeff has owned the product as a completely web-based application subsidiary company called UST Global Media Services and expanded its customers to Warner Bros. and Universal.

In the small-world category, Jeff is working at Universal now with someone who worked on the original TVIS team at the time they bought the first iteration of *The Studio System*. He's replacing their current system, which is clearly still based on system from long ago.

The vision continues to inch ever closer to reality. "The Warner Bros. Business Affairs Department still runs on spreadsheets, which hold crucial information needed by the Head of Production. It's time to change and I happen to have the system that will fix it. It's finally time for these guys to do the job cheaper and more efficiently.

"After the studios are on board, we can extend *Concept to Camera* out to other organizations and create an ecosystem that supports multiple shows from multiple producers, who can staff a film in a particular location from a database of talent in that location. Ideally, we'll be supported by the guilds, the agencies, the talent and the below-the-line locals. To bring the idea to fruition, we will disrupt the industry in a way never seen before.

"One of the common objections, anti-trust issues, is not a problem because customers don't have their data on the same box, and I don't have access to any of it. The studios administer the data creation and security. It's our servers and our application, but I don't know what's in it."

There is one unexpected problem from the most recent production company contenders: "A Netflix executive thought this 'new thing' was way too old. It's true that Netflix production is shiny and new and maybe unhampered by Hollywood tradition. They know that the studios have software that's twenty years old.

"My plan is to finish our Dealpoints module first. It's designed for documenting production staff contracts, which honestly don't ever look the same from person to person or show to show, making automation tricky. Then, we'll go back and show the Netflix team the new user interface. That may get me a foothold with them.

"Amazon's hesitation is different. They're very cost conscious, and while they were impressed with my pitch, they don't want to pay for it. I'm not worried. They'll eventually see the light.

"I will promote this until I can't do it anymore. It's flattering that we can't handle all the work we have now. Once Warner Bros. is done, there is a line of customers waiting for us."

--- Interview 11/2017

CHAPTER 13

JOSET COOK: I Only Worked for Nice People From Then On

Joset Cook sat outside a writer's office in the production bungalow for Universal's popular series, *Miami Vice*. She was one of the first writer's assistants we trained in how to use their newly arrived personal computers, and possibly our best, most eager student.

The initial application that most shows took on was script preparation. Prior to this, scripts were dictated or written by hand or on a typewriter by the writer, then handed off to the writer's assistant, who was responsible for creating a final document in the correct format, usually on a typewriter. The TVIS team trained producers, writers and assistants in the sometimes-arcane methods of the first round of script software available to the industry.

After the training was completed, members of my team spent a lot of time in production offices, working to solve problems; sometimes helping out for hours. For *Miami Vice*, Joset became our lifeline. The scripts were prepared in L.A., but the show was shot on location in Miami. She dealt long distance with short deadlines.

The rules for properly formatting a script were and are unique, especially when there are multiple revisions. Little has changed over the decades as the rules became the norm. What did change with the arrival of script software is the workflow that's used to ensure consistent formatting and preparation of final shooting scripts. Especially in television, the writer's assistant is under constant time pressures to send scripts out to waiting cast and crew. Nothing gets done unless and until the script is approved, copied and distributed. Literally everyone uses it as the bible for how to do their job.

The scripts for *Vice* were often late, forcing the preparation staff to work through the night to get them ready for the next day's shooting. I was sent to Miami to train the local staff at the beginning of season two and learned firsthand how hard the job could be.

I found myself doing some of the required juggling to get the latest revisions completed as quickly as we could. Joset kept the pages coming from back in L.A.

I don't know if you've heard the expression that goes something like: "Working on a TV show becomes your life." There is literally no time to do anything else while a show is shooting. I worked in production offices very briefly, but came to admire everyone [especially those like Joset] who could deliver accurate work in such a pressure cooker.

Joset and I connected outside the office, and we're still friends today. I left Universal in 1990 to move to Oregon and try something else for a while, before moving back to L.A. in 2004. She stayed, continued to work for television writers, including Daniel Pyne and those who supported Executive Producer Dick Wolf [*Law and Order*, among other series], and then retired.

She fascinates me because she was able to work under all that pressure and still produce accurate work time and time again. She was a sought-after employee because she could be counted on to deliver with a positive attitude. I admire her quick intelligence, ability to absorb new information and willingness to implement changes she identified as good for the show. Plus, she taught me many things I needed to know about how a production office was really run.

Joset's Story
Joset Cook knew that singing would be part of her future from the time she was four or five. "My mother and her sisters sang around the house, and I wanted to be a singer, too. I sang all the time. I listened to Kay Starr and learned to sing from that.

"In my opinion, if you see what a natural interest is for a child, you should nurture it. If you're lucky, you're given a gift.

Music came easily to me. I played a French horn in high
school, even though I can't read music. I could play something
someone played for me."

She started singing professionally when she was seventeen.
Her first job was as the featured singer for The Counterpoints.
She remembers how tricky the job could become. "We performed at the Sans nightclub, and because I was under age,
when the police would arrive, I'd have to hide in the bathroom. We sang there and at The Deck and The Cove near Kent
State University in my home state of Ohio.

"I didn't start college until I was thirty, so I missed the 60s
campus protests because I was working. We performed a couple of nights a week. I sang with the group until I got married
the first time and moved away. We sang everything but opera:
rock 'n' roll, country, everything. Dave Morris, a friend of the
band, used to record our stuff, but I don't have any recordings.
He says he still has them but hasn't transferred them to CD
yet. I keep waiting.

"Over time, I worked with various other groups. I know now
that I became an entirely different person later in my life. At
first, if someone wanted to watch me sing, I lit up. I didn't just
stand there and sing. That part of me was extroverted. But, like
most entertainers, that's not normally me in other parts of my
life. Today, I'm my more naturally introverted self."

When she married, Joset moved to Toledo from her
hometown, actually to the tiny village of Mogadore, twenty
miles east of Akron.

"After the move to Toledo, I stopped singing for a time. My
husband was a disc jockey—he's now in the Radio Hall of
Fame. When he worked at station WTOD, their Social Director asked me to go with her to an audition for *Anything Goes* at
the Canton Players Guild. When the director asked the group
if there was anyone else who wanted to audition, she pointed
at me and said, 'She does.' I really didn't want to do it.

"I hadn't prepared anything, but I sang *Chances Are* and got a
standing ovation. They called me and gave me the lead. But my
husband's cousin Roger Sharp was in New York on NBC, and
we planned to go for a visit at the same time. I wanted to go, so

I turned down the role. I wish now that I had taken the job because I love live theater.

"My expanded family was also musically inclined. My husband's sister was a good friend. Her daughter, Lisa Howard, is a big deal on Broadway—she plays a leading role *in Margaritaville* right now. I guess certain families have abilities."

When she arrived in N.Y., Joset quickly fell in love. She went to the theater where Barbra Streisand was going to perform. "Wow," she thought to herself. "That's cool." She saw her first Broadway shows on a later trip she took by herself at the age of twenty-one, *Man of La Mancha* and *Hair.*

"When I got divorced, I moved back home. About two years later, I married again and had a child, a son. Then I divorced again.

"I didn't sing with anyone during most of the time when I was still in Ohio. Instead, I went to work for Sensormatic Electronics Corporation. They make the clip-on things that prevent clothing theft before it's sold in the store. I worked in the marketing department, writing publicity and also in the computer department. I managed the team that worked with a pool of twenty-seven Dictaphones and transcribed the content. I used the computer system to print brochures.

"When they moved their offices to Hollywood, Florida, they took all their executives. I was the only other employee that went with them. By then, I had started singing again with a band called Spectrum in Ohio. I left that behind for the move.

"I loved Florida. I was actually born there, but we moved when I was very young. I worked for Sensormatic for a few years and then moved to work for a different marketing company. That's when I was singing with the show band called Seventh House. We played at the Marco Polo and Mr. T's. I liked marketing, but singing was still my passion.

"I quit eventually because I got po'd at the guy running the band. It was time to go and change my life. I left both jobs and moved to work for two different bond houses, Matthews and Wright, and Hibbard, O'Connor and Weeks.

"I lived in Lauderdale Lakes for over three years, but left after another dumb choice. I was sure I wouldn't get married again until I went home for a visit, so I decided to go. While there, I saw a woman who was my friend in school. Her son, to whom I was attracted back then, came over and I found out he was newly divorced. We hooked up, and I married him and moved back to Ohio again. Big mistake!"

After her last divorce, Joset began living at home with her parents. "While still in Ohio, I went back to singing with a group of three guys in a band called Changes. We wound up working at the Langmoore Country Club [now the Pickwick Country Club] every weekend.

"During the week, we worked at La Cuisina in Massillin, Ohio. When we arrived, there would be lots of cars, but very few people were inside! One night, the two guys who owned the place let us leave our equipment there. The restaurant burned down as a result of arson. Our music, sound system, keyboard—all was destroyed. The FBI contacted us, and we learned that the place was a gambling establishment run by the Mafia.

"I was so unhappy living in Ohio. I missed the sunshine and dreamed about the ocean. I wanted to live where the sun shines all the time, but I felt that I couldn't go home again to Florida because it wouldn't be the same. That left California. I moved with my son and no job, arriving in L.A. in July 1977."

Joset's first California job was as an internship specialist for the California School of Professional Psychology. "That was my major in college, so I felt qualified to help kids get their Masters and find internships. When the job ended, I solved my long commuting problem by moving to Friedman, Rosenthal and Nell as a Junior Accountant. I qualified for that job because I knew bookkeeping from a class in high school."

Mitsui Manufacturer's Bank was her next employer. She ran the New Accounts and CD department. Next, she moved to work for executives at Hospital Affiliates International. While there, she got to know the Hospital Administrator at Encino Hospital. When he offered her a job, she moved one more time.

"Most jobs bored me after about six months. After the hospital, I went to Chuck Easton Construction and prepared their advertising brochures. Their company was most often hired to build wings for hospitals. My role was to meet with the hospital and sell them on using our company.

"Next, I worked for a guy named Jerry, who published books of recipes. He created the books himself and sold them. He also wrote children's books.

"I was still bored, so when an opportunity to get into showbiz appeared, I was thrilled. A friend named Harry Shannon wrote screenplays, and I typed them for him in my spare time. That's how I learned script format."

Her boss at the book company came to her one day and announced, "I guess this is it. I'm moving my offices to Riverside, and I assume you don't want to go. This is your last day."

Joset was furious and got up and left right then. "I received a small severance, but didn't know what I was going to do."

When she first moved to L.A., Joset promised herself, "I don't know how, but one day I will work in the entertainment industry." This was the moment. She bought copies of the Hollywood Reporter and Variety to see if there were jobs she could apply for. While she was looking them over, her phone rang.

"It was a guy I knew from Encino Hospital. He asked what I was doing and then told me that his girlfriend had just left *Hill Street Blues* and the job was available. I interviewed for it and got it. I was in! Just that easy. Helping my friend type scripts gave me a leg up. In life, you seem to be set up for things and then you're prepared when the right thing comes along. That's not just a coincidence.

"I interviewed with Producer Stephen Bochco's assistant. I loved typing, so they showed me their MBI machine, which was used to format scripts. They asked if I could do it. When I said yes, I sort of exaggerated. They sent people for two-week classes to learn the machine. I taught myself in two days because I wanted to keep the job!"

Despite her thrill at being 'in Hollywood,' Joset found that working on *Hill Street* was awful.

"It was a boys' club. I worked incredible hours. When I left, I promised myself I wouldn't put up with that again. Stephen was always nice to me, but the attitude of the other guys was ugly. My son's bike was stolen one day, and Stephen bought him another one. I never forgot that.

"The rest of them did things that today would be on the #Me-Too list for sure. For example, they hired one female writer. They scheduled meetings and didn't tell her. It was horrible."

Joset next worked with writer David Milch, who would later create *Deadwood*.

"I loved him, too. He was crazy in his way—an English professor, but not always a together man. When he was dictating a script to me one day, I interrupted to say, 'I'm sorry. I didn't get that.' He got up and left the room. He did come back and apologize, but it was a bit scary. I came to understand that I had interrupted his train of thought.

"I left *Hill Street* because I was tired of the treatment. I took a job on *Miami Vice* with Dan Pyne, who is such a wonderful guy. I only worked for nice people from then on."

As an expert with script software, Joset was assigned to train several other assistants at various times. "One day, I was assigned to train the script backup on *Miami Vice*. I went really slowly and explained things to her multiple times. I know it's hard to learn something new, so I was patient. I left for half an hour so she could see what she could do. When I returned, I expected to answer her questions, but nothing had been done.

"Oh gosh, did I go too fast? What don't you understand?" I quickly said.

"I can't type," she finally admitted.

"I don't know who hired her, but I told her typing was required to do the job. I offered to find her something else to do, but she didn't want anything else. I told the writers she couldn't do the job. I had no choice.

"Dan and I left the show because he disagreed with Executive Producer Michael Mann. We moved to work with John Mankiewicz on his first scripted reality cop show. Then Dan did a series of shows and feature films, *including Pacific Heights* and another film, *White Sands*, which was followed by *The Hard Way*. He wrote the movie *Doc Hollywood*, which starred Michael J. Fox.

"We spent time working in Santa Fe and then Dan bought a house there. I also love Sante Fe and almost retired there."

Joset worked for Dan for a total of eight years. "When he went to Paramount, I couldn't transfer because I needed the Universal pension. I got a job at *Law and Order* for writer Robert Nathan and Tony Ganz, the president of the Film Division at Wolf Films. When Robert left, I went to work for Reggie Rock Blythewood at *N.Y. Undercover.*

"When I was looking for my next assignment, I asked for information about any openings, but was told there was someone else up for the only job available. Still, I asked if they'd pass my résumé to the new co-executive producer, Kathy McCormick. I didn't hear anything, and then one day, I saw her in the hall."

Joset introduced herself and Kathy said, "Come on over. You're hired."

"She told me later she thought I was the person she'd been told to hire. I really wasn't popular after that! Kathy was great to work for and we're still close friends."

Joset retired from Universal in 2006 and moved to Ohio for six years to be near her grandson. Once again, she found the Ohio weather depressing and is now back in L.A. for the sunshine.

She summarizes her Hollywood career like this: "I liked working for writers, and I thought it was doing a good service to be the best assistant I could be. I made sure they didn't have to worry about stuff getting done. They could just write."

Most importantly for someone like Joset, as a writer's assistant she didn't get bored after six months in the business. "Every day was different in that job. No two days were at all predictable. It was never boring. I lucked out."

--- Interview 8/2018

CHAPTER 14

CHARLES FLOYD JOHNSON: George Lucas Called

Hawaii is my favorite place on the planet, and working with Supervising Producer Charles Johnson in the Hawaii production office of *Magnum P.I.* was like going to summer camp. I first visited Hawaii in 1974, but it completely captivated me again in 1987. My hotel room was on the beach at the base of Diamond Head, with a balcony and a spectacular view of blue waves. I checked in and headed for the office.

The guard at the Honolulu studio gate gave me directions to a bungalow not far from the entrance. There was but a single sound stage in those days. And, of course, all around me was the lush, lush Hawaiian tropical green.

This trip was my first to work with a show on location, and I must say that working long hours in paradise was not a hardship!

Charles led a staff on the hit series with a positive attitude and a willingness to try something new. He let me know he was eager to help me get acclimated so that I could install the PCs approved by the studio. When I arrived to set up equipment and connect the network linking the remote office to the mainland office, I felt welcomed by everyone. They also responded well to the software I installed for them.

His longevity in the business is not surprising to me. Meetings with Charles always included laughter. He made work fun and I value that ability above most others. One of the few African American executives I met during those years, he succeeded because he's a joy to work with and an expert team motivator.

We've stayed in touch over the years. He continued to produce shows for *Magnum* creator and Executive Producer Don Bellisario and is currently credited as an Executive Producer on *NCIS*, one of TV's longest running series.

You couldn't do better than to emulate Charles Johnson's perpetual positive and giving nature while under the immense pressure of creating a TV series episode every week. I was fortunate to learn by observing him early in my career.

Charles' Story

Charles Floyd Johnson was one of those people who had a fascination with the creation of entertainment almost from his beginning.

"By the time I was in the first grade, I loved both TV and film and wanted to learn everything about them. I didn't know how to create TV and didn't know anyone who made the shows, but it looked like something I should do.

"By the fifth and sixth grade, I was going to movies all the time. This was in the 50s, and I went to the Saturday matinees to see serials starring Superman and numerous cowboys. When I was twelve or thirteen, I began seeing movies of all kinds, especially ones with minority actors like Sidney Poitier and Dorothy Dandridge. I don't know where my interest came from, but it kept growing."

An only child, Charles was born in Camden, NJ, but grew up in a small town in Delaware. His mom was a teacher and his dad worked in real estate for the military. By high school, he was involved in everything—the band, the choir and the drama club. "I wasn't always good at it, but I constantly participated in plays at both the high school and Sunday school.

"My early high school years were segregated. When I was fifteen, my parents decided to search for a boarding school where I could learn alongside white students. They didn't want to send me close to home, so I landed in a school on Long Island called Stonybrook College Preparatory. Stonybrook University was just being built then. I was the only African American student. Eventually, there were a couple more. In addition to classes, I did what drama activities were available.

"By college, I was convinced I wanted to be in entertainment in some way. I went to Howard University in DC, after first debating Brown or UPenn. Howard appealed to me because I'd been in an all-white environment until then and wanted a change. My parents were wonderful about it. I thought they'd object since they'd sent me to a white boarding school."

Instead they told him, "If that's where you want to be, we support you."

Charles joined the Drama Club, the Howard Players, which was well-known even then, and acted in plays for the first two of his college years.

His parents didn't want him to major in drama because they felt it would be hard to get a job. Taking their advice, he chose political science and minored in history and education—because of his mom's profession.

After college, he thought about going to the Neighborhood Playhouse, run by Sanford Meisner, creator of the Meisner Acting Technique, but hesitated to make a commitment.

Again, his parents said, "Are you sure? Why don't you go to a graduate school for a solid education first?"

Charles decided they might be right. "I didn't know what my place in entertainment should be, so I went off to law school at Howard. I resisted at first because my dream was to conquer New York."

Instead, Charles agreed to do one semester of grad school before making a final decision. In the end, he finished law school and passed the bar in DC.

Life intervened before he could embark on a career in the law. "I got drafted in the late '60s, was sent to training and got orders to Vietnam. I didn't go because I'd earned a law degree, and the Army needed lawyers to prosecute soldiers going AWOL on the East Coast. I didn't end up doing that, because the assignment was for four years, two more than my initial commitment. I was allowed to go to Fort Dix as a Courts and Boards Officer and run the admin office for special courts-martial. Eventually, I became a defense lawyer because they were so understaffed. I handled more than 300 cases in a year and half and was very good at it, learning a lot about trials and working within the military legal system.

"When I was discharged, I got married to someone I knew in college. She was an art teacher in DC, so I returned there for three years to work for the US Copyright Office, located in the Library of Congress, as an attorney adviser. The job was literally 9 to 5. We took set breaks and lunch hours.

"During a convention, I met one of the justices of the Swedish Supreme Court, who invited me to travel to Stockholm. He told me I could stay in Europe if I got a grant he recommended. I came up with a topic to pursue and did get the grant to work for the Swedish Ministry of Justice. After leaving Stockholm, I was asked to go to a UNESCO conference, which sent me to Paris for two weeks. I applied and was offered a UNESCO job in their Copyright Division, which meant I received my security clearance at the age of 29."

He turned down the job when it was formally offered.

"I began to feel that I wasn't doing what I needed to do. I didn't want to be thirty and not doing what I just knew was right for me. My predictable work schedule in DC allowed me to be involved in plays in my spare time. I signed up for community theater roles and performed in maybe twenty productions in two and a half years. That's when the bug really hit me. I decided—after doing some government films and small TV roles—that I needed to go to New York or California. My marriage lasted only five years, so I became free and unencumbered. I could go to California, and I went."

Charles didn't know anyone in California, but he arrived in 1971, ready to change his life. He'd used some of his time at the Copyright Office to read their copies of Variety and The Hollywood Reporter. From those, he learned about L.A. acting schools and agents. Some of the schools accepted funding from the GI Bill. He felt he had options.

"I was in California for a couple of weeks to see if I liked it. I did, of course. I went to Universal, used the 'Steven Spielberg method' for sneaking onto the lot and visited a couple of stages and ate in the commissary. I immediately decided a studio was where I wanted to work.

"Six months after I arrived, a fledgling actor friend told me her husband was moving to a job with Universal Business Affairs. She set me up for lunch with him and I met his boss, Paul Miller. They first tried to get me into the Mail Room, but I was rejected because they thought I had completed too much education. Eventually, the position was mine as they decided to relent and finally hire me. I'd been in California for almost a year already!

"Three days after I started in the Mail Room, a job opened up in Business Affairs. The EEOC was pushing minority hires at the time, which helped. The job in Business Affairs lasted for three and a half TV seasons. We managed business for sixteen hours of TV. It was crazy. I met Roy Huggins [*The Fugitive*], Jack Laird [*Night Gallery*] and other producers, and was soon attracted to what I learned about the job of production coordinator. In the middle of my fourth season, I got the assignment I craved on one of Roy's shows, the huge hit called *Rockford Files*, starring James Garner.

"I worked on other Roy Huggins shows. While I was still on *Rockford*, Meta Rosenberg, Jim Garner's agent and producer, butted heads with Roy. Jim chose Meta, which meant that everyone on Roy's side was out. An assistant friend of mine asked them to consider me for one of the open positions. The next day, I was an Associate Producer. I was promoted to Co-Producer when David Chase, who would go on to create and produce *The Sopranos*, was approached to work on Rockford. He wanted to be a Co-Producer, so they gave the title to both of us.

"This was in 1976, when procedurals were all the rage. *Rockford* was nominated for an Emmy and won. I won my first Emmy as one of the producers in that season."

Charles didn't know it then, but there would be more TV detectives in his future and he would earn credits on multiple long-running shows. Given an opportunity as part of the EEOC initiative, he never looked back. He stayed on *Rockford* until 1981, learning everything he could about how to make a show.

He left when Garner needed to end the series due to health problems. The studio was not happy about it, but agreed to wrap after five and a half seasons.

By this time, Charles had become valuable to Universal as a proven team member and they wanted to keep him. He remembers, "They put me on the second pilot shot for *Simon and Simon*. It sold and became a long-running hit, but without me. I did a pilot with Telly Savalas that didn't sell, a third pilot that also didn't sell and a TV movie with Lynda Carter during the same period, so I was busy.

"When I was free again, Jim Garner and his agent brought me to Warner Bros. to work on an update of the classic Maverick, to be called *Bret Maverick*.

"Then I was out of work for three months. I didn't get a job on *Cagney and Lacey*, which was too bad and continued to wait for something to pop up.

"One day the phone did ring. It was Don Bellisario asking me to come work on *Magnum, P.I.* Universal was having problems because Tom Selleck wanted Don to be in Hawaii and Don needed to stay in Hollywood. They specifically wanted someone who had worked on *Rockford*, and I was the only *Rockford* producer available. They felt the two shows had a similar tone, so I would have an easier time joining the established crew. And it was Hawaii! Of course I went."

Charles worked on the show from 1983 to 1988. During that time, his title evolved from Producer to Supervising Producer in Hawaii and finally to Co-Executive Producer. The show was nominated for several Emmys, but didn't win. He ran an upbeat production and further honed his abilities to juggle all the moving parts of a TV series. Since they shot in the islands, he also maintained long distance communications with the studio in L.A., as well as with creator Don Bellisario. Doing all of that well was sometimes a delicate task to be sure.

After *Magnum* wrapped, Charles didn't have to look far for his next professional gig. "Tom wanted me and another *Magnum* Producer to run his new production company, TWS Productions. People wanted to be associated with Tom, so we found plenty of work.

"Our first project was a *Rashamon* idea for a series told from multiple perspectives, like in that famous film. Before the series sold, Tom got a call with an offer to work with Burt Reynolds, who wanted to star in a series to shoot in Florida called

BL Stryker. Burt told Universal that he wanted to be associated with Tom's people because he thought we knew how to include humor in a dramatic concept.

"We met with a most charming Burt, who was trying to get his career back on track at the time. We signed on and did the show for two years. Tom and Burt's partnership was not exactly a marriage made in heaven, which resulted in Tom reducing his role in the show while keeping his executive producer title.

"At the end of the second season, Burt got the offer for *Evening Shade* and moved to that show. I had decided not to return anyway, since working with Burt could be problematic. A nice man, but when he got himself in trouble, we had to pull him out of it."

In 1992, Charles was asked to move to one of Don Bellisario's popular series, *Quantum Leap*, because the show was having budget issues. The studio came up with the idea, and he worked with Don again. It was a good match because they complemented each other's styles well.

"Don can be a tough task master, but I've interfaced with him for such a long time that our relationship works," he explains.

"While I was doing *Quantum Leap*, George Lucas called. He wanted me to come to Skywalker Ranch to talk about a project that he couldn't name until I visited. I didn't know why he wanted to meet with me since I didn't really do features. Most curious, I went, of course, and found out he wanted to do *The Tuskegee Airmen* and needed a black producer, writer and director. I was in his office because his personal assistant had researched African-American producers and my name came up. Incredible.

"I signed on as producer, but we didn't shoot the movie until 2008, and it was finally released in 2012 as *Red Tails*. We worked on it for twenty years because we could never get a script that George liked. Plus, the *Star Wars* prequels kept him distracted and delayed our project."

After *Quantum Leap*, Charles signed on, at Universal's request, to get the old team together to reboot *Rockford Files*. The studio ordered two seasons, which turned out to be eight two-hour films over a two-year period.

"In 1996, I again got a call from Don Bellisario and soon joined his series *JAG*. They were having trouble on NBC, which ended up canceling it after one season. CBS picked it up, and they asked me if I could get someone to finish *Rockford* and move to Paramount for *JAG*, an unexpected job that lasted for nine years. Then it spun off into *NCIS* in 2003. At the same time, another Bellisario show called First Monday began, and I did that one, too. *First Monday* is gone, but I'm still here on *NCIS* sixteen years later. We have an expert team that continues to create a popular show."

Charles could do the rest on his laurels thing, but that's not his way. He's not waiting until he can retire to get started on new projects.

"The truth is," he admits, "I am getting tired and feeling the itch to pursue different ideas. I'm developing a play for Broadway, a remake of *The Owl and the Pussycat*. It's not been done in the theater since the 1964 version, with Alan Alda and Diana Sands. We optioned the rights from the author's widow, but we need two big names to commit in order to make the venture a success.

"In 2015, I did a documentary about someone I admire greatly: Congressman John Lewis. The film is called *John Lewis: Get in the Way*. He was wonderful to work with and is, of course, a civil rights legend. I'm now trying to develop a miniseries about him based on the book he wrote called *Walking in the Wind*. The executive who was the development person for George Lucas when we worked together remained my friend, and she and I are big Lewis fans. She brought the book to me with plans for a six- to eight-hour miniseries. It has occurred to me that the Obamas have just made a deal with Netflix and are looking for a project. Hmm.... That would be great.

"I'm also working on a memoir. A friend, Denise Nicholas, who starred in the Room 222 series and is a published writer, teaches a memoir class and I'm attending. She wrote the brilliant *Fresh Water Road* about the civil rights movement and has many secrets to teach me."

And, just because he can, he's teaching a course in Film and TV at Georgia Southern University. "One of my college classmates is a professor there, and I lectured at seminars for him in the past. They asked me to teach a class and, since I wanted to learn about teaching as a possible retirement activity, I agreed. I go to Georgia once a month and teach for two to three hours. The rest of the work is online."

Charles is grateful for the opportunities he's been given. One of the nice guys in Hollywood, he likely paved the way for more than one minority entertainment hopeful to succeed. And now his students are lucky to be learning from him. Creating entertainment is not easy, even if he makes it look so most days. He has his own secrets to reveal about how to thrive in the TV business.

--- Interview 5/2019

CHAPTER 15

SHARON MAHONEY: We're All Just Walking Each Other Home—Ram Dass

Sharon Mahoney killed it in *Shades of Grey*. She entered the room at our auditions, and we were immediately struck by her beauty and warmth. I was part of the casting team and agreed that we wanted her as the female lead in our show.

Not only would I come to know her as just plain nice, she was a serious actress, not overly impressed with either herself or the glamour of Hollywood. Blessed with a gorgeous head of thick, wavy, red hair, she also has vivid green eyes and a broad, welcoming smile that made you want to smile back. The part she read for was described as "a woman with style, class and a presence that made her a match for Dorian Grey." [The show's lead, described as "the most charismatic male pop star in the universe."]

As I got to know her, I realized she had what it took to be a professional actor in Hollywood. By the time she came to *Shades*, she'd succeeded in musical theater in her native Chicago and appeared in multiple commercials. New to Southern California, she hadn't found her break yet.

Sharon was instrumental in setting the tone for a mostly happy, collaborative cast and crew. There were moments of great stress, as with any creative endeavor, but everyone wanted to be there and showed up for rehearsals and performances.

I learned later that most of the cast knew from the beginning that the show had flaws. They were pros, and we were still learning. Most of us were working on our first official theater production. But the actors liked us and they liked the music. In Sharon's case, she sang the show-stealing torch song early in Act 2. It was one of the best moments in the whole experience.

Sharon and I connect every so often and keep each other updated on our lives. She hasn't gotten the big break she deserves yet. I saw her in guest roles in TV series and in a few more commercials over the years. She worked steadily in regional theater. Eventually, she found a great guy and got married. They moved to an L.A.-area town that was not in the middle of the Hollywood action. She took a job in his family's business and settled down.

When I last saw her, she shared that she and her husband were separated. "We mutually agreed it was best to end the marriage, and we figured out how to remain very good friends," she told me.

I learned a lot from Sharon about how to be beautiful, talented and genuinely nice. I'm not close with many actors, but, as one of the first I ever worked with, I would have to say that Sharon spoiled me. She was never a diva—although she played a diva in our show.

I know there are many more talented people in Hollywood than jobs. It's not always the ones who deserve the break that get it. I admire people who can go after it in spite of the odds.

Sharon's Story

As a second grader, Sharon Mahoney was chosen as one of a few kids to perform in the local high school's musical. "I don't remember if I asked to do it, or I was chosen by my teacher, but it started the ball rolling for me and taught me that I loved singing and musicals."

When in high school, she became involved in the choir, talent shows and musicals. She was also a jock, playing basketball during her freshman and sophomore years.

"I decided that I wanted to be more girly and feminine, so in my junior year I dumped the sports and joined the Pom Pom squad [more a dance team than anything]. It had nothing to do with popularity, but everything to do with softening and feeling more feminine and maybe, in the process, going on a date with a boy!"

Sharon planned to go to college with a double major in Voice and Broadcast Journalism.

"Between sophomore and junior year, I auditioned and was hired for Marriott's Great America Theme Park. I did five to six shows a day for the summer. The choreographer did industrial shows and ultimately sent me to St. Louis to be team captain of a performance ensemble on a riverboat on the Mississippi River. I sang and danced in a musical revue-type show and waited tables. I worked in the theme park until I was eighteen and then on the riverboat for an additional year after that."

She graduated high school early so she could continue the theme park shows. "I missed the senior year experience and my graduation and decided not to go college right away. Given the chance, I would redo those years just for the friendships and connections I missed."

Her family objected to her choice to delay higher education. She was a straight-A student, and they felt she was destined for college. Sharon explains it this way: "There were five of us. My sister was the first born; a brainiac and a singer. She chose the intellectual path rather than the artistic and, as the second-born with a similar talent, they thought I'd be just like her. People thought I'd lost my marbles, but I thought if I'm being offered the jobs, I should take them and then go to school. It would be many years later when I finally went to Santa Monica City College for two years."

When she was twenty, Sharon moved back to Chicago and began booking commercials.

"I sort of committed to acting, even though that wasn't the original plan, and I wasn't as trained in acting as I was in voice. I took acting classes, waited tables and did odd jobs—like performing as a dancing 7-Up can."

In acting classes, Sharon learned a new emotional vocabulary. She wanted to feel things deeply and decided to take a range of classes, including Shakespeare, scene study, on-camera techniques and improvisation, at the famed Second City.

"I got financial help from my folks, who didn't understand, but generously chose to back me. They were conflicted: wanting to help me but not wanting to support a 'pie in the sky' attitude. So my dad offered to pay for an undergraduate education, with the stipulation that I study something practical. When I asked him if he would still pay if I studied musical theater, his answer was no.

"His pragmatic, financial, long-range planner personality was so at odds with what I was trying to do that he just couldn't wrap his brain around it, though he REALLY tried. He thought entertainers were people goofing off and playing around, maybe because they didn't have other skills. He thought I was wasting the gifts God gave me.

"But I felt I was following a passion, which was also God-given, so I chose to go against the grain and risk very important relationships to pursue a career in the arts."

Sharon did OK in musical theater and industrial films for Arthur Andersen Training Films, which was part of the big accounting firm. She fostered her interest in being a newscaster/host under the umbrella of the industrial films.

"I loved hosting, and was consistently told that I was a trustworthy person who warmly informed the viewer."

Ironically, she would later audition for a lot of roles as a newscaster and the casting directors often said she seemed so natural they wondered why she didn't pursue a career in that field. At times, she wondered the same!

Sharon left Chicago after an opportunity came for a role on *All My Children*. Her agent was uber-aggressive and wanted to put her on tape. After that, they flew her to New York for a screen test.

"Everything that could go wrong did. I flew out the night before, and an electrical problem at O'Hare meant planes couldn't leave on time. We were #77 in line and one of the last flights out. I arrived in New York at 3 am and found they'd given away my hotel room. I felt in way over my head, but I booked the soap. They sent me home to pack. Before I could move, they decided they didn't want a redhead and canceled the contract. Welcome to showbiz."

Seeing a setback as a crossroads moment, she realized that if she was good enough for the soap, maybe she was good enough for more than Chicago. L.A. offered film and TV at a level that Chicago didn't at the time, and felt maybe a little more doable than the intimidating New York.

"I don't know where I got that feeling. Somehow, I convinced my dad, who was head of Sara Lee and in contact with ad agencies, to get me an interview with a talent agent. He subsidized a two-week trip to meet a couple of agents, and I was off. Dad's willingness to help me with the agent thing was a huge gesture. He was reaching way outside of his comfort zone and I knew it. I was profoundly grateful to him.

"Years after I moved to L.A., my father actually took singing lessons so he could one day sing a duet with his daughter. After one of his lessons, he told me he realized this was really hard work. He acknowledged my talent, work ethic and courage. He confirmed misgivings about my career choice, which is why his decision to help, to ultimately admire and have pride in what I was doing, will always mean more to me than any credit on my résumé.

"By the end of the two weeks in L.A., I attracted enough interest that I knew I should stay and give it a try."

Sharon moved to California in the fall of 1988 at the age of 23. In the mid-90's, she went back to New York for three weeks to audition for musicals on Broadway and hold meetings with her commercial agent.

"The producer feedback was that I was talented with a great look. But I felt like a fish out of water, so I returned to L.A. From that point on, I thought it would be great to work on Broadway if I was a good fit for a project, but my home base would be in L.A., and my focus would be the film and TV world.

"After just a few months in L.A., I quickly realized the consequences of my choices. I was up against others with a built-in network from college or simply a stronger résumé based on the work they did in those formative years. I was an outlier, a lesser-known commodity and, therefore, a riskier hire.

"Success in the film and TV business is a lot about who you know, but the theater scene in L.A. was not so much that way. Yes, it helped if you worked with certain directors or came from a reputable school, but getting hired in theater wasn't as tough here as, say, New York or Chicago. I don't want to blame circumstances I created with the choices that ultimately made it more difficult for me to break in. Based on those choices, I needed to work harder networking, meeting people and selling myself; all things I was not very good at doing.

"L.A. felt like the right environment for me. I liked the weather, the lifestyle, the space it offered, both literally and metaphorically, the ability to learn, struggle and grow with a bit more breathing room than I felt I would have in New York.

"I was booking little jobs and losing out on even more. I got to final calls for almost everything, but would then lose the role. All the while, I kept getting that same feedback: "You're very interesting with a very interesting look." It was nice but really not all that helpful if I couldn't book the gigs. Still, the responses were enough to keep me motivated. I was learning the definition of patience and persistence; paying my dues. I continued to study and audition daily.

"There were so many talented people around me, and I felt I really needed to excel to stand out. I was a good singer, a good actor, a good comedienne, a good improviser but I was not GREAT at any of them, at least not in my opinion. The standards I set for myself carried far more weight in determining whether or not I would book a job. My confidence level turned out to be more important than the opinions of all the producers, directors, agents and managers. 'I'm the unknown who's not remarkable enough' was the story I told myself."

With her track record in commercials, Sharon booked enough to make a modest living. She earned her SAG pension and health insurance and was quite busy at the Redondo Civic Light Opera and the La Mirada Theater.

"I would occasionally book shows and a national commercial at the same time. Often, it was either/or. I couldn't take both jobs. My director for *My Fair Lady* let me go to San Francisco to shoot a commercial, but that was rare. I made more money in the early 90's, but from 1988 to 1998 I stayed pretty busy."

That same time period also presented its share of challenges, especially a manager who made bonehead moves.

"For example, she focused on getting me a role on *Seinfeld*, trying to make a big break happen quickly. I didn't agree, but she continued pursuing what she thought was best, all the while telling me she was submitting me for all kinds of projects ... which she was not. I learned years later that the casting director of Friends liked me and called my manager to offer me a small recurring role on the Teri Hatcher series, *Lois and Clark*. My manager turned it down without ever telling me about the offer.

"She did the same when an offer for a recurring role on *Days of our Lives* came through. I would later learn the degree to which she didn't want me doing roles that were 'too small.'

"The real damage occurred when she actually spoke to these casting directors and declined the offers. She told them I didn't want the work; that I wanted to focus on bigger, more impressive roles. So the rap on me was that I was spoiled and arrogant. This was so not me! I especially loved the idea of being a member of an ensemble cast. Success in this business has a lot do with building momentum and relationships. She put a wrench in that process at a critical juncture."

Sharon eventually fired the manager for being too aggressive, but the damage was done. "In the overall scheme of things, this experience was a tiny blip on the screen, but at the time, it felt like an injustice. I was unaware of what was happening behind the scenes so, from my vantage point, I just thought I wasn't good enough to get the ball rolling.

"By the time I learned all of this, there was nothing I could do to repair the past or un-ring that bell for several casting directors. All I could do was keep moving forward and show who I really was to those that would give me a chance. Those opportunities were becoming fewer and farther between. I kept trying, but my confidence had taken a hit. By 2002 and

2003, I was still auditioning, primarily for commercials, but I wasn't booking."

She was running out of money, with no reward in sight. "I needed to earn a living and create some opportunities where I could find reward and accomplishment. I left acting completely and started with real estate.

"I like being focused, as opposed to multi-tasking, so I focused on real estate in the same way as acting—by taking courses and working with top people. In 2004, my agent said goodbye 'until I could fully commit.' Most of the commercial work consisted of pharmaceutical ads and things I wasn't interested in selling, so it wasn't hard to walk away.

"I sold real estate, got married and then worked with my husband's company as the Marketing Director. A decade went by. In 2012, I left that life, got new head shots and tried to start commercials again. I couldn't even get an agent. My résumé was too old and, more importantly, my heart wasn't in it.

"I believe what's meant to be will be. There's some flexibility within that, but I learned that if I feel like I'm smashing my head into a brick wall, then I need to turn and face a new direction. I need to continue creating, growing and thriving, not just surviving."

Today, Sharon is focused on taking care of her dogs [one with special needs], while she discovers and develops new passions. She's excited for this period of growth and transition.

"I don't know exactly what I'm going to do, but I know one avenue will be a deeper spiritual practice. Back when I was a kid, I remember being in church, in confession, and asking the pastor why Catholics were better than Lutherans, who were better than so and so. I didn't understand why the differences mattered. I was fascinated by what so many religions had in common. I went on to study Buddhism, Judaism, various denominations in Christianity, but never really practiced. Now, I'm coming back to wanting a dedicated and more rigorous practice, putting the theory into action.

"I want the journey to be sacred, and I'm working to make it so. I'm grateful to have the freedom and time to reflect and dig deeper.

"There's a wonderful saying from Ram Dass: 'We're all just walking each other home.' Our commonality, our humanness and this need for connection inspire me.

"A fellow cast member once told me that I had 'a voice he could rest his heart in.' That stunning compliment meant more to me than he'll ever know.

"Having a positive impact like that was the reason I performed. Those generous people who shared such kind words over the years really buoyed me and kept me going, especially when the insecurities would creep in."

Sharon further summarizes what she's learned like this: "So far, it seems life has happened in ten year blocks for me. I've realized that the call to acting is not there any longer. I would like to uplift others and make a positive impact, however large or small, by being of service in some way.

"I admit I don't know where I'm going and that's OK for now. I've learned to ease up on myself and let go of perfectionism—probably one of my greatest achievements."

--- Interview 6/2018

PART IV: A Break From L.A. in Portland, Oregon, and New York City

I had been at Universal for over five years when I realized something I never expected to confront. I maybe wanted a change from L.A.

I still loved the job, but the city itself was too familiar somehow. There weren't enough new experiences to satisfy my thirst for variety. That may sound crazy, but I felt new scenery was what I wanted. It was time to shake up my life again. Several of my friends suddenly moved to Oregon, looking for a change themselves. They encouraged me to consider relocating with them.

After a visit up there, I agreed that new scenery in a location where I had friends was just what I needed. I could even consider starting my own consulting company and taking a break from the Monday to Friday schedule.

I made the move in 1990 amid the interactive media boom in entertainment.

As part of my move to Portland, I took six months off to get acclimated. The break was fantastic, my first ever since I became an adult. When I started to itch to go back to work, I looked for freelance projects as a designer or assignments as project manager for interactive CD-ROMS or websites. I contacted the Oregon Film Office and began meeting people in the entertainment community. Jobs did come to me as a result. Some contracts took me back and forth to L.A. I accepted opportunities to work at Universal, where people knew me best. I guess that means I never truly left!

My first Oregon contract was for a soon-to-be friend and colleague named Steve Gehlen, who called me in for an interview because my résumé included time at the major

124

studios. Steve is a talented web designer, interactive marketing expert, technology guru and banjo player in his own band. He and I would work together on multiple projects during my time in Oregon.

I love his energy and enthusiasm for all things entertainment and creativity. We volunteered to help launch the Portland Creative Conference, a highly successful annual event that is still going today—with Steve as its Chairman. I became a Board member in the early years and looked forward to spending the last weekend in September listening to some of the best creative minds in entertainment, art and new media talk about their work. It was impossible to attend the event and not feel refreshed and energized, ready to explore new creative ideas.

Steve and I collaborated with game designer Kellyn Beeck on projects ranging from CD-ROMs to interactive marketing. Kellyn taught me how games are structured, which I found fascinating even though I don't play them myself very often. I admired his career. He found a way to work on projects he cared about and sometimes made decisions that seemed like setbacks, but which were actually the way forward to what fed his passion. I guess you could say we're both driven by what we intuitively know is right for us.

For example, in approximately 1996, I accepted a contract offer from Peter Siegel that took me to Manhattan, of all places. I'd never wanted to go there, but he was adamant that I "must come." I decided to trust him.

The project was to convert a ground-breaking Compuserve site called Entertainment Drive into a website called eDrive. The founders of the company were young, sharp and committed to their mission. The vision was large and the time to create the site somewhat smaller. We only launched a portion of it on the original schedule, and the debut was successful. Opening night included a star-studded event planned weeks in advance. The highest profile celebrity in attendance was Cindy Crawford, who showed up, smiled, chatted for a few minutes for the photographers and then left. The next morning, we went back to work to finish the site.

One of my assignments at eDrive was to assist in the booth on the red carpet for the premiere of the movie *Hercules* at the Disney Theater in Times Square, which we were to cover live on the Internet. Once was enough for me. I admire the people who work in publicity for Hollywood and the celebrities who participate, but that end of the business is not for me.

After the eDrive contract ended, I stayed in Manhattan for a few months, partnering with Jeffrey King, one of the eDrive co-founders, in a startup venture. We acted as consultants for other startups who needed websites as part of their business.

Unfortunately, none of the companies we joined hit it big. We collaborated with more celebrities. Basketball star Isaiah Thomas was attached to a venture that aimed to deliver online gift certificates. It failed through no fault of his. The lesson I learned from my startup experiences is that the personality and competence of the company's founder determines success or failure. The business may be innovative and timely, but if the person running it can't or won't lead, the project doesn't succeed.

I loved the website design and the variety of clients and topics I encountered while running my business, but hated the need to always be looking for the next gig. The uncertainty of cash flow in our consulting partnership led me to decide to return to a full time job.

Back to Portland I went for a job at a most promising startup called Cenquest, which had funding to create online masters degree classes for the University of Texas. We would shoot original video, create animations, design the course experience and work with professors to incorporate the content required for each subject. I became the Director of Production for the courses, a perfect job for me because it used all my skills from Hollywood production and interactive media. My team included Rosie McGee as Multimeda Producer. She came from a unique background on the team supporting the Grateful Dead and was highly creative herself. She's turned her passion into a retirement career as the Dead's storyteller and historian.

The road to success for this new company was murky. I had another lesson to learn about the insecurity of startups. Once venture capital funding enters the picture, professional company builders show up, and often the initial spark that made the company a great place to work is obliterated. That was my experience at Cenquest. I was laid off when my management style was no longer preferred at the company. It was traumatic, but turmoil was not unexpected as long as I continued working with startups.

I chose another route and, in 2000, accepted a position in Portland at Hollywood Entertainment, working for the Director of their website team—Steve Gehlen! My title was Executive Producer, which I loved. Steve trusted me to help carry his vision for Hollywood's online presence.

Hollywood Entertainment owned the Hollywood Video stores, and the website they bought to serve as the foundations for their site, called Reel.com, was a leader in online movie and TV content. I was in heaven. My team included Content Editor Franny French and writers, graphics designers, programmers, game players and movie reviewers. I even wrote several reviews myself, for films like *Moonstruck* and TV DVDs like *24* and *The West Wing*.

I stayed with Hollywood Video in Portland for four years, until the weather finally got me down and I knew what I needed to do—go back to L.A.

CHAPTER 16

STEVE GEHLEN: I Wanted a Job at Nike That Didn't Exist Yet

Steve Gehlen arranged to meet me after he read a newspaper story about my work in IT for Universal. He reached out shortly after I moved to Portland, Oregon, in 1990. Like me, he's passionate about movies and computers and is immersed in both to this day.

We soon met for our first lunch, talked about our mutual interests and found many similar goals. When a new project was approved at his company, PacificCorp Financial Services, he hired me for the team. Not an entertainment project, but a perfect chance for us to get to know each other better. I learned how wonderful it was to work with him and introduced him to volunteering at the Portland Creative Conference, where we both served on the Board of Directors. Founded by Claymation pioneer Will Vinton, the Conference spotlights the best in creativity in all fields at each year's event. Steve's first assignment was at the registration table in 1991, the Conference's second year.

Steve and I shared a desire to contribute to interactive media projects and worked together on several. We met Kellyn Beeck, who added us to a team assigned to build an interactive CD-ROM about Buddhism. Other joint efforts took advantage of the budding interest in interactive media in Hollywood. Our interactive studio tour design was a bit ahead of its time. It was eventually built, but unfortunately not by us. We pitched an electronic press kit project to Universal for the film *Jurassic Park*. Ultimately, they built it in-house.

We didn't give up. In fact, Steve became determined to create his own position for a company he identified as in need of his interactive media industry knowledge. My admiration for him only increased when he persisted and positioned himself to leap forward in his career. He convinced Nike to hire him in time to produce their Olympics website for the 1996 games.

Meanwhile, I accepted a contract to help launch a new entertainment site in New York and our paths diverged for a time.

Steve called me again when he accepted a job with Hollywood Entertainment, owner of the Hollywood Video chain of stores. His challenge was closing down the Bay Area offices for the movie site Reel.com and moving production of the site and its content to the Hollywood Entertainment Corp offices just outside Portland. He asked for my help to get up and running, because he said he trusted that I could be counted on to manage the details. Of course, I agreed to help.

I eventually became an employee, taking over the team when Steve left. That job gave me the best official opportunity to date to exercise my writing skills. I wrote movie reviews and industry articles, in addition to managing the site's technology and operations.

Today, in addition to serving as the Chairman of the Portland Creative Conference [also known as Cre8con] and being responsible for reviving it after it was dormant during the early 2000's, Steve continues to be influential in the Portland media community. He's figured out how to pursue his passion through a series of interactive entertainment positions while remaining in his favorite city, raising a family and achieving excellence in digital marketing. He currently leads the team that launched the ecommerce digital marketing presence for a major Oregon retail chain.

Steve's Story
Steve Gehlen is always trying to combine both left- and right-brain activities. When he started college, he knew he wanted to make movies. By studying film at the University of Oregon and immersing himself in subjects like Film Theory, Film History, TV, and Radio, he learned the basics and acquired behind-the-scenes knowledge.

He satisfied his right brain with music. "I was in a band in high school and college. We recorded two albums and put them out on cassette. The band, called Runnin' Wild, specialized in bluegrass.

"In my senior year and into college, I also played with a country band called Front Row Revival. I was into the Oak Ridge Boys, who sang fabulous four-part harmonies, which we emulated. There was another band of our peers in high school playing rock music. I came up with the idea to combine the two bands to play country rock. I loved having nine of us playing together on stage at the same time!"

During college, Steve majored in Film Studies and enjoyed learning about L.A. and its position at the center of the film industry. "But I wondered if I would be happy living there. I grew up in a small town and didn't want to be a starving artist in L.A. Independent film wasn't a thing at the time. My sense was that if you majored in film, you either worked in Hollywood or in local TV."

To broaden his choices, Steve took a computer science elective and simply loved it. The big deal for programmers in training in 1982 was called the *Hello World* program. "For me, when the computer printed out those words on the teletype after I submitted punch cards, I was hooked because I could tell a machine what to say."

Soon after, he added Computer Science as a second major. He wrote his first large-scale software application during his fifth year in college, when he focused on the senior-level computer classes.

"The summer before, I got a job writing software for a company in San Francisco, where my brother lived. I wrote code for them, and then, during my school year, as a moonlighter. I started their programming work at midnight, after classes and homework were finished."

He quickly saw the possibilities with technology. "If my career was in computers, I could be more flexible about where I lived and worked and still enjoy film and music as a hobby. When I graduated in 1985, I expected to work for the same company I was already coding for, Imagimedia Technologies. One night, I had a dream in which I walked into their office and all their furniture was gone. I asked the office manager what happened and she said they'd run out of money."

The very next day, they dealt him his first career disappointment in real life when they called to tell him, "We can't hire you full time because we aren't making enough money."

Steve's hopes were dashed for real. "It was devastating. I thought I had a guaranteed job right out of college and all of a sudden it was gone."

His alternate plan was a position where he could introduce microcomputer technology into a company. "I took a job at Norpac Foods as a Microcomputer Manager. My parents worked there, and my teenage summer job was working on the plant floor. I was thankful because at least I was starting an Information Technology career."

One advantage of his choice was that he made good money soon after college. His next opportunity was at PacifiCorp Financial Services, a subsidiary of the large electric utility PacifiCorp. His title was again Microcomputer Manager, but for a larger organization.

"At night and on weekends, I did theater production sound design and directing. One of my mentors started a theater camp for high school students, and I did sound design for the plays and taught there during the summer.

"Around this time I read a book called The Media Lab, by Nicholas Negroponte, head of the MIT Media Lab at the time. The book explained how video and audio media could be combined with digital technology. I recognized that this was the way to my future because I knew both."

Thinking again about moving to L.A., he actually created the entire application package to apply to the USC Film School in 1987. He'd read about George Lucas and Walter Murch and knew it was the place for serious film students. "I earned a high GPA and GREs and several reference letters. I realized I actually might get in! I also realized that, at that time in my life, I wouldn't know how to make the decision if I got accepted. I never mailed it. Classic fear of success."

He did eventually send an application to the MIT Media Lab. He didn't get in.

"I also produced, directed and edited a documentary called *One for the Arts*, about that summer theater camp. It was nominated in 1993 for the Oregon Media Production Association [OMPA] Cascade Award for the Best Documentary created in Oregon. I didn't win, but going to the ceremony as a nominee was really fun and validating.

"To exercise my writing impulses, I collaborated on a screenplay with a friend, David McGinnis. I thought it would be more fun to co-write than try it on my own. To prepare, I read screenwriting books, took workshops and read a lot of screenplays. I didn't take the time to shop the finished product, but I learned the writing process, which proved priceless.

"As a music outlet, I set up a recording studio in my home and invited my old band mates and music teacher to come over once a month to write and record original music. Each December, I mixed the tracks and made cassettes to give to friends and family. It was a perfect creative outlet, with no pressure except to have fun and enjoy the process."

Finally, in 1991, Steve accepted that his best option was to go into digital media to combine his computer-centric day job and creative moonlighting interests. But the technology was still nascent. He wanted to stay in Portland, so he needed to identify who in town would be most likely to get into digital media. There was really only one answer: Nike.

"My goal became getting a job at Nike, the closest thing to a movie studio in Oregon. They shot great commercials and print ads using high-end marketing materials, as well as video loops in retail outlets.

"I wanted a job at Nike that didn't exist yet. I didn't know anyone there. To get noticed I started the Portland Chapter of the Microcomputer Managers Association and recruited someone at Nike IT to join the local Board. We initiated monthly meetings. After a year of this, my Board connection told me that he had a job opening on his team that he wanted to talk to me about.

"He said his team was expanding and needed a microcomputer engineer. I would set standards for hardware and software and manage training.

"I told him that my goal was to work in digital media. He confirmed that there was no job at Nike with that role, but then said that if I helped him get his department started, in six to nine months he would help me get what I wanted. In almost exactly nine months, I presented digital media opportunities for Nike to my boss and throughout the company. I recommended Nike video games, CD-ROMS and online services. During an annual IT event, I received an annual Just Do It award for pioneering thinking in digital innovation.

"In my twelfth presentation, I talked with the Global VP of Marketing. I knew a relative of his, so that got me into his office. We were scheduled for an hour, and he was still asking questions an hour and twenty minutes later. He let me know that in two weeks he was starting a department called New Business Development, with a mission to create new products and services. He invited me to join him, which I did! It was a dream come true."

That was a huge turning point for Steve. He stayed in the role for just over a year and was mentioned in an Ad Age article called *Who's in Charge of New Media at Major Brands?* The team was Steve, two others and the VP to whom they reported. The VP reported directly to the President, which gave them visibility and clout.

"I put together business plans for new products and services which my boss presented to his boss and CEO Phil Knight. The first innovation we proposed was video games because that was where the revenue was. I worked with Athlete Relations and the legal team, as well as our game development partners.

"The initial scheduled New Business pitch meeting from the group was for inflatable basketballs and footballs. The executives loved it. Next was our time to pitch. The response to our video games idea came back: 'Not a good fit.'

"Nike was about real physical activity, not computer games people sat down to play. A subsequent digital media pitch for a CD-Rom sports reference title about Nike athletes, including video clips, was put in the 'Not a fit' category for the same reason as the video games."

Steve needed something truly different. After the next New Business pitch—for sports watches—was approved, he got to work to get his first green light.

"I talked with America Online because I thought the best bet for revenue would be a Nike Forum on their platform. At the time, AOL was signing content deals with influential media properties like the television networks and Disney. Users paid a monthly subscription that was shared with the media partner based on time spent on the forum. I envisioned live sessions with Nike athletes, which wasn't yet being done.

"The final draft business plan got a thumbs up from my boss. The pitch meeting returned another decline. We now had three strikes.

"After eighteen months of trying, my VP admitted that Nike executives were comfortable with new sports equipment, but not digital products. He decided to rename the department as the Nike Equipment Division and told me I needed to find something else to do."

This was mid-1995, and Steve told the New Business VP that if he didn't need to worry about revenue in his next position, he'd like to work on Nike's first website. Other major brands had launched websites, but Nike wasn't there yet. He told the Marketing VP, "I can put together a website and lead a development team for you. I know how to do that." He actually didn't, but he talked the talk very well, and she took him into her department.

"I'll never forget one of our first regular meetings, which was to be about how to get the project funded. I entered her office to find one of my ex-IT guys at her computer. When I asked what he was doing, he said, 'She wants me to uninstall her Netscape web browser.' I was floored. Here I was about to try to talk her into something that she just literally asked to have removed from her computer. I thought my job was over before it started."

He began the meeting by asking who might have extra money in their budget to fund the company's website. Her advice was to talk to the head of Global PR, who had a healthy budget and needed a good way to serve members of the press with information about Nike athletes competing in the 1996 Summer Olympic Games.

That sounded exciting. "I knew that I could help with that goal. I told him that with a site on the World Wide Web we could publish athlete stories, images, and event results for the global press to download and re-publish for themselves. After I made my pitch, the project was funded! I had the green light to produce the first Nike.com because I was in the right place at the right time with a mix of technical and creative skills that was still unique at that moment.

Steve needed to find external expertise to build the site, which was going to be technically complex because he wanted to serve near-real-time results from the Olympic Games. "At that time, I couldn't find one single agency that I felt had both the technical and creative chops to get the job done on the level people would expect of Nike. So, I hired two agencies and managed them as a collaboration."

His success in landing this opportunity was not well received in some quarters, to put it mildly. "I was the guy who got the golden ticket to pioneer Nike's first website, but I wasn't the only person competing for the job. I started to get arrows in my back. Someone was successful with a campaign that labeled me difficult to work with because they wanted my job."

After the Olympic games, Nike still thought of Nike.com as an Olympics site. As a result, Steve couldn't get funding for phase two. "I presented a transitional plan for an ongoing brand that was rejected. The site went dark for awhile. That would be unthinkable now, but it was a different time."

He was asked to give a presentation at the Oregon Multimedia Alliance about how Nike.com was able to provide near-real-time results when IBM's official Olympics website crashed. After he finished, Hugh Macworth handed him a business card. Steve assumed Hugh wanted to sell him something because vendors were always pitching their business to people who worked at Nike. Instead Hugh wanted to talk to Steve about a job opportunity.

"He was the CEO of a startup called Digimarc, which made digital watermark technology to track online usage of copyrighted materials. They already had Adobe as a customer. Soon after, when the politics got really challenging at Nike, my position was eliminated. I called Hugh, who said, 'I can't promise to make you rich, but a startup like this will most likely help to put your newborn son through college.' I went to work at Digimarc as an online web application producer, managing development.

"I left after eighteen months because Hugh had left the company, and it was changing direction and management style. I struggled to fit in. When I left, I had Digimarc stock options, but then the stock market crashed. Eventually, the share value came back enough that I sold them and saved the funds for college for my kids. Hugh's prophecy came true."

From the negative experience at Digimarc, Steve learned that money alone is not the right reason to take a job. "I sat back and thought: what would be the most fun on the web right now, regardless of the financial opportunity? For me, that was to create a website about movies.

"The only company in Portland that would make that possible was Hollywood Entertainment Corporation, owner of the Hollywood Video nationwide chain of stores. I checked them out. They had just hired Jeff Yapp, formerly from 20th Century Fox Home Video, as their new President. I wanted to know what his vision was, so I sent him a letter, introduced myself, and offered to create Hollywood Video's website. He agreed to meet me, and after a few conversations ended up creating a new position for me as leader of the website creation team.

"During the dot.com bubble, Hollywood Entertainment acquired the Reel.com movie website. When the bubble burst in 2000, I took over the content and site operations teams. I remember one Sunday night, I was ready to go to a movie with my wife when Jeff Yapp called."

He asked, "What are you doing right now? Tomorrow we're going to announce that we're laying off most of the staff at Reel.com. We want you to go down to Emeryville, CA, and keep the site going."

Steve asked if he could think about it. "On Monday, I accepted the challenge. Of course, people were prepared to not like me and not cooperate because I represented the company that laid off their co-workers. I did what I do, which is be authentic and collaborative. I pulled it off and people ended up supporting me.

"That same year, I was asked to take over the Portland Creative Conference by Will Vinton, who co-founded the event in 1990, which was super flattering. Will was influential in the creative community in Portland and in Hollywood because he was the founder of Claymation, which he used to produce the highly successful California Raisins commercials. I called Board members to gauge support. I was so busy. Could I even give it the necessary commitment? I eventually decided not to do it because I was spending a lot of time in the Bay area keeping Reel.com alive."

Steve pursued other ideas at Hollywood Entertainment. One involved leveraging extended domain names, including .tv. "Streaming was starting to be talked about and video on demand was new. I registered hollywoodvideo.tv because it seemed to me that more people would stream TV before movies. Basically, I wanted to license a bunch of TV shows and create Hulu or Netflix way before they were started.

"If I'd been more savvy, had more power and believed in myself a bit more, I might have been able to sell these ideas. Part of what still held me back was that I wanted to stay in Portland. I still think it's worth it, but it held me back."

Without warning, he met a different challenge. "I got severe tinnitus. It hit after concerts, was really distracting and became a medical issue, almost debilitating. I developed a depression at one point. I saw doctors, who told me things like 'the medical community only knows 10% of what it needs to know about tinnitus.' I was told that I had the worst type, Category 4.

"I went to the tinnitus clinic at OHSU [Oregon Health Sciences University]. They told me that the goal would be to have it be like a wedding ring. When you first wear it, you notice it. But after a while, you don't even think about it. That's where you have to get with tinnitus.

"I embarked on a personal journey that included meditation and self-talk, biofeedback, and counseling sessions. I came out of it with insights and perspectives that combined Eastern and Western philosophies. I was raised Catholic, and what I learned during this period is that prayer and intentional meditation are the same thing and that spirituality and quantum physics are in complete alignment. I learned that I can affect reality with my thoughts and had been doing it most of my life. That got me past the tinnitus, but gave me so much more.

In the wake of this experience, Steve founded three non-profit organizations. First was the Internet Strategy Forum, which became a national professional organization with Board members from IBM, Intel, Disney, Universal, and VISA. This evolved into a full-time job as the Executive Director of the organization. He also founded Keeping the Arts, which funds youth arts education programs in Oregon. The third group was Oregon Creative Industries, a trade association.

"These successes were followed by a period in his life where he took a break. "My mother-in-law, one of my favorite people, died. Then, my dad had back surgery that didn't go well. He suffered strokes and realized he would have to live his life in a wheelchair. He gave up, stopped eating and melted away. That was hard. He taught me persistence, so it seemed out of character for him to give up on living. I couldn't wrap my head around it and concluded that he must have mentally disconnected after a stroke.

"I needed to recharge, so I quit my volunteer activities. Three years later, in 2015, I re-started my work on the Portland Creative Conference by positioning it as a fundraiser for Keeping the Arts. I just love it now. It's getting better and better. We've given over $165,000 to support youth arts programs throughout the state of Oregon."

For his next salaried position, Steve chose to run Global Digital Commerce and Marketing for Icebreaker Clothing for three and a half years. "They're based in New Zealand, and I visited the headquarters there six times, which was amazing. This was the biggest web team I'd managed, fourteen people supporting a global ecommerce site."

Now he's hiring a new team and building a site from scratch again. "I accepted an offer to be Digital Commerce and Marketing Director for the Coastal Farm and Ranch retail chain in Oregon and Washington.

"Plus, I spend time raising two great kids. Both of them won the Champion of Character Award at the K-8 school they attended. When I was asked to name my greatest accomplishments during the interview for my new job, I easily replied: raising my kids, plus founding the national Internet Strategy Forum and producing the first Nike.com website."

--- Interview 7/2018

CHAPTER 17

KELLYN BEECK: My Interest Is the Story of the Game Rather Than the Technology

As an interactive media freelancer, I accepted contracts with different businesses. To introduce myself to the Portland area after moving there in 1990, I made connections through the Oregon Film Office, where I rightly assumed my experience in Hollywood would get me through intriguing doors. One of my projects involved the design of a new interactive CD-ROM called *The Magic of Tibet*. Kellyn Beeck was on the team.

He was a successful game producer, with multiple published titles to his credit, while I knew very little about how games were designed and built. He taught me both, and showed me what it's like to combine creativity with success because you have faith in yourself.

The *Tibet* project would be a game that shed light on Tibetan religious traditions, comparing them to other major world religions. Our subject matter expert was Robert Thurman, a theology professor at Fordham University in New York. He was the founder of Tibet House and a personal friend of the Dalai Lama—and Uma Thurman's father.

The project gave me the chance to research religions, which was unplanned but fascinating. I learned volumes about the Dalai Lama, the Potala Palace in Tibet and how mandalas were used to express the stories of the faithful. All of this was to be part of the game we were building.

The Magic of Tibet was never completed. The CD-ROM marketplace window was short, and the title never attracted enough money to proceed with production, which was too bad.

On the plus side, it was a high-octane project that exposed me to talented and diverse people, while allowing me to learn and extend my skills in interactive media. Kellyn was a visionary for the game play elements. He was challenging to work with because he knew so much more about gaming than I did. He also happened to be one of the most congenial people I'd ever met.

His track record of successful game design and production included titles like *Defender of the Crown* and *The Seventh Guest* series, both hugely popular in their day. He also believed that work should be fun, something I'd supported for my whole career.

The available space on a CD allowed games, marketing materials and reference titles to be built around collections of knowledge. Access to the data could be achieved via gaming and/or using standard reference tools like search and keyword tagging.

We were enticed by the possibilities for this technology as a new marketing avenue for movies and TV. With my technical knowledge, I understood what it took to build a whole new way of presenting data. Kellyn collaborated with Steve Gehlen and me to create the design for an interactive press kit for the Universal film *Jurassic Park*. Unfortunately, the studios weren't racing to get involved, so I was forced to look elsewhere for paying projects.

Kellyn moved on to work for other game companies and even for Microsoft for a time.

When I worked with James Sheldon on the research for what was to be his autobiography, Kellyn agreed there was substantial potential. The stories James could tell were universally of interest and should be written down. We wrote a book proposal that we pitched to a publisher, but received no response. James eventually published his book himself many years later through an independent publishing house. He was never quite sure anyone would want to read it, but our enthusiasm and the proposal we delivered helped to push him along.

Collaborating with Kellyn was simply great. I'd do it again anytime.

Kellyn's Story

Kellyn Beeck went to college with the idea of making a difference. He wanted to learn to be a journalist; to write and tell important stories.

"I grew up in the Watergate era. My mother was a pianist, my father an engineer and inventor. I saw that the ideas of formulas and stories are not that far apart. A formula tells a story and is the solution to a mystery. That perspective always appealed to me—it's the 'something' that connects computers and games for me."

He explains another angle on his history that drove an interest in coding. "My mother is descended from George Washington's family. His fascination with codes interested me. That's where it started."

When Kellyn graduated from college, he realized he still needed to take computer classes. "I was hooked on the idea of computer gaming. I wanted to stay in school and get a Computer Science masters degree. As soon as I learned Assembly language, I started writing games.

"I was offered a job at an ABC affiliate, a large station in Virginia, and saw an opportunity to actually be a journalist as originally planned. I quickly accepted, quit school and went there to work for almost five years.

"The anchor at my new work home, Jim Kincaid, was a former White House correspondent and Ted Koppel's best friend. It was like getting another graduate degree in storytelling to learn from him because Jim is the best I've ever met.

"Mark Twain is my favorite storyteller, and Jim liked him, too. He ended each newscast with a story. In one of them, he told viewers about what happened when he was injured while covering Vietnam. At the time, he and Ted Koppel were ABC correspondents. Jim was reporting on a battle from a helicopter that was shot down. He survived, but his back was broken. He spent almost a year in the hospital in Hong Kong. Every week, Ted came to visit with a book for him to read, generally from the newsroom library. He came one week without a book. Jim complained that he'd be bored without a book to read. 'You've read every English book we have,' Ted replied.

"He had a photographic memory, so Jim was pretty sure that was accurate. Actually, the only one left was the Encyclopedia Britannica. Ted began bringing him volumes and Jim read the whole thing.

"Years later, that reading is what made him such an asset in the newsroom. He could remember a lot of the content, sometimes verbatim. If you needed something on a deadline, you asked Jim. He was a wonderful mentor for me.

"I was still programming games as a hobby, and sold my first one to the head of R&D at Atari, who was leaving to start his own company. That success gave me the impetus to focus time on digital storytelling.

"My interest has always been in the story more than the technology. I went first to Silicon Valley after my time in Virginia. I wanted to start my own company, which would become Cineplay, and tell stories in the games we sold. San Francisco was too expensive, so I moved to Portland, Oregon. The PBS station there needed help, and I worked for them part time while building the game *Defender of the Crown* in partnership with a friend who knew the California Raisins creator and Portland resident, Will Vinton. Will owned the only computer in a production studio in 1990. No one else had one. He bought his own Mac, since the company wouldn't give him the budget, and used it as a creative tool.

"He eventually bought Cineplay—they were buying everything with their expansion cash flow from the *California Raisins* stop-motion animation success."

While Will's venture into computer games didn't go well, they did hire Kellyn to help build their first computer animation studio. "We basically designed and laid out how the studio could be operational. The plan included computers, software and people. A recipe for starting that business."

Kellyn left before they began using the technology. His next venture was at Trilobyte in Jacksonville, OR. "We finished *The Seventh Guest*, which turned out to be hugely popular. I was essentially a senior producer. My actual title was fancier, but I was really a producer.

"The founders were a programmer and an artist who designed and built the game. At the height of their stardom, I felt like I was producing the Beatles or something. We did a press tour as they started the follow-up title, *The Eleventh Hour*. They were booked at the Wall Street Journal with writer Walt Mossberg, and with the New York Times and Entertainment Weekly. They got a lot of press.

"Microsoft co-founder Paul Allen invested and eventually bought Trilobyte altogether. We went on to create the technology used at Paul's startup Starwave, which became ESPN.com."

One of the Trilobyte partners, Graham Devine, invented a video screening technology based on an obscure formula. "Because of my father's invention successes, I understood how to take new technologies to market and was the engineering manager when we created the publicly available version. This technology was also sold to the Paul Allen Group.

"I felt like I was in the right place at Trilobyte as long as I could exercise my creative instincts. As time went on, however, there was less time for me to focus on creativity.

"I think of my career in terms of projects. I wanted to do *Defender of the Crown*, *Rocket Ranger* and *Centurion* as a game designer. Moving on to animation projects and then *Seventh Guest* and its sequel, *Eleventh Hour*, made sense to me. But managing the Trilobyte stars and their technology inventions didn't quite cut it for the long term.

"I was offered the opportunity to work on the next project in Chris Taylor's *Total Annihilation* series, and I jumped at it. He's an inventor and a unique creative force in gaming. We did several projects over the years, including *Supreme Commander* and the *Dungeon Siege* series. I came on board full time when Chris started his own company, Gas Powered Games.

"That company was also eventually sold. The buyer was a Russian company called War Gaming. Their claims to fame were the games *World of Tanks* and *World of Warships*, both in the virtual world game genre. War gaming is today one of the world's biggest gaming markets.

"I've also worked with Tensen, the Chinese gaming company. Both these assignments gave me insights into new cultures. They do things so differently. Emphasis in their world is on the group, not the individual, like here.

"During that same period, I decided that the time was right to fulfill a promise I'd made long ago to finish grad school and started an online/on-campus degree program at Boston University. It was a tremendous experience that provided an excellent way to get me up to date on technology. When my career began, I was coding assembly language on the platforms of that era. Now it was ancient history. The BU program does a good job of giving students a crucial update.

"It was partially because of this that Microsoft recruited me to help them with the Windows 10 release, which was top secret at the time. Windows 10 and the Xbox were joined at the hip, which is the connection to my gaming résumé. Microsoft was concerned about Xbox security and hackers because the Internet had become a dangerous place in 2010 and 2011. They wanted to hire people who could speak to the developers, which was the key to making the software secure.

"Bill Gates invented the idea of the trustworthy computer. The innovation I was part of was to ensure security for everyone in the software creation process, including developers. By the time I arrived, team training, taught by Adam Shostack, who wrote a book on the topic, was complete. This project may sound like another detour from creative design for me, but one of the reasons it worked is that I enjoyed spending time with the teams, helping them look for security holes. It was interesting detective work. I wrote white papers and invented defensive depth scheme ransomware."

Today, Kellyn is a high-priced consultant helping people who want advice on security architecture or solving security problems. He works for Accenture, one of the major management consulting companies, whose clients are Fortune 100. He's also still in the games business on the side, working with his brother, and still does work for Microsoft on occasion.

"A lot of my career, I worked for myself on multiple projects simultaneously. When I worked on a CD-ROM title called *Magic of Tibet*, I was set to meet Uma Thurman, who signed up to work on the game produced by her father, Robert Thurman, the foremost Tibet expert in the US. The meeting never happened because the game wasn't picked up for development, but not for lack of trying on our part.

"We talked to MGM and got an offer from the people who worked with us on *Defender of the Crown* to make another game, with actor John Heard. We did make that one. It did OK when it was released."

Kellyn moved back to Portland from Seattle a few years ago. "I never really left Portland. When I worked in Seattle, I rented an apartment there and kept my house in Portland. My wife works in a school in Beaverton, Oregon, and we're raising our kids here.

"There is something else that I've become fascinated with recently. My daughter just graduated from college as a laboratory researcher who wants to create a cure for cancer. I think she and others are on the path, but it's not one that was expected. It will focus on the immune system and helping the body to defeat cancer at the cell level, and it's beginning to be shown to work in the laboratory. They can attach something to a protein molecule that goes into the blood stream and attaches to cancer cells.

"The brain research that's happening now is creative and interesting to me. Proteins are most fascinating. Memories are not what we thought, for example. They're proteins. When you remember you're rebuilding the memory using proteins. If you have the right proteins, your memory will be picture perfect! I should be that lucky."

--- Interview 4/2019

CHAPTER 18

JEFFREY KING: I Assumed the Best Title Ever—Chief Strategy Officer

I never wanted to move to New York City, and I'd never heard of Entertainment Drive when the contract to work on their website launch was offered to me.

Peter Siegel was leading the project, and I was eventually convinced to join the team. The deal was nice—it's a truism that the best way to live in super-expensive Manhattan is on someone else's nickel. Since eDrive was paying both a salary and all expenses, I finally said, "OK. I'll come for six months."

Which is how I met Jeffrey King. Although he's clearly intelligent and a fast learner, that's not the first thing most people notice about the eDrive co-founder. I'd never worked with someone so physically magnetic before. He showed me what it's like to be allowed in a room because you just plain look good.

Jeffrey and his business partner welcomed me with the proverbial open arms. I quickly understood that they were quite inexperienced with websites and needed us to do everything to make their launch happen. It was a typically tension-filled countdown to the big launch party. They didn't realize how much work their vision entailed.

I told them that we couldn't launch more than a small portion of the site by their deadline. To their credit, they took my advice and launched a much smaller site with pages that dependably worked and showed the excellence to come. The launch party included lots of press and even an appearance by Cindy Crawford. eDrive HAD to look perfect that night. Jeffrey and I missed most of the event. We were back in his office hand-holding the site to support his partner's very public presentation. It was one of the most anxiety-producing and yet totally fun events in my career. Of course, that's because we pulled it off. Whew!

Jeffrey took on multiple projects after our work at eDrive ended. For one of them, I hired him to join me at Hollywood Entertainment in Portland, where he encouraged them to meet the challenge of Hollywood's digital transition. They didn't listen, and he moved on to work in politics, something I would not have expected, but where he fit right in.

I admire his intelligence, his caring nature and, yes, his charismatic smile. We connect every so often, and it's that wonderful kind of friendship you have with someone where it feels like you just spoke yesterday, even though it may have been years.

Jeffrey's Story
Founding eDrive was not his career vision when Jeffrey King started out. After growing up in St. Louis, he decided to attend Pitzer College, one of L.A.'s Claremont Colleges. Pitzer at the time was an elite liberal arts college for well-off smart kids who didn't apply themselves in high school.

He was influenced there by a professor who impressed upon him the fact that the Japanese would out-compete the US because their educational system was so much better. "The effect on me was a decision that I should learn Japanese and be a powerful international businessman. I wanted to know about international trade as a quick path to wealth and power. I studied Japanese and international business at Pitzer for one semester. It wasn't for me."

After next working in St. Louis for a summer, he realized the Monday-to-Friday grind wasn't for him either. He located a more congenial environment at the University of Wisconsin— a good school and totally different from Pitzer or St. Louis. He decided to go.

On a whim, Jeffrey tried an acting class at his new school and was quickly hooked. "Toward the middle of the intro class, you were required to audition for the advanced class. I, of course, had to do that. On audition day, the room was sterile and the woman in charge was intimidating. I made it through the first sentence and realized I didn't know what came next. Instead, I showed my genuine despair and frustration, just what was required by the scene! Eventually, the words came to me. I don't recall any of it now, but I was invited to join the program and that was that."

One of the best-known Hollywood startup clichés gave Jeffrey his next success. A professor knew a friend who was the dog sitter for an agent and introduced him.

They hit it off and the agent told him, "I'll send you out tomorrow."

"I went to the audition and got a callback. Of course, I decided to move to New York to be one of the gritty actors, not the *Beverly Hills 90210* kind. I took a job as a waiter and failed at it. I got a bunch of callbacks but didn't close on most parts. I did well at the challenge of the initial audition, but the pressure of the callback made me try too hard. They would ask me for 'less.'"

At some point during this process, Jeffrey was introduced to a future mentor, who ran his own agency and would become the initiator of eDrive. They went to dinner and at the end of the meal, he pitched his dining partner on hiring him. "I wanted to learn how he did what he did, what happened on the inside. It was the right connection at the right moment."

Jeffrey's new job required him to work harder than ever in his life. Through his agency, his partner represented actor Ben Vereen and placed publicity on the Compuserve online service. CompuServe was the cheapest way to communicate internationally about Vereen's international bookings.

"You could send emails anywhere in the world using their service. I could communicate by email for pennies." Jeffrey could see that their work would become more global in short order—one of the first technology disruptions coming for businesses everywhere.

"We offered to help CompuServe develop what they'd already built as the first online entertainment area, called *Mr. Showbiz.*

I wrote most of the pitch to expand that brand to launch an entertainment forum with a connection to the industry via the agency's access to influencers. We were the first to digitize press kits, which worked because publishing rights were cleared and the studios were OK with expanded distribution. They also gave us clips from their new movies, and we put them online."

No one then knew how big the online audience would be. On CompuServe, they focused on free stuff. Jeffrey traveled to L.A. to establish studio connections for the fledgling idea. He was thrilled with his first meeting on the Fox lot with their Online Activities Program Manager, whose entire office was full of VHS tapes and stacks of photos. A gold mine for CompuServe.

That trip resulted in a deal for Jeffrey and team to cover the Oscars in 1994 as the first online site to do that. The 'webcast' was a success and contributed to their cachet in the industry.

"Before long, we hit a glitch when we heard arguments that our site wasn't allowed to make money off promotional material in this way. Our response was that we were also promoting the products. We got a savvy agent who became the New York pro who knew most about digital rights and helped us push our position. It was not easy, though. Fox started saying they would put their stuff only on the Delphi service, which they were invested in. Our agent countered that the talent contracts required that press kits could only be used for promotion and that the studio couldn't make money from them."

CompuServe eventually prevailed, but didn't make headway at Disney until the lead-up to the launch of *The Lion King*.

"We saw the rough cut of the film during a pre-Oscars planning trip to L.A. Disney brought in animals, including a giraffe, to the space where the screening was held. Roger Ebert sat right behind me. I also met Nathan Lane. Then Jeffrey Katzenberg walked out on stage, followed by a trainer with a lion.

"The film was great. They sent us a package of trailers and we digitized them all. The story we heard is that it went to company Chairman Jeffrey Katzenberg to approve us using the materials. He gave permission, which was the financial beginning of Entertainment Drive [eDrive]. We acquired the rights to *The Lion King,* published a ground-breaking piece of software called the eDrive Movie Viewer and webcast live coverage of the Oscars, all in 1994."

The eDrive Movie Viewer was an early VCR-style controller for viewing videos in Windows. Originally written to play sexy videos on the computer, eDrive acquired it specifically to distribute the *The Lion King* clips. Again, Jeffrey made a deal. He talked the developer into adding a video start button to the original viewer and the revised result became the eDrive Movie Viewer.

Jeffrey's efforts paid off. "On the day it launched with the *The Lion King* clips, eDrive brought down the CompuServe network. The lesson for me was how to leverage what the developer did. Life sometimes delivers good things in roundabout packages."

Their next online coup came from a connection to All American Television, the syndicator of *Baywatch.* Jeffrey went to their offices and entered the conference room to dead silence.

"They weren't expecting a 24-year-old from CompuServe. I was to speak first, so I walked over to the guy who was obviously in charge and said, 'So, is this the *Baywatch* audition?' He laughed and all was well. We made the deal for series material on our site. He called me 'the Johnny Cash of online' because I wore black."

At the Oscars, eDrive was stashed in the print-press room, since no one really knew what the new guys were about, and another lucky break materialized. "Tom Hanks won that year for *Philadelphia* and gave a speech about his acting teacher and tolerance for the gay community—the one that was the basis for the movie *In & Out.*

"Then he stopped in our room. eDrive users were sending us questions. My partner raised his hand and said there was a kid asking about what to do if your friends make fun of someone who is gay. Hanks stopped and made everyone listen to his answer. It was incredible. We're typing as fast as we could to send it out 'live.' A teacher at the kid's school put it up for the students to see. That was the first prestigious example that our content was not fluff."

By the mid-nineties, eDrive was making money, mostly from the Viewer, and the company was a big deal at CompuServe. In 1995, Jeffrey met Jerry Yang of Yahoo before they went public. He agreed to cover multiple awards shows and created celebrity interviews for the service.

"We interviewed Ed McMahon. I didn't really know of him, but I was ready with my list of questions. A driver took me up into the Hollywood Hills to McMahon's house. On the stairwell were portraits of McMahon and his family done in the style of Andy Warhol."

eDrive was established in its niche, but just a bit too early for the major online tipping point. Jeffrey's experience with Jerry Yang and Yahoo convinced him that their site had to be on the Internet.

"We told CompuServe that if they invested, we would expand onto the Internet, and they did in 1996. AOL was starting its rise at the time. Yahoo went public and it was crazy in the business immediately. CompuServe was protective of their brand and wanted eDrive content to be exclusive to their service, even on the web. Legally, they needed an arms-length relationship with us because their position was that they weren't responsible for the content in their forums. For their investment, CompuServe got a minority share and made money with us."

When the website launched in 1996, eDrive was named one of the Top 100 sites on the Internet by PC Magazine. The site was eventually sold to OneWorld. By then, the team also managed celebrity sites for people like Cindy Crawford, and controlled a large database of valuable content.

In 1997, Jeffrey started a company called Alkemy and focused on business development for startups, including one partially backed by basketball star Isaiah Thomas. Unfortunately, none of the companies Alkemy supported was ultimately successful. He learned the hard way just how important the personality and eccentricities of a startup's founder are.

"It could have happened for us. Some of our eDrive friends did end up making millions."

Jeffrey moved on to other projects. He co-produced a documentary about Cuba and took it to film festivals. Along the way, he spent a lot of money, thinking there would always be more. After all, he was part of the cool young Internet crowd attending trendy conferences. But everything he worked on just missed, mostly because the people involved didn't live up to their billing. It was still early for many internet ideas, so venture money needed to last until early was over, and most companies couldn't make it.

"In the late 90's, I lived the Manhattan life and met people with amazing backgrounds. In 1998, money was still moving into the Internet when I met a broker for a small investment bank. I learned later that it was also on the grayer side, a *Wolf of Wall Street* kind of business. What I saw was that he was making ridiculous money.

"I started feeding him info about the Internet, and from my connections and experiences at conferences. He asked for my thoughts about a company called Real Networks. I joined a conference call with his client and didn't charge for the time. When we talked, the stock was at $11. It went up, split and then went up some more. After the split it was still higher than $11. His client made $2.4 million on the trade! I got lunch."

In spite of this bad experience, Jeffrey decided he could succeed on the money side. Again, his connections worked, and he met a congressman from Cleveland named Edward Feighan, who ran a lucrative roll-up of specialty insurance companies.

"He asked me to introduce him to up-and-coming Internet service companies and paid me a small retainer. We selected nine companies after looking around for two years. There were nice, hip, downtown New York creative shops—and even a NASA-scientist founded data shop."

During this time, Jeffrey assumed what he now calls the best title ever—Chief Strategy Officer. "Edward wrote the business plan and raised the money. He asked me what I wanted for my efforts. I was 29 and told him that my plan was to be a millionaire by the time I turned 30. He said, 'OK.' I should have asked for more! The package included a signing bonus, stock, salary and options. I thought I was set for life.

"Then the Internet bubble burst. The hippest downtown New York shop on our list was owned by three guys who weren't making much money. Edward offered each of them $1 million to sell to him. They kept asking for more. He really wanted to make the deal, but he was out. Without them and with the collapsing industry, the whole deal fell apart for us."

The next three years were dark for Jeffrey. In 2000 and 2001, he spent the rest of his money and became quite depressed.

"I was in Manhattan. The city's ambiance was great for a bit after the pull-together feeling that followed 9/11. Then, it got uglier. In 2003 I left and went to Portland, Oregon, where most of my family was living. The eDrive site development manager had returned to Portland, and she offered me a job at Hollywood Entertainment, the owner of the Hollywood Video stores. I quickly saw the writing on the wall about Netflix and the disappearing video rental business.

"Soon, I'd created a road map for them that recommended increasing digital interaction and migrating customers to a digital experience.

"I told them: 'You need to engage with your customers, move them online and make them repeat visitors.' Ultimately, they chose other options and died with the rest of the video rental businesses."

Following that, Jeffrey got into politics. "A friend of my brother's was Chief of Staff to a member of the City Council in Portland. I loved *The West Wing*, so was happy to work on a few campaigns. I raised money and met some Capitol Hill people, including someone with a policy idea to use institutional investments to drive energy sustainability. I tried to bring everyone together and ended up working on a program to emphasize sustainable investing."

His new passion led him to define a strategy for investing in proactive clean-energy projects. Again, he was a bit early to the market. He learned about the world of state treasurers, who, it turns out, do not do budgets, but mostly run the banking side of state finances—investing state money and borrowing.

The work was similar in many ways to what he'd done in Manhattan in the Internet entertainment world. He came to know people in sustainability and clean energy and helped them develop business opportunities. "The actual political-campaign work was not for me," he explains.

One of the sustainability people connected him to Pacific Crest Securities and their head of New Products. They wanted to create an expert network. "It was a good job for me—assessing people and helping them become part of a money-making venture. They hired me, and we collected 75 experts in the first six months. Very few public securities prioritized clean energy as a major item on their balance sheets. We found the pioneers."

The experts included the chief lobbyist for the Sierra Club. "He wasn't an ideologue. He was passionate and practical, which was important in 2007."

There was also the rise of Barack Obama and a focus on climate change—and cap and trade. The investment community paid attention. Clean energy pros worked with Jeffrey to put them in the expert network, where they could be compensated for their knowledge. "As Obama became more likely to win, people I knew became his advisers. Then the economy collapsed and there was money to drive clean energy trends as part of the financial stimulus package.

"In another 'aha' moment for me, the analyst for clean energy at Pacific Crest wrote a report on the solar industry for investors. He listed the states that implemented good renewable energy standards and which companies sold there. He also listed the states that didn't, and specifically noted states where, even if they had momentum, it wasn't reliable because the political or policy environment wasn't stable. We could pitch states on being on the good list, not the bad list, by helping them attract outside investment to improve their position."

During that empowering 2008 campaign, Jeffrey met a guy who ran the Indiana operation for Obama. "I was invited to help out. The primary lines were long, and the campaign managed the crowd. I was assigned crowd control, a horrible job for me. It meant I was the last person who could go to the Stevie Wonder concert that night, for one thing. We made it at the very last second.

"When Obama came out on stage, it was a pivotal moment. I was sitting next to a group of black church women, who viewed the event as a religious experience. I knew then that I wanted to do what I could for his game-changing campaign.

"To get attention from a campaign, you have to be in an important state or have a lot of money. Oregon, where I currently lived, was not important enough. To get the campaign's attention, we created successful fundraisers in Portland and Seattle. The draw was the network of people that came. We raised $75,000."

Jeffrey's opportunity was to take the group from the fundraiser, keep them together and grow them into a national network of business leaders that could be used to grow business opportunities and for advocacy. "The Obama people bought it. We called it the Clean Economy Network."

He's been working with them since 2009. "Now that the Republicans have taken over in Washington, I don't know what's next. My passion for viable sustainability options is still there; I hope our momentum can find a home and keep going."

More power to you, Jeffrey.

--- Interview 4/2017

CHAPTER 19

ROSIE MCGEE: Turn Off Your Cell Phone and Smoke a Big Doobie

Cenquest was a Portland, Oregon-based venture-funded startup with ambitious goals and a small, talented staff. Rosie McGee was the most helpful, and most colorful, person I met there.

I soon learned where the color came from, and that she was a proverbial fountain of expertise in many areas. She impressed me as the best kind of loyal friend, particularly to the woman founder of Cenquest, who was surrounded by more strait-laced business types.

Rosie was the Office Manager when I was hired to lead the team charged with creating Cenquest online graduate courses. Soon after I started, Rosie became the company's Multimedia Producer, directing the production of rich media for the CDs that augmented the online portions of the courses.

When a layoff and other difficulties forced her departure from Cenquest, she took a unique job working for the concessionaire at Grand Canyon National Park. "It seemed really cool to be paid to live there year round," she explained. I visited her once and was treated to an insider's look at the place where the word 'awesome' really means something.

After seven years at the Canyon, Rosie moved to the San Francisco Bay Area to manage a new museum being built to celebrate the rock music scene of the sixties. And she wrote her memoir. It's titled *Dancing With The Dead—A Photographic Memoir* because Rosie literally danced on stage at Grateful Dead concerts in their iconic, early days. Her ten years of stories are illustrated with 200 of her own photos.

She lived, traveled and worked with the Dead, as their friend and travel agent, frequently with camera in hand. Her book is about that time in her life.

Because interest in the Grateful Dead is higher than ever today—there are over 1.5 million Deadheads—she built a traveling storyteller career in retirement. Her photographs of the time are sought after, and have appeared in numerous books, films, magazines and on TV, including in the recent 4-part Martin Scorsese mini-series. As a trusted historian of the band's early days, she is often invited to speak at academic conferences, at libraries and in university classes.

I can confirm that she's never lost her independent perspective. Today, she lives in Portland, near her two grandchildren, whom she adores. She's sporting teal hair and, when she's not on call for Grateful Dead-related activities, she's busy taking more photographs and creating gorgeous painted rocks.

Rosie encouraged me to write my own memoir at a time when I didn't fully comprehend the idea. Thanks, Rosie.

Rosie's Story
Rosie McGee was born in Paris to French parents. They wanted to emigrate and soon succeeded in coming to the US. She and her 9-year-old sister first saw New York harbor from the deck of the ocean liner Liberté when she was five.

They chose where to live after arriving by flipping a coin to decide between Denver and San Francisco, according to family lore. It wasn't quite that simple. To be an immigrant at the time, you needed a sponsor. Rosie's family was originally sponsored via her father's offer of a job as a UN translator, which allowed them to board the ship bound for America. The job evaporated while the family was en route. A sponsor in Sausalito stepped up, so San Francisco became the city of choice.

Rosie's intelligence and curiosity helped her to graduate high school at sixteen. "I acted in plays in the drama scene in middle school and high school. When I graduated, I attended a summer drama workshop at San Francisco State. At the end of the eight weeks, they gave scholarships to students accepted into the Theater Department. It was known as really good then, and I was thrilled to be able to go there.

"I was naïve, and in college too young. I lasted for only the year of my scholarship.

"I also wanted to move out of my home, but my parents thought I was too young at seventeen. I thought they were boring, while I was adventurous."

Rosie's unconventional nature won out. She dropped out of school, got a job as a typist at a detective agency, and began devoting energies to theater work, biding her time and saving her money so she could move out.

"I would do what I could to get home late, leading a double life. I became a fixture in local theater in North Beach, where I hung out at the Coffee Gallery and was introduced to the music scene. I loved folk music and open-mic nights at the coffee houses.

"My other life allowed me to meet Howard Hesseman—later of *WKRP in Cincinnati*—the bartender at the CG. He also appeared with The Committee, an improv comedy group in North Beach. Through Howard, I met Tom Donahue, a Top 40 radio DJ. Tom later pioneered the underground FM radio scene. He offered me a job that paid enough that I could move out of my parents' house at last. I had just turned nineteen."

Tom also managed a record company called Autumn Records and produced Top 40 rock shows at the Cow Palace, including the Beatles last show at Candlestick Park and the Stones concert in 1964. Rosie worked backstage logistics for him, leaving theater behind for unheard-of access to glorious music.

"I started in theater as an actor, but with really bad stage fright. Behind the scenes action was where my heart felt at home. During my year at SF State, I rotated from job to job for multiple live productions. I ran the lighting console and acted as stage manager. I really am a techie at heart, so I was great at the light board. The curtain goes up and it's magic time. You have to perform in real time and live in the moment. It's fantasy and I still love it."

She was eventually forced to work in some non-music jobs. "Tom fired me because I started smoking weed. Some of the people around him were veterans who could do their jobs while high. I assumed I was like them, but it didn't work out so well for me. I remained friends with him for many years, but I didn't work there after that."

By 1966, Rosie was living with Grateful Dead band member Phil Lesh and initially wasn't working a job.

"After 1967's so-called 'Summer of Love' destroyed Haight-Ashbury, the Dead moved out of the city to Marin County, splitting up for the first time into various households. Phil and I rented a cabin in Fairfax and lived by ourselves—after living with the band for two and a half years. We lived together another couple of years, and then split up. I stayed at the heart of their scene by working as the Dead's travel agent and French interpreter on tours of Europe, and continued to dance onstage."

She took on a job as the Grateful Dead's bookkeeper for a short time and started working part-time in the office for the Youngbloods. She also worked for Alembic, the company providing the Dead's sound system, live recording and guitar modifications. Later, she worked for the Doobie Brothers.

"Once you are in that music business circle and known, you can get openings. I worked at a variety of jobs until 1974, when I met the man I would marry, moved to Taos and came back two years later. We were poverty-stricken and couldn't survive the winters when there was no work. We returned to the Bay Area, where I could at least get a job with one of the bands. Greg was a carpenter and could do handyman things. I again worked for the Dead's travel agency. I was welcomed, but it was much less intense than the early years.

"Greg and I traveled to Bali and Southeast Asia. We were gone for three months and, after we returned, I got pregnant. We hung around Marin and struggled. Then came the period where we lived in a lifeboat in Sausalito. We were eventually evicted from the boat, moved into a school bus and then to my husband's brother's property in the mountains outside of Laytonville, a tiny town way north up Highway 101, in the redwoods. I had an infant, but our property came with no electricity or phone. It snowed in the winter."

Rosie lived there for eighteen months and then came back.

"I bailed from Greg and that untenable mountain environment and moved back to civilization in Santa Rosa with my son. I worked again for Alembic, which had moved there and was building high-end electric guitars and basses. I was finally able to get my own place, and Greg rejoined me. When my son was 4, I left Greg for the second and final time. That was when I went back to the well again and worked as a travel agent for Jefferson Starship. I really didn't want to work for 'straight' companies."

Rosie's history in the music business ended in 1978, after amazing opportunities. On three different occasions, her job was travel agent for rock bands. First, for the agency opened by Bob Weir's girlfriend in 1973, which supported travel for the Dead and others, like Jesse Colin Young and New Riders of the Purple Sage. The agency made it affordable for wives and girlfriends to go on the road. Because it was an 'in-house' agency, commissions paid stayed in the coffers of the band.

"Later, I worked for the Doobie Brothers—first in their manager's office, and then as their travel agent. Next, I was a travel agent for the Jefferson Starship. It kept me in the music scene, where I was very comfortable. All these years later, it's still like an old shoe."

Fast forward to 1991. Greg moved to Eugene, Oregon. Rosie did the previously unthinkable—leaving the music scene in the Bay Area—and followed so their son could be near both parents. She moved to Portland and for a time took more conventional jobs.

"You do what you have to do. We shared custody, more or less, but I had to work and also raise my kid. I worked for high-tech companies as an office manager or in operations and facilities management. I started at Cenquest when it was very new, as the initial employee. It was the first fun I'd found in quite a long time.

"I found the CEO's first office space and did what it took to form the company physically. As the company got bigger, I got more directly involved in the work of creating graduate-level online classes and became the Multimedia Producer. It was rewarding in that it blended my organizational, creative, visual, facilities and writing skills. I hired actors, worked on the lighting and managed the set. We worked under a minimal budget, but we had a great time."

When the company hit hard times, Rosie got laid off and ended up on unemployment. Her son was grown, which meant she could sell her house before the equity was gone and take a $7 an hour job at the Grand Canyon.

"I met a whole new reality, living in a dorm room, for example.

"After seven years, I was hired to be the Ops Manager for a rock 'n' roll museum in California. Instead of building slowly with the money they raised, they hired high-priced architects, designers, consultants. Metallica played at one of their benefits. When they funded an expensive branding retreat weekend with some of the money from the benefit, I knew the end was imminent. I was laid off after three months, along with three quarters of the remaining staff. There were more consultants on retainer than employees on payroll."

Today, Rosie has time to reflect on all that propelled her, and she's content. "Immersion in the music business allowed me to attend lots of concerts. I was lucky to see the top performers of the moment without ever buying tickets. I attended Janis Joplin's performances at the Monterey Pop Festival and the Fillmore East in New York. She was absolutely mesmerizing. I lost playing pool with her once."

Once again, Rosie has slipped on that familiar old shoe and is immersed in work that benefits from the never-ending following of the Grateful Dead. "We had no idea the band would attract such a durable audience. At the beginning, they just wanted to play, have fun and feed their families. There was no need to be famous, but they became more and more well known. Serious money didn't come until much later, long after I left."

No one is more surprised than Rosie that she wrote a book. "I dragged the boxes of my Grateful Dead photos around without a plan for a long time. Eventually, I became aware that my photos were valuable as historical documents. It wasn't until I began organizing the photos while I was living at the Grand Canyon that the idea happened. A friend of mine there, who was a Dead fan, was always asking me to tell stories. I didn't mind, and would sit with him in my kitchen, talking about those long-ago days.

"One day, he said, 'You <u>have</u> to write a book! You owe it to us!'

"So, I began creating a brain dump of stories and images with no editing or plan. I wrote one every couple of weeks and, after awhile, I had a bunch of stories."

Her life with the Dead and her memories of the years from 1964 to 1974 are the subject of the book, *Dancing With The Dead*, published in July 2012.

"As devastating as the failure of the California music museum and the loss of my job there was, I took some of the severance and went to Santa Fe for four months and wrote the book I had in mind. I arrived in the middle of winter. No TV, just me and my computer and my memories."

She conducted research to confirm things like dates and some circumstances. "I wanted to write my memories of how I saw and understood things at that time. Readers should feel like they were there with me. For example, what I remembered as the trigger for leaving Phil Lesh I now know didn't happen until 1970, but I left him in 1969. I was 100% sure of the wrong year. I've never fully cleared that up in my head.

"I tried for six or eight months to get an agent, leveraging intros to three big-time New York agents from friends who were published authors. That guaranteed they would at least read the proposal. They gave me feedback but no deal. I started my own publishing company, got an ISBN number series and a bar code to identify the book.

"My first publication was an e-book for Kindle, Nook and other options. I found the publishing opportunity through a service that required me to create a Word file with processed color photos. I spent four months editing, even paid a professional editor. She helped with the order of stories, too.

"It took another full year to figure out how to publish the print book. I reprocessed all 200 images to optimize for black and white, and released the print version on Amazon in 2013.

"One more year later, a long distance trucker asked me about an audio book. I found a producer and recorded my book in his home studio for Audible.com. It took three exhausting five-hour days to record. But who better to read these stories than me?

"These days, I'm out there in demand as a traveling storyteller. I've come to understand that it's one of my roles as a tribal elder. I tell the stories so the history doesn't get lost."

Rosie knew it was up to her to market the book. She started by doing photo presentations and reading short excerpts. On her own initiative, she scheduled appearances in small cafes, where she would pass out her card with instructions about how to find the book online. The first showcase was in Petaluma, California. Maybe 30 people showed up—26 were her friends.

"At that first one, I dealt with my fear of public speaking. Now I totally embrace and love it. I can be called on spontaneously to get up and talk to people, but it took time to learn to relax.

"I was invited to make my photo presentation at the Orpheum Theater in Flagstaff, as an opening act for a Dead tribute band. Once I published the print edition, I could include book signings and photo sales at my events. Just recently, I did a presentation, signing and photo sale at a local library."

She used social media and the photos to sell the book. The signings promoted licensing of the photos. "It's all about name recognition. I have a Facebook page with nearly 5,000 fans, and I send out a newsletter. I'm on Twitter. I do radio interviews. Half of my business income comes from licensing photos for other people's projects—books, films, magazines. There was a recent 4-hour film produced by Martin Scorsese that includes 28 photos of mine in it. Several times during the San Francisco premiere, one of my photos was the only thing on the screen for a few seconds. That was cool!

"I think the Director, Amir Bar-Lev, did a masterful job of showing the people and events that represented the larger whole. I recommend watching it all at once—all six episodes. Watch three, break for a 20-minute intermission, then watch the rest. Turn off your cell phone and smoke a big doobie. Let it take you there."

Rosie feels that, "It's remarkable that my business generates profit. At least I make my own schedule and that's a joy." Her range of events is increasing. She traveled back East for a couple of shows with Phil Lesh and his band. "That audience is my people."

And, "In August 2018, I'll be there for the second time at the Jerry Garcia Day event held in a park in his childhood neighborhood. They only allow a handful of vendors, and I'm one of them because I'm family.

"East Coast Dead Heads are huge fans who keep asking me to come back. One event is in a library in upstate New York. Another is for the Association for Jewish Philanthropy."

Interest in The Grateful Dead continues to grow beyond Rosie's expectations. There are over 400 tribute bands in the US alone. The music became a genre that is interpreted by different kinds of musicians, from jazz to bluegrass to country.

"You can even go to a pure bluegrass festival and there will be a few Dead tunes in the mix. The lifestyle and community ethos of 'be kind to each other, take care of each other and get high together' will never disappear. I will say 'yes' when asked to join in."

Rosie is increasingly invited to speak at academic conferences. "That's a whole area that's mind-boggling. At first, it was difficult to accept that academics were studying my misspent youth. That I was their source material.

"I was invited to the American Pop Culture Association's big annual conference in Albuquerque. One of their subject tracks is Grateful Dead Studies. I thought it was totally weird. After all, they are dispassionately studying what was my passion in my youth. For three years, I didn't go. Finally, I went for two years in a row. This past year was the 50th anniversary of the Summer of Love and I had to be there."

She's presented at the California Historical Society and at a Northwestern University symposium in San Francisco. "I looked around the room and everyone was wearing corduroy jackets with elbow patches and was there to present papers they would publish to get ahead at their schools. I spoke about what a disaster the Summer of Love turned out to be for the neighborhood. They were fascinated.

"I've met hundreds of new people and, either online or in person, connected with the most enthusiastic fans. A great many are under twenty-five. I tell them stories about when the band stopped in 1995, when Jerry Garcia died, and they're enthralled. They call me things like 'tribal grandmother.' It helps me to accept that there's value in what I do.

"The most common thing they say to me is, 'thank you' for sharing my stories and photos with them. There aren't many opportunities for that kind of validation in life."

--- Interview 7/2018

CHAPTER 20

FRANNY FRENCH:
Everything You Need Is Right Beside You

Franny French is the first full-time writer to work directly for me. I hired her when I was Executive Producer for Hollywood Entertainment's Reel.com website. The only team member who worked exclusively with words, she kept the site alive with reviews and commentary about each week's new movie and TV titles in the Hollywood Video stores. Her strength is her ability to blend creative talent with well-organized management of herself and others.

The team included multiple site builders, user experience experts and graphics designers. Her role was key to attracting visitors to Reel.com, who were there to learn about Hollywood and be lured into the stores to rent videos.

She loves to write and is good at it. After she led successful brainstorming sessions, the team had a list of multiple options for the next set of business and creative stories for future articles. Franny also pitched her own stories. We both enjoyed the freedom to populate the site with intriguing, unique articles about Hollywood.

She is an easy-to-like team member and someone I admire immensely.

Franny's Story
Franny French grew up in a theatrical family. Her mother was an actress; her father a painter. Her parents split up when she was a baby, and her mother raised her as a Christian Scientist.

Since she was seventeen, Franny wanted to be a writer. That year, her favorite class in school was English, of course. Her love of storytelling might have begun when the class read The Stranger by Camus. She related to the main character in particular.

"I found it weird. The author wrote, 'Today, my mother died.' Then he talked about why he doesn't care. I was surprised that you could write about something other than the story and liked that you had to work to understand it. I knew that's what I wanted to do."

Predictably, Franny was an English major in college as the first step to pursuing that dream. She always liked books, but now ideas about herself as a serious intellectual were being validated.

"Luckily, you grow out of that. I feel now that I'm becoming less mature with every decade."

She went to the Borough of Manhattan Community College for a year after high school. Ashamed that she was in a community college, she didn't tell anyone where she was. She transferred to Hunter College in year two, but didn't want to be there either. "Both were necessary for me and not really bad, but I wanted a campus and a serious academic challenge. I earned good grades, so I got into Barnard in 1985, after writing a great college essay. Even though it was one of the most expensive colleges in the area, I didn't think past getting in, and definitely didn't think about how I would pay for it.

"After the first two weeks, they asked for money and said if I couldn't pay, I needed to apply for a scholarship. To get the funding, they would need to see my parents' tax returns, or I had to write something about why I couldn't provide them. At the time, I wasn't talking to my parents, and I didn't think they'd even filed their taxes.

"I wrote the letter. I wasn't comfortable talking about my strange background, but I wrote about it anyway. They next thing I know, I'm called to the financial aid office. The woman I met there was very emotional, telling me my letter was so moving. They gave me a full ride. I don't think it hit me how much I did to help myself. I was mostly embarrassed instead. That's when I learned that there is power in what you write."

Franny did well at Barnard, even though she thought she was in over her head at first. She worked hard and got excellent grades. After graduation, she and her best friend got jobs with the Department of Housing, Preservation and Development, which was responsible for renovating abandoned buildings in New York City for homeless people to live in. It seemed like a great program, but they came to see that no one was actually doing anything. Sometimes, she visited places where there was no floor yet. The lesson: "Hey, don't ever just walk into a building. Always look first."

She invented work for herself to keep busy on the job. Others were older and just skating by. She managed to stay a year.

"My next job was at NYU for eighteen months as a student coordinator in the Creative Writing Program. I met a lot of famous people. Later to be Pulitzer-Prize-winning poet Sharon Olds was my boss. Galway Kinnel was teaching there. E.L. Doctorow became a friend even though he was much older. I met writers at different levels of their fame, including novelist Peter Carey from Australia, who later became a Booker Prize winner. I was so excited to be there with these successful people. They were bitching about how books made into movies are never good. I didn't understand how that could ever be a problem!

"Working hard and being methodical about things is my preferred operating method. I'm a persistent Capricorn and a late bloomer. I liked that the people at NYU were so respectful of me. They wanted to hear what I had to say, even though they were way ahead of me on the path I wanted to travel. I felt wealthy because I was spending time with them."

Franny next moved to Oregon to get her Masters in English at Portland State University [PSU]. "I wanted to do the PhD also, but decided I didn't need that. Instead, I pitched myself as a freelance writer as I entered my early 30's. It was the beginning of the .com boom in the '90s, and I began by writing restaurant and movie reviews for the website CitySearch. I knew someone who was a writer there and at the local newspaper Willamette Week. He wanted me to write at the paper, too. Like everything in most careers, it's all word of mouth.

"Willamette Week paid a dime a word in those days. I wasn't happy with that idea. Didn't Dickens get a nickel a word? But there were only so many writing gigs in town, so I did it.

"My boyfriend, and now ex-husband, worked for Portland Arts and Lectures, where I again hobnobbed with famous people. There were drinks with Garrison Keillor and David Sedaris and conversations with Doris Kearns Goodwin. It was great to meet them, but no friendships took hold."

She loved writing movie reviews because she could attend the movie in the middle of the day and write about it later. "Some of my reviews are actually quite good! I felt kind of important in the club of people who are critics. There's a responsibility that comes with it that I took seriously. To me, a bad review of a restaurant was painful. Writing a snarky bad movie review could be a weird kind of pleasure, but it's definitely more fun to write a good review.

"Citysearch liked my writing submissions and offered me a full-time job. I took it. I liked the people and the startup. I got only $1,000 more than my first job out of college, but there were perks like free haircuts or a stay at an inn I was reviewing. I generally ate for free. It was a fun job in that way."

Then the .com bust followed the boom, and she was laid off. It took a year and a half to find the next job, at Hollywood Entertainment, where Franny started in 2003.

"I worked for the best boss ever there. When she left, it was hard to imagine working for someone else. One example of her approach: The day I started working, I had the flu. I came in to work, and she sent me home. Soon after I arrived back at my house, I fainted into my bathroom window and broke it with my head. Thankfully, the curtain was between the window and my head so there was no glass actually in my head. I went to the hospital instead of spending the day at home.

"At Hollywood Entertainment, I wrote movie reviews for Reel.com, a highly respected movie and TV site. It was an awesome job. The site was wonderful. It was tied to the Hollywood Video stores, but many didn't know that—only in the fine print was the site branded with Hollywood

Entertainment. In my opinion, the company didn't really understand what they had. The owner didn't make ecommerce money from the site, so he left us alone. Thus, Reel.com became a movie content website before it was a marketing site. Our reviews were respected because of where they were published. I hired a pool of freelancers who wrote most of the reviews, but there was time for me to write some myself and post features about topics of interest to our audience.

"After my first boss left, I cycled through six male bosses. They went through every male on the team, but never promoted me. I felt smarter than the guys. I started being vocal about it and made plans to give my notice and move to another job. One of the executives took me into his office and offered me the job to run the team. He said, 'You're going to have to really work hard to prove yourself.' Men were never asked for that. I listened, but turned it down."

Franny worked next in healthcare as a senior editor. It wasn't creative, but it was a good job. "The work gave me my first crack at being a professional editor, and I found I preferred it. I feel like I'm good at it. I like to take someone's piece of work and make it better.

"When I was working in health insurance, I went to lunch one day with a coworker. Turned out, we had a very similar situation in terms of our parentage. Her mother was an artist; her dad was the actor Jan Michael Vincent. What a crazy, small world."

Franny left health care and worked for an events company. "That year almost killed me. I'm hesitant to ever go back to corporate America now. It's just not the right path for me. It's easier in some ways, but it makes me miserable. I hate commuting and being in an office. With freelancing, I can have unconventional hours, but I make less money. Still, it's OK.

"The more life I live, I realize being wealthy is an emotional liability that doesn't bring happiness. I like my life and don't want to get away from what I have: quiet, pretty, positive. It's good to have just what you need. I try not to worry about anything. It helps that I sometimes get life-affirming messages from my head. At that crazy events job, the message was 'relax.' I held onto it. I sat on a park bench one day and a plaque on the ground next to it read, "Relax." Now the message I get is, 'Everything you need is right beside you.' And it is, quite literally, a lot of the time.

"Most of the writing I do today is fiction, and recently I began writing another novel. I've finished three so far, including a literary crime fiction novel with my sister called, *The Time It Takes to Drown*. I never thought I'd write a mystery, but the story combines several threads and is an overall good tale.

"Sometimes now when I write, I have an experience where things are just happening and I don't know where they come from as I put words on screen. It's like I'm reading the story as I write it. I generally know where a book is going, but I don't always know how it's going to get there.

"For a story where the main character attempts suicide by drowning, the scene sort of wrote itself. The action is so far outside my realm of experience that I looked up how a change of heart can happen in the case of attempted suicide, because the character saves herself at the final moment in the story. But, wait, there's an undertow, and she almost drowns because she can't get out. But then she does. The story retreats two months and goes on from there. I didn't know when I started writing that there would be a suicide attempt in this story at all.

"Another time, I wrote a scene where there's a knock on the door and someone's there, but I wasn't sure who was there as I started writing."

After she rewrote the beginning of the suicide story, Franny gave the revision to her writing group for feedback. "They loved it. They said they wished they didn't know what they already knew about the story. It feels vulnerable to write like that."

The Time It Takes to Drown incorporates many things that happened to Franny and her sister, who's been a nonfiction writer for a long time. "I helped her learn to write scenes and change fact to fiction. It took time for her to see that what really happened doesn't need to be relevant.

"I'd never collaborated like that before. We worked via Skype and phone, and each wrote different chapters. We did it in a year and a half, which is very fast for me.

"I didn't know it would take so long into my life to get published. My expectation of early success came because Norman Mailer was friends with my family. The adults usually got drunk when he was around. He was attracted to my godmother, who went on a date with him when I was twenty and living in New York City. He was married at the time. She asked if they could use my apartment for the afternoon. I agreed.

"Since I knew I wanted to be a writer, I asked my godmother if I could meet him before the date, and then I would leave them alone. I had seen him before, but not since I was eight. He was still the most famous writer I knew. He came and huffed and puffed up to the fifth floor walk-up that was my little apartment. 'So, you want to be a writer. How old are you?' he said. 'Twenty,' I replied. 'I hit it big at twenty two,' he shot back. 'You have two more years.'"

She left the two of them in her apartment for their only date.

One of Franny's goals in life is to be friends with famous people. "My fantasy is that Reese Witherspoon's company loves me and my book. We'd hang out. I'd love to be friends with Ann Patchett, who has a bookstore in Nashville now. My sister and I wrote a mystery novel and maybe it will be in her store. In my fantasy, Ann says, 'I love you guys. Come on over to hang out and have dinner with my husband and me.' I'm in my perfect space.

"Literature saved me from having no passion. I'm still trying to write the kind of books I want to read. My mission is to be a famous writer who gives voice to the me at seventeen. If I'd known I would get to fifty-five and still be trying to sell novels, I wouldn't have believed it could work out that way.

"I know now that part of getting older is the realization that life never works out like you thought it would. In my case, it's gotten better, and writing is my joy. I'm very much compelled to write these days."

--- Interview 4/2019

PART V: Dream Job at 20th Century Fox—Again

I began looking for a way to move back to L.A. in 2001. The job at Hollywood Video in Portland was fun, but I realized that the weather in Oregon was not for me. Six months of every year it's cloudy and damp, which made me crave the California sun.

With my connections, I booked interviews and started the process to confirm a job at Warner Bros. that I thought would be perfect. Unfortunately, the horrific attacks on 9/11 changed everything and affected me in unexpected ways. The studios retrenched and were no longer interested in moving people to L.A. for open positions. My possible new job was given to someone internal, and other interviews dried up. It would take three more years for me to find a way back to Southern California.

The opportunity came via an offer to be a Disney.com Executive Producer. Working for Disney wasn't on my list because friends who'd worked there told me that it might not always be sugar and spice on the inside. But, the people who wanted to hire me were lovely. They seemed excited that I could bring my collaborative, people-focused management style to their team, and they paid to move me from Portland. I found a townhouse to buy and began working at the Disney.com offices in North Hollywood. We weren't on the Disney lot, but I was treated to a comprehensive tour, including the offices of the Imagineering group. Those folks are among the most innovative in the world. What they do is incredible.

I lasted six months at Disney. It turned out they really didn't want my management style, which was more disruptive than they expected. I tried and they tried, but it just wasn't working. To their credit, they agreed it was as much their fault as mine and gave me three months paid to find a new job inside Disney or elsewhere.

Three months wasn't long enough to find my best fit. I spent an additional two months looking, until Tom Tralongo, a friend of many years, made me an offer to go to Fox.

He said, "I don't have a management opening, but you can come here as a Business Analyst. I know you'll be a manager before long."

I took his offer and started working as an analyst for the application that tracked international distribution licensing deals, learning from IT analysts Sheila Liao and Ashish Bhatt and business experts Mark Morrison and Scott Gregg about a whole new arm of the TV business. I found myself more engaged than I'd expected because it wasn't production. Again, the people were great and I fit right in. Tom's easy-going management style made for a freeing transition after the mismatch at Disney.

I was assigned to Alison Lyons' team next. An excellent motivator, she was responsible for the online digital sales and marketing initiatives that eventually would become the first features of FoxFast.

The FoxFast project was formally born when International Distribution President Mark Kaner decided to build a best-of-breed digital distribution system. Two of his executives, John Koscheka, SVP of Distribution Services, and Mike Bessolo, Marketing SVP, agreed to go bold with the digital file creation, logistical and communications vision for the new website. Marketing expert Justin Primo, whose job it is to assist licensees with efforts to promote Fox titles on their services, taught me how marketing was done in international locations.

The project would turn out to be perhaps the most challenging of my career. It prioritized three main goals: (1) create a digital video viewing network accessible from anywhere in the world, (2) provide self-service and on-demand features as a selling point to attract broadcast customers to Fox titles, and (3) innovate an updated marketing platform to spread the word about popular TV shows and movies in Fox's deep library.

The first goal for the new site was international reach and 24/7 availability. Internet services were just beginning to surface in some parts of the world, and we pushed communications capabilities that gave Fox customers access that other studios hadn't yet decided to match.

Five FoxFast IT team members from our consulting contract with PB Systems made my life easier. All were trained in computer engineering. They were and are extremely capable. Ramesh Gurram, Umesh Mandadapu, Ashish Bhatt, and Nag Mantena were crucial to the success of the technical design and development from the very beginning. Koundinya Gadamsetty's specialty is testing. His QA [quality assurance] excellence made it possible for me to trust that what we launched would work. When he said, "Go," we went.

Our team enthusiastically collaborated with the best technical minds in the studio, people who were defining ways to deliver digital video in the different formats required in various parts of the world.

As the site grew, we added team members, including business analysts Larry Owens and Ken Mihara, who joined us a few years before I left.

It was a blessed environment. After my boss, Alison Lyons, left the project to move to her next position, I was put in charge of one of the best teams I've ever managed. To a person, they valued excellence, trust and a focus on customer service.

As the first phase of the project, the offshore team in India built a central database to support two sites: FoxPress, which was already up and running, and which became a proof-of-concept for the initial vision and the FoxNow digital promo viewing app. Each was a front-end portal, or window, into the data in the database, which was named DAPR, or the Digital Asset Product Repository. DAPR would evolve to support several more services as the site grew.

FoxPilots, was launched in 2007. It allowed licensees and potential licensees to view pilot episodes of upcoming Fox series as part of their decision-making process for acquiring new fall shows each spring. The site was available on demand, 24/7, regardless of where the customer was in the world.

Next, we created the Fox Screening Room to provide the same service for episodes and films available from the Fox library.

Technology for storing the videos, securing access for customers and providing on-demand viewing gave Fox a market advantage because no one had demonstrated using digital video as a commodity in that way. All the studios were talking about it. I loved being part of it.

Perhaps the biggest innovation we tackled was digital distribution of full-length broadcast quality program videos. Not only are these files massive in size, each must be available in multiple formats because customers can use different technologies on their internal systems. After acquiring the huge storage capacity needed, we created what is arguably still the most customer-friendly delivery network for broadcast quality files.

There were some who doubted the service could hold up under the stress of customer demands. I won't say there weren't issues, but basically it worked. And worked securely, which was of utmost importance. The content we shipped via Internet connections was the company's intellectual property. Its protection is a must.

All the studios now provide a digital supply-chain service, thereby eliminating the need to ship titles around the world on tape or DVD. Savings in both delivery time and cost justified the launch and maintenance investments.

I retired from Fox in May 2016, and was replaced by Nag Mantena, who was my lieutenant for the last several years of my tenure. He did a better job than I did, and that's a wonderful thing. In fact, he's been promoted to Technology VP West Coast for new Fox, the company created to house the remaining entities when Disney purchased large sections of the former 20th Century Fox. Ken Mihara is the current FoxFast team leader, and he's proven himself to be a wonderful leadership example.

The rest of the team has remained together now that the Disney purchase is complete. FoxFast continues to provide first class customer service and digital innovation. Why wouldn't Disney absorb a successful team and the people who keep it that way?

For me, working on FoxFast was fun, fulfilling and fantastic. I wasn't working in TV production, but I was in the room when the design and launch of the first high-quality digital video was made available to an international customer base. I can't emphasize enough how great it is to be not just supported but encouraged by management to break ground every time we conceived a new service. I collaborated with the best business and technical minds and led a team that achieved great things. What a perfect preface to retirement.

CHAPTER 21

TOM TRALONGO: I'd Rather Be on the Front of the Wave Than the Back

W hen he hired me as a Senior Analyst at 20th Century Fox in 2005, Tom Tralongo saved my career.

We'd known each other for a long time—since we both worked at the studios in a previous life in the early 80s—so it was natural that I would contact him to let him know I was looking for something different.

Tom had been rehired at Fox as a director in the International TV Distribution IT group. Several teams reported to him, but there were no manager openings. Instead, he offered me an in as an analyst. As he talked about the environment and culture at Fox, it sounded like heaven to me after the stress of Disney.com.

Plus, I knew Tom and knew that he and I would work well together. The people around you hold the key to satisfaction in any job, and Tom's style was very much to my liking. I met a few more of the people on his team and decided to take the offer.

It was one of the best decisions I ever made. After working for a time as an analyst, I was promoted to lead the team assigned to build the new FoxFast website.

Tom put me in a position to enjoy one of the most productive times in my career. He supported me and ran interference when executives in other areas tried to make our life harder. He encouraged my style of team management, which is based on nurturing people who want to come to work and who love their work. He gave us credit for what we built. I am eternally grateful for the opportunity to work for him.

We are both retired now and remain involved and connected to the entertainment industry. We've moved on to the freedom to construct new lives. Lucky to live through the digital startup era in TV, we're looking forward to what's next.

Tom's Story
Tom Tralongo's path to a future after childhood wasn't exactly clear. Nobody in his family had gone to college. He says he was an average high school student but graduated in due course. He initially expected to work in newspapers, until he found out what that paid. He switched to a psychology major—until he found out he'd need a PhD to earn a living.

"I took my first job at GE as a morning and evening janitor. That got me a day job in the mail room while at night I went to community college. More importantly, it provided free access to what companies paid money for in acquiring computer power. I learned to program in Fortran and COBOL."

He's never forgotten the initial attraction to computing. One of his passions today is old computers. He has Fortran compilers and is searching for access to a PL1 compiler.

"At the time, there was a woman who oversaw one of the elite tech groups at GE who almost daily asked me where I was going to study next. I'm not sure why, even to this day, but I told her I wanted to attend UCLA."

He applied and was accepted. Once there, he used the mediocre [his word] computer skills he'd learned at GE to run all the stats for his professors. Through a series of almost circumstantial personal relationships, he connected with a small company in Santa Monica and was hired as the programmer and operator, working with a smart kid who taught him more stuff, including the DYL-260 reporting system and the IBM DOS Job Control Language [JCL] and operating system.

Tom didn't transition to entertainment because of a passion for it. He simply wanted more opportunity and to work in a larger corporate environment, even though he'd taken no business classes in college.

"I responded to an ad for help at Fox, which coincidentally needed DYL-260 and JCL experience. It turned out that my boss, Beverly Stone, recently lost her boss, who had been killed in a robber. She needed someone to help her in the technical area and hired me for my first studio position. My Apple experience on a computer at home was useful when they needed someone to help them transition from Apples to the new Microsoft PC.

"I didn't understand the studios at all when I started. My only exposure to the film business came from my high school journalism days when we reviewed little motion pictures, not the blockbusters. Movies like Between the Lines with Jeff Goldblum. And anything by Woody Allen. The ethos, if not the vibe, of entertainment was part of my life, but I didn't know what a studio was until I'd worked there for a year."

He spent twenty-three years at Fox.

"I enjoyed a charmed career. When you are in computer support, you're asked to help with all kinds of problems and end up learning every part of the business. The question is always: Is the problem the program, the person or the hardware?

"One day, one of Fox's overseas financial experts called about a report. He said all the accounting was wrong and asked me to run new reports on different databases to help him figure it out. I wrote a first report that took the whole machine down, but I eventually identified the accounting problem. I learned how to properly analyze a solution that way, with wonderful mentors in my corner who steered me in ever more productive directions."

As he took on more roles, Tom learned more about the business. After one new assignment, he found something he didn't want to do—support a group called Corporate Fixed Assets.

"I didn't want to know anything about it, but I had to learn it. I was lucky in that I never did just one thing. It was more fun learning about grips and gaffers on a production when I went to work in the Fox Facilities group. I developed relationships in the Sound and Set Lighting departments and built the first PC network at the studio for the International Theatrical group."

He left Fox the first time when he acknowledged that he was a Psych major trying to make it in computers and wanted to get more education about his new business focus.

"My research told me that Cal State Northridge allowed master's degree work credits for two years of employment. I signed up.

"I couldn't live on the college wages, so I went back to work after a few months. The second time I left, I started my own business. I'd just built the Fox International Theatrical System, which gave me the opportunity to offer consulting services. I eventually landed at Warner Bros., where I consulted for them, starting in 1990. I also provided expertise for the development of several non-entertainment systems for other companies.

Then a Warner executive reached out and asked him, "Do you want to consider doing a job in Television?"

As part of the merger with Lorimar Telepictures, many of the Warner Bros. people had been fired. Tom felt ready to go back to a big company, but his background was in Theatrical, not TV. He decided the offer was telling him it was time to learn more.

"I was at Warner reporting to TV, not IT, for the next five years. IT hated my role because it was in the business unit, but that structure allowed me to have access to information and conversations that would never have occurred had I been in IT, so I loved it.

"They flew me all over the world, and I learned about international sales from the sales execs who lived it. I also read contracts. The Warner Bros. channel HBO was fighting with everyone at the time, and I learned the legal intricacies of how it worked out. The people I met were the best. For me, taking a back seat on the technical side of the business was perfect. TV was more fun and complex in the legal world than Theatrical.

"I connected with the first Dreamworks CIO, Lynn Jacobs, and accepted her offer to join the company after she proposed a salary I could take. She'd worked at Universal and was known at Stephen Spielberg's Amblin Productions. They wanted a woman CIO at Dreamworks and hired her. She was great at analytical thought. If all she had to do was critique a project, she would have been great and in her element."

When he joined Dreamworks, the company had a Disney mentality: people there believed that everyone should want to work with them. His title encompassed all things International—Theatrical, Home Entertainment [HE] and TV. He pretended to know HE even though he hadn't really worked on projects in that business yet.

"I was there four years. I worked for Hal Richardson, who was the counterpart to Fox International TV Distribution President Mark Kaner. In my opinion, Hal is the only Kaner contemporary, both as a human being and as someone who knows his shit about Television. Later, when I wanted to build bigger systems and Dreamworks didn't have enough product to fund them, Hal hooked me up with Michael Grindon and Peter Iacono at Sony. I interviewed and took a job consulting for Sony for a year.

"I'd actually had Sony experience when they were in Burbank back in the days of Columbia/Tri-Star. When I arrived at Sony this time, people I knew from a decade earlier were still there.

"Then, I remarried, gained two stepchildren and needed a job with insurance. I called Fox's Peter Levinsohn, a longtime friend. Multiple people, including Mark Kaner, Marion Edwards, Mark Rosenbaum and Greg Yen, all interviewed me at Fox. I got the gig.

"I did know my TV stuff by then. I could tell IT I knew all about the technology infrastructure. PPV [Pay Per View] was just starting. New pay deals were being made, and someone had to represent them in IT. I was there at the right time, knowing the technologies. I also knew how to read the contracts with countries in Europe. At that point, the leverage was with the distributors.

"I helped my fellow IT people to 'get' what we were doing and understand that the technology supports the business. You can know database design and how to build systems that work, but you MUST know the business you're working in. For a long time, there was nothing new in theatrical until digital projection. Now every eighteen months, or sometimes less, some new tech alters TV. We were there to implement it for a time—PPV, VOD, Internet, all of it."

Tom led the team that launched FoxFast. He is proud of the fact that: "The FoxFast site changed that business forever.

"In 2014, I decided to retire. I was tired and told my bosses in the middle of 2013 that I was thinking about it. I didn't want to drop the FoxFast group and needed to plan a transition. I also didn't want to continue to fight the political battles coming in IT. I knew there was not another big project coming for Mark Kaner's group and realized an opportunity to stop working and retire early as a result.

"My dad asked me to do better than he did, and I was grateful to retire before he did. I knew that next I wanted to fight for something, not defend something that already existed."

Since his retirement, Tom's career is a variation of what he'd hoped would happen. "About a month before we started the end paperwork at Fox, I got an email from a recruiter at Sony. My counterpart there was mercurial, but she really knows TV. The email said they were interested and two VP positions were open. I didn't want that, though. I really wanted to run the place. Plus, I wasn't out of Fox yet. I ended up with a consulting contract at Sony and later met the people who got the jobs I passed on.

"I'm grateful for the wonderful teams at Dreamworks and Fox. They deserve the credit. They did the building, and I gave them room to do it. I made a good living, but that wasn't what was ultimately satisfying.

"Even so, post-retirement is not what I thought. Life transitions have a way of springing up unforeseen. Until my stepdaughter is out of college, I may keep consulting. Besides, I like to work. Even if I'm not sharp like I used to be perhaps.

"I'm aware that entertainment will not exist like it was any longer. We'll be dinosaurs soon. I'd rather be on the front of the wave than the back. On to the next thing even if it turns out to not be quite as rewarding as what we did before."

--- Interview 1/2019

CHAPTER 22

SHEILA LIAO: A Career Forged by Amazing Mentors

Sheila Liao became my friend for life on the day I experienced a strange feeling in the middle of a Fox staff meeting. She happened to be sitting next to me and could see that something was wrong. I didn't know what it was. I just knew my heart was beating fast, and I felt light-headed. Given my family history of heart issues, I thought, "Uh oh. Here it comes."

I left the meeting to try to walk it off. After a few minutes, Sheila followed me into the hallway. I was sitting on a chair trying to tell myself everything was OK. She calmly said, "Do you want me to call the paramedics?"

Something made me say, "Yes, please."

Help soon arrived. They told me my heart rate was seriously elevated and that they wanted to transport me to the hospital. For some reason, I wasn't scared exactly. I just said, "OK."

By the time I was in the ambulance, I felt much better. Sheila offered to ride with me to the hospital, and I was grateful to have her there.

Here is where I tell you that, I swear, on the way to the emergency room, my ambulance had an accident! They apparently clipped the side mirror of a car as they were turning a corner. The owner of the car was less than happy and insisted that they all stop to file a report.

One of the EMT's told me they called for another ambulance to take me the rest of the way. The entire drive was probably less than 2 miles and it took us over an hour!

Sheila kept me calm until we arrived in the Emergency Room. I was seen quickly and told they wanted to monitor me. It then took several hours of multiple tests and doctor visits before they recommended I stay overnight for more observation. Sheila called home and told them she would be late. She stayed until I was moved to my room for the night. I'll never forget how much easier the whole experience was with someone to talk to who was on my side.

Long story short-ish, I left the hospital the next morning. There had been no heart attack—just a panic attack they said, although I couldn't imagine what I was panicked about. I did a few more outpatient tests, but whatever it was was gone and has never returned.

I met Sheila when she was a business analyst on my initial team at Fox during my second stint there from 2005 to 2016. She was working on a different project for the team, so when we had direct interaction in meetings or planning sessions, I learned that she's cheerful and positive, a wonderful team player.

After my heart scare, we began having periodic lunches. We discussed her family and her desire to move up in the ranks of Fox IT. We shared advice: for me, about retirement and issues with my work; for her, the unfortunate news that her marriage was falling apart.

We're friends to this day and will stay connected if I have anything to say about it.

Sheila's Story
Sheila Liao grew up in the Philippines and left for the US when she was fifteen. She has fond memories of "walking in the rain. I do miss the warm rain, which L.A. doesn't have."

She graduated pre-med from UCLA. While there, she worked in the fundraising office for the UCLA Hospital. She wanted to be close to the medical world, so she stuck with it for the rest of her college experience, eventually accepting that she was tired of medicine, and tired of being poor.

She felt greatly relieved to conclude, "I'm not going to pursue this. It's just too exhausting."

When she graduated, she moved to New York, a place she'd always wanted to live. She found the city harder than she'd expected, but stayed for almost two years.

"I was ready to pursue a graduate degree back in L.A. The UCLA fundraising office offered me a position, so I returned to philanthropy. While I considered whether to take the placement test for the MBA, the group underwent a massive reorganization. Michael Ovitz, the super-agent, was trying to be a benefactor for the office and brought in a woman who was not philanthropic, in my opinion, but rather a political campaign strategist with a mission to re-do everything.

"My new boss laid off people and changed the tone to one I considered to be negative. She pitted me against another admin person to determine which of us should be in the new Director position. It was horrible.

"When I was recruited by Gina Brogi, who ran the Finance Department in Fox Television Distribution, I responded positively. She was looking for someone to manage her Access databases. I knew Access because I'd created the database that managed donors for the UCLA annual donor fund."

Sheila started work at Fox in 1999. "I wasn't pursuing entertainment, but technology. I was thrilled to be there and liked Gina and the other team members." She's been at Fox ever since.

"At first, I was sure it was the wrong place for me. I had no finance or entertainment background. I'd never read television contracts before. The learning curve was so steep. The person who originally built the Access database stayed on as a consultant to train me, and she was frustrated by my lack of knowledge. I was self-trained in Access, but that wasn't enough for the needs of the position. The concepts were foreign to me. Many days, I came home and cried. My husband didn't understand what I was trying to do and couldn't provide more than general support. I had to learn everything that first year about finance, contracts, and coding to execute financial modeling and forecasts.

"I put in long hours and, then, in the first budget season, there were more hours, followed by more stress. My trainer was getting frustrated because I knew nothing really. It was so painful and I knew no one to turn to. The IT team was not involved because the CFO at the time didn't use IT. It was the hardest thing I've ever done. The concepts, the hours and the programming—all of it. I felt stupid.

"I stuck it out because I liked the people. I was part of a young team that was fun and smart. I thought studio executives would be screaming and abusive. But everyone was nice— from President Mark Kaner on down.

"The trainer finally left and said, 'Just let her do it.' My management was, thankfully, very supportive. Ultimately, there was satisfaction because I did it when required."

Sheila and her team were successful in the end. She analyzes her part in that as a limited contribution: "I could support the system and produce data, but I couldn't help with the analysis.

"When the TV Distribution IT group started two new contract systems they named Tuscany and Provence, for Domestic Syndication and Pay TV, respectively, I expressed interest and was told I could stay with Finance or go into IT, where they wanted business analysts. I liked the opportunity, so I said, 'OK, I'll try that.' My experience did not include building systems, but why not? I think of myself as a Forrest Gump. I stumble and then do well because I work at it. Once in a position, I dig in and do my best.

"Tom Tralongo, the IT Director at the time, was friendly and open, which meant I was fine working for him. My career has been forged by amazing mentors who are very strong in their fields. I'm fortunate that I worked with such good people who watched out for me. They saw that I could do the job, often before I did, and mentored me in that direction."

In her new role, Sheila learned what requirements documents are. It was now the year 2000 and not everyone needed a computer science degree to be a business analyst. "I was able to create my version of the position and write my first requirements document. I knew the business side so well after two years in the finance group that I felt I had a leg up when presenting Tuscany technical requirements to the IT team.

However, the team leader destroyed my first attempt. I cried again.

"From his perspective, he didn't want to work with people who didn't know what they were doing. He had a system to build. He needed to architect the best system, and he wanted the best requirements. Part of my later success is because of his toughness. He taught me how to build systems and be a business analyst.

"As Tuscany finished and we began to define the Provence system, it was another tense time for me, another steep learning curve. I worked with an analyst named JP, who is so good at what he does that I aimed to perform at that level. We spent long hours together, but enjoyed ourselves. After we launched Provence, I went to the Paris office for the deployment, which was wonderful.

"I was now 32, and my husband was asking when he would see me at home again. When I got pregnant because I wanted two kids before 35, my priorities shifted."

After her maternity leave, Sheila returned to work, but a few months later realized she wanted to spend time with her baby. She quit to be a full-time mom.

"In less than a year, I was back asking for part-time hours and was able to start working from home. I knew I wanted to be pregnant again before 35, so planned to make it all work together. Toward the end of my second pregnancy, I stopped working again, this time for two years.

"My ex-husband was also in IT. During this whole time, he kept getting laid off. After my first child, his latest layoff came as we had just bought a house. When my daughter was young, he lost his job again. I felt like it was time to go back to work. My COBRA insurance was about to end and the cost of private insurance would be out of reach for us. At first, I went back into analyst work part time. Then someone left and I took the open position in TV Distribution IT to get benefits."

In 2009, Sheila left TV Distribution for Home Entertainment to design systems for production support. She was promoted to Manager and then Director and Executive Director.

"I took a demotion after that to Senior Business Analyst and began to work from home part time again. It was a challenge because the Home Entertainment Division was managed like the Wild West. Design was done by VPs who didn't know the details. My boss wanted to keep the users happy, but he wanted to build his own design, regardless of their needs. I did complete one project, a system for royalty statements."

At this point in her career, Sheila is trying to be more strategic. "I'm grateful to have a career forged by multiple amazing mentors. The big thing coming is where I'll be in Fox after the Disney transition. If I'm in control, I want to stay as a senior analyst working from home for three more years. I don't need to be VP or Executive Director to feel fulfilled. I just want enough money for the right life balance. I can also go back to the business side of the studio, but that's not something I've done much thinking about yet. I may pick up my medical interests and return to a career in nursing, for example. I will probably end up in IT—perhaps at a different studio.

"My decisions are driven by my children. My daughter is in the eighth grade. When she's in high school, I want to be here. I'll have options, but don't want to pursue them until I'm finished being the mom I want to be."

--- Interview 4/2019

CHAPTER 23

ALISON LYONS: If You're Not Having Fun on the Job, Something's Not Right

Alison Lyons treats everyone the same. If you're on her team, she believes you can do great work and gives you the room to do it. She finds ways to assign team members to the work they like best, which is hugely appreciated.

She became my project manager soon after I started working at Fox for the second time. She knew I liked working with movie and TV content over general business any day and let me play to my strengths. I was thrilled because her projects were more interesting than those of my previous team, and she seemed to be having fun at her job.

Our business connections liked working with Alison's team because she was always smiling and her team was interested in learning as much as possible about their challenges, which led to software that improved daily results.

The team's mission was to work with the Marketing groups to create websites for titles that were being promoted to international broadcast licensees. It was through her that I met the people who would appoint me to manage the FoxFast team.

Any manager could benefit from watching Alison work. She's a supportive team leader who brings out the most in each individual on her team.

Alison's Story
"When I started college, I wanted to be a software developer. That guided me for three years."

Alison Lyons attended the University of Florida and majored in engineering because there was no specific degree in computer science at the time. She soon realized she wasn't cut out for the core courses, changed majors in her junior year and graduated with a math degree that delivered on her computer goal. EDS, a large technology consulting company, hired her as a developer. They were hiring people with any degree and putting them through their programmer boot camp.

"They called us systems engineers, then advanced systems engineers. I moved to California after training and was hired by EDS manager Barry Hayden, who is now also at Fox.

"The change allowed me to leave the EDS office in Ohio and live near the ocean in Los Angeles. I was definitely lucky, because when the company spends three years training you, you could be sent anywhere. I went to Pennsylvania for a year as part of my training program, a cool opportunity because I worked at a GMAC [General Motors Acceptance Corporation] office to learn their business. I was embedded everywhere, even repossessing cars with them."

Alison thrived when learning new businesses, something she continued to do after her move to California in 1993. Moving from successful project to successful project would be the pattern for her career, and the reason she became an in-demand manager who melds diverse people into highly functioning teams.

"For the next three years, I worked on yet another EDS account in California and rose to the role of project manager. To increase my challenges, I quit to become a contractor at the drug company Amgen, and then was hired there. This time, I did not have a good experience.

"The issues at Amgen existed in my immediate chain of command. They were enduring multiple transitions and became the laziest bunch of workers. There were only two products to manage at the time, so they could get away with it. I like to get stuff done, so I hated the atmosphere.

"Their project methodology was immature. When I tried to initiate changes, there was a lot of resistance. I learned the hard way that I wasn't yet great in people skills when I alienated some without understanding the impact. On the plus side, I had only known the EDS way of doing things, so the work at Amgen broadened my knowledge about how to procure hardware and software licenses. I also wrote my first RFP [request for proposal] there."

She'd never aimed for an entertainment career; however, when EDS people she knew in California got contracts at Sony, they gave her a way out of the Amgen misery by urging her to join them.

"I went from a negative place to a new role leading a data conversion project for a major studio. It was wonderful. I immediately became more productive and grateful to be in the right place again. We contributed to the infamous Y2K projects that almost every company endured while planning the transition to the year 2000. When it was over in November 1999, I left the team."

Companies were crazy to hire for the new century, and another studio soon recruited her. She started at Fox the first time in December of 1999.

"It was challenging to be the newbie, because it was clear I wasn't in a position to help. The fit didn't work, so I quit my first project there.

"I briefly went back to Amgen because management had changed and it was a much better experience. I did one project, which allowed me to work from home three to four days a week, a rarity at that time. They hired a big consulting company and wanted me always on site, but I didn't want to do that again. In another case of serendipity, I got a call from someone I worked with at Sony who wanted me for his project at Fox. I wasn't sure I wanted to go back.

"When he said, 'Name your price,' I named it, and he said, 'OK.' I moved to Fox again in November of 2000."

It was a fortuitous decision. At first, she worked on data conversions for a system named Tuscany, which was a contract management system for International TV

Distribution. Then, she transferred to a new team and a new project, also financial, called Prophet, learning all the while.

"I've been at Fox ever since, as a contractor for the first four years and then as an employee. They pegged me to lead the design of two new sites, the FoxEST and FoxVOD marketing sites for the Electronic Sell-Through [customer download of video for later playback] and video-on-demand businesses. I'd never done stuff like that before, nor had I built an external-facing website. I joined a good team, and we had a great vendor who provided the skills and knowledge I didn't yet have—all the components of a perfect job for me.

"After those sites were launched, I worked on the company's first digital screening room, which was for the annual May screenings, held each year by the L.A. production community to show new Fall programs to international buyers. Online screening was not a thing yet, so we were breaking new ground."

The project after that didn't get funding right away and she was miserable again.

"I was fortunate enough to be able to work in another group for a while, but I went to my boss and told him I wasn't the person to do the project. I asked him, 'Is there something else, or should I look for another job?'

"He was great. An exec in TV needed a project lead person for a short-term project. I did that for six months, after which my boss came back to me with a choice. 'This has to stop,' he explained. My floating to another department meant he would be down one headcount for the duration. He wanted to be able to fill the gap on his team."

Alison tried to calm her nerves at the news. "I was freaked out. What was to happen to me?"

To investigate her options, she, for the one and only time in her career, went to HR. "I told them my boss needed me to find another job and asked them where to start.

"Their response was that I didn't need to find another job because I was now assigned to the CIO as his special projects person! After three to four months, I went back to another IT group and worked on digital projects for Home Entertainment. I was moving a lot, but thrilled I was working!"

She was offered a job managing international contract administration for a non-IT group at Fox. "I was excited to do something so different and outside the borders of IT.

"At the same time, I also split up with my 17-year personal partner—an unbelievably stressful time. To add to the stress, there was someone difficult working for me. Perhaps not surprisingly, I developed physical symptoms. I decided I didn't want to live like that anymore."

Alison knew she needed a change and came up with the idea of moving to her weekend place in San Diego. "It's so different from L.A. I thought a lot about how to do it and came up with the idea to fill an open analyst position in my group and ask Fox to replace me as the manager. I gave them three options for how it could work and submitted them in writing.

"I began my pitch by saying that I was moving and that I had ideas about how I could move and still work for Fox. The first option for them was to decline my pitch and I would leave the company. The second option was to keep me as a temp for six months to train my replacement. Option number three was to let me take a step down and work from San Diego as an analyst at a lower salary. To make that transition work, I recommended a friend for my current job."

Her boss went for option three. Her friend was hired, and Alison lived in San Diego full-time.

"I stayed in the new position for a year. Then, yet again, Fox reorganized and my new management didn't want a remote employee. I went to L.A. the next week and asked everyone for options. An IT manager I knew said, 'I'll take you.' She assigned me to an amazing group and we worked very well together. There was another reorganization and another transfer, and then another one."

Alison will tell you that this type of job changing, especially in a remote role, takes confidence and the ability to build good relationships—and a company that recognizes your value in many guises.

"It's not always about moving up. It takes going through failures and times when you are miserable. You have to adapt and be flexible. What I have been able to do since I took that reduced, remote role and lower pay is eye-opening. I have lots of extra time in my life and reduced stress. Even though I've been promoted and am a manager again, it's still much better than before.

"I've always liked to have a team that works well together, and I enjoy working with the users to solve a problem. I want to care a bit about the application, but it's not a priority. An accounting system is not interesting, but making it work can be satisfying. I worked on systems that don't get a lot of use and that's not very satisfying, but I love poking around in data. The process is simple but the subject may not be. A question comes to you and you research and analyze it. You come up with a hypothesis and test it.

"I can do what I do almost anywhere, which is amazing. I went from the auto industry to biotech to entertainment and learned different businesses. It's what's cool about IT. You can apply the same logic to moving between divisions at a company like Fox. You learn about all aspects of the business and know more about the details of the work than most people in any given department. That's valuable.

"I wasn't one to keep up with the techie world because I never embraced the tech side as much as the business side of whatever project I was on. I often feel out of depth in a techie discussion."

She does acknowledge that it's most interesting to work in entertainment. "It's fun that the data is about TV and movies. It's relatable. If you're not having fun on the job, then something's not right."

IT processes continue to evolve, and Alison evolves with them. "I moved forward to the Agile software development methodology, where development is based on daily project scrum meetings attended by the whole team to review progress. It's better than the more traditional waterfall method of developing features in parallel in a black hole until testing and delivery. On an Agile project, the team is constantly talking, which enhances the shared identity of the group.

"When I left the full-time management position in L.A. and moved to San Diego, my life suddenly accommodated more things. In the first year, for example, I went for a lot of walks because I got a dog. I enjoyed much more outside time when the sun was shining. No more missing the daylight on short winter days. I could notice birds, flowers, my garden. I didn't realize how important that was. I ate three meals a day at home. In L.A., I ate out or in the office most of the time.

"At first, it was difficult to make new friends in a new place without an office to go to every day. After a while, I found friends on meetup.com. I joined the local women's club and eventually became the president. It's been great, and I'm even doing a little too much. When I worked in L.A., I had money and no time. Now I have less money and more time.

"Someday, I'd like to find a way to work part time and do more along the lines of my new pro bono work for a local group in San Diego.

"I need my current income level to build up retirement savings and for insurance. But I understand more about why people downsize when they retire. The goal could be to pay down or off the mortgage, for example.

"Today, I logged out at 6 pm, and I generally say 'yabba dabba do' like Fred Flintstone.

"I'm not guilty if I don't keep working. The only other thing I did when I worked all the time was the gym. That's how I managed the stress. I've kept that up and it's still important to me.

"Work starts at 9 am. The commute is short. I can leave the house at 7 am, go to the bay and paddle around for an hour and get home in time to log on at 9. That's the best!"

--- Interview 9/2017

CHAPTER 24

SCOTT GREGG: I'm Really Good at Business Class With a Cocktail

In his role as business subject matter expert [SME], Scott Gregg always came to the table with a positive attitude, which may be even more crucial to a project's success than his expertise.

We first worked together on the Tuscany and Avalon systems in Fox International TV Distribution. It was comforting to know that my business liaison was so knowledgeable, so willing to help and such a darn nice guy. I admire Scott for his ability to bring people together to launch complex, satisfying IT systems.

In short, he's charged with administering Fox license agreements with broadcasters all over the world. He and I worked together between 2004 and 2016, and I relied on him as the primary business executive sponsor for IT projects in his area. His deep, broad knowledge of the subject was crucial to the effectiveness of what we built.

As a key part of one of the best-managed business groups I've ever collaborated with, we quickly learned to trust each other's judgment. I never knew him to raise his voice or treat anyone disrespectfully.

He's an extraordinary example of how to succeed as an executive through competence, empathy and patience.

Scott's Story
Scott Gregg was born in Colorado and attended a small, semi-private college near Lincoln, Nebraska. While completing a BA

in Theater, he found time for an internship with a performing arts center in Denver, via its conservatory for training actors.

"My first job was as an apprentice stage manager. That didn't really work out, so I stayed a season, maybe two, as the purchasing agent for sets, props and costumes. They hired me as the tour manager on an original musical called 'Quilters' that incorporated regional productions in Colorado, Wyoming and Arizona. When they submitted it in competition at the Edinburgh Theater Festival, I was the tour manager."

Ultimately, he worked for two and a half years as Assistant Director and Ad Administrator at the theater, handling payroll, insurance and general business functions. It didn't pay well, so "on a wing and a prayer," he moved to California with his partner, where he began temping at the studios.

"My first Hollywood job was for producer Dino Di Laurentiis, in the personnel department. After that, it was back to temping and an assignment at MGM assisting Bob Branson, himself an assistant for a new executive who once ran Universal's International TV Distribution group. It was a move that served as the foundation for the rest of my career in entertainment.

"One day I went into Bob's office, puzzled because he was somehow different. Out of the blue, he asked where I had gone to school. It turns out he and his wife also went to a small school in Nebraska. I was flattered to learn next that he wanted to recommend me for a full-time position for his boss, as an official Assistant to the Head of International Distribution at MGM. Was it just because I chose the right school? How lucky could I be?"

In an at-the-time unrelated coincidence, Branson also recommended a woman named Marion Edwards for an MGM position. She would go on to assume the position of President of Fox International Television Distribution and be Scott's boss there. "There's that 'small world' and 'you never know where the next big thing will come from' phenomenon in action," he explains.

While at MGM, Scott was promoted to a sales role, selling residential pay-per-view in the era of the Request TV service. He was responsible for Eastern European free TV markets.

"When MGM was sold in 1993, Marion went to Fox to work with Jim Gianopulos, and I followed my boss to Playboy Entertainment. The sales group there was much smaller—only two salespeople handled the entire world. What a great experience for me, with tons of travel and tons of work. Because it was Playboy, everything we sold had to be aired in late night, which complicated sales pitches. Even so, I loved learning all about how TV distribution worked internationally."

A little over three years later, in 1996, Marion called and asked Scott to come to Fox. The job she offered wasn't a sales role, but for divisional administration, assisting with licensee contract negotiations. Eventually, his role was expanded to encompass everything from contracts for New World film product to computer systems development.

He's worked at Fox for over twenty years. New divisions have been added to his area of responsibility, including Fox Channels, which has its own sales group. "We recently added a whole new business when Fox assumed sales support for National Geographic titles and content like the wildly popular 'The Walking Dead,' which came to us through a Fox Networks Group deal with the production company AMC. Our role begins when the show's initial exhibition window on the network is over. Our second window sales group sells it to free TV and SVOD [subscription video on demand] licensees worldwide."

Scott recently added the role of liaison with IT for development of Nat Geo applications. He also collaborates with a stand-alone company in the UK where international employees work to administer licensing deals. In the category of new wrinkles that leverage his knowledge, he was asked to provide data to the EU and UK commissions that were reviewing purchase of British media giant Sky by 21st Century Fox.

"The Sky deal was a complex, controversial proposal that, if successful, would result in a mega-merger that the approving bodies in England were not sure they wanted. Our information was provided to clarify the advantages and help push the deal to completion.

"I have sometimes felt that I didn't have the correct background for the projects I worked on. The challenge of succeeding anyway allowed me to use my horse sense and problem solving abilities to best advantage. I fell in love with dealing with clients in diverse countries around the world, each with its own market rules. I found that the quirks of multiple cultures fascinate me. Who would have thunk it?

"My job is often conversations with Paris, the UK, Italy and Germany in the morning, then Sao Paulo in the afternoon. Then Sydney later in the day. My favorite part of the world is Europe, possibly because it's where I've traveled the most. If I could live in Europe, I would choose the UK."

Scott's role requires travel to two TV sales markets in Europe each year, Mipcom in October and MipTV in April, with stops in the Paris and London Fox offices. There is a planned new office in Milan, and he will eventually stop there as well.

"When we launch the new Tuscany office, I will visit Italy again.

"We've just begun traveling in support of a healthy content business in China. The government is omnipresent, of course, and the financial terms of our deals require that money stay in China. But, the size of the business is potentially super-lucrative, especially for theatrical titles ... more than TV or streaming—so far.

"I give people that interview for jobs in our group the following advice: You have to have a weird gene that makes you completely obsessed with 100% accuracy. We review deals and model them in a sophisticated IT system. There can't be mistakes. Bad data in will equal bad data out.

"I also tell them it will help if they get a kick out of successfully meeting the challenges of ever-evolving deal structures. I'm never bored because the deals are never the same."

It's not all deals that easily close, of course, as Fox and the industry undergo massive shifts in audience and viewing habits.

"Internally, working with other divisions has been challenging because we're all trying to figure it out. The mentality in Fox Distribution is to focus on cooperation and sharing, but that's not necessarily the culture in other divisions at the company."

Scott is the beneficiary of good fortune, hard work and, especially, a good reputation.

"In the current very challenging entertainment space, every studio is contemplating how to compete with Netflix and Amazon. A Disney-owned Fox must also compete with Hulu, which Disney now owns. The streaming companies compete with their own original content that streams solely on their services. They don't need our distribution business."

One way the studios are responding is by funding their own direct-to-consumer groups. Disney announced its entry. CBS already has the All Access service.

"What is our future? The Fox Networks side of the business owns a massive international presence with BskyB, Sky Deutsche and Sky Italia, which together have 22 million subscribers. They have proposed the launch of a direct-to-consumer SVOD channel [subscription video on demand]. Some of our Free TV licensees are creating SVOD services for their consumers. In Asia, FoxPlus is an existing SVOD service and we license to FNG [Fox Network Group] Asia for that service. There are multiple models in development for both first-run and library content. It can get quite confusing.

"We also have to keep our linear business going. What I'm finding is an evolutionary growth in my career as a result of all the upheaval. New projects are often ones I'm uniquely qualified to counsel, plus it helps keep me relevant. I know this company very well, which means a lot to me. I've begun promoting others in my group to allow them to handle more of the day-to-day tasks, while I find bandwidth for the new projects. It's still a great ride."

He's anticipating what could come next. "I've learned that I'm really good at business class with a cocktail! I want to stay productive, but if this job evolves to something without real direction, I am confident there'll be something else to do.

"I worked once for a crop duster, spraying pesticides in Colorado. My dad was a pilot, so we knew planes. If I had to, I could land planes. But I didn't like it and didn't want to pursue it at the time—or now. I also worked at a guest dude ranch more than one summer. I've done a wild bunch of things. When opportunities presented themselves, I often went for it.

"My father and I watched the 2017 eclipse from the top of a mountain in Vail. I recently told grade school friends that being in Colorado is being home, even though I've lived in California since 1986.

"Eventually, I plan for a retirement in both Colorado and California. For now, I maintain really good friendships all over the world. I've met great people everywhere that I have the privilege of working with and knowing. I'm ready to leave for my next sales meeting in a few weeks. Don't ask me when I want to stop—I don't."

--- Interview 12/2017

CHAPTER 25

MARK MORRISON:
Reinventing Myself in
China

In the years after I left Fox, Mark Morrison experienced a situation similar to one I had endured before in my career.

New management relegated him to the sidelines and eventually laid him off. It's tough to go from being a respected team member to something less for reasons beyond your control. He mourned, and then accepted the opportunity to rethink his career and his life. What he did next is a fascinating example of how to reinvent yourself.

I met him when he became my tutor in my role as business analyst for his main contract application, called Avalon, in 2005. He was an experienced TV distribution services manager for Fox International TV Distribution. His patience helped me to succeed in a somewhat touchy political environment, for which I was, and am, grateful.

After I moved from supporting Avalon to working on the FoxFast project, Mark continued to be involved with my team as a subject matter expert for how Fox shipped movie and TV content to broadcast licensees. We counted on him to know what customers and the international sales team wanted and needed, as well as how to streamline current and proposed processes for both analog and digital materials. He helped us test the new website and encouraged customers to see the advantages of what we'd built.

When his tenure at Fox ended, Mark decided to do something about as different as you can imagine. He's living and working in China. Fulfilling a dream he's nurtured since college, he teaches at a university there, and says he loves it.

As the one and only person I know who followed an ambition to live in China, he's an example of what's possible if you listen to your best instincts.

Mark's Story

Mark Morrison began his career by pursuing an interest in broadcasting, although it wasn't his first passion. As far as he's concerned, "Most of the people in the entertainment industry are in the industry by chance. So, I am typical in that way."

His college degree resulted from a double major in broadcasting and theater, which he felt would provide him with the skills needed for directing film.

On the broadcasting side, he mostly studied radio and television news, neither of which were what he really wanted to do. He liked the idea of working in radio, but there were limited opportunities. His ideal job in those days would have been at the public radio station in the university town of Mt. Pleasant, Michigan. Theater became his passion. He both worked backstage and acted on stage, which supported the creativity he craved.

Like many who graduate from college and want to see more of the world, Mark decided he would move to Chicago, New York, San Francisco or Los Angeles after graduation. "I went first to San Francisco because a lot of my friends migrated there after university. There were at least ten of us living there at the same time.

"I stayed for nine years, trying acting in commercials and theater. There was zero pay for the theater stuff, but it was fun.

"I also worked with a performance artist named Frank Garvey, which really exercised my creative muscles. I eventually went back to school in San Francisco and obtained a master's degree in Social and Cultural Anthropology."

With the hope of better paydays after obtaining his master's, Mark relocated to L.A. Unfortunately, he felt that L.A. completely sucked the creativity right out of him. Not quite ready to give up on the city, however, he changed direction and accepted what seemed a cool job at Twentieth Century

Fox as a temp for the VP in charge of International Television Distribution.

"I stuck with it even though it wasn't what I wanted. At least, my foot was in the door in a leading company. What we did wasn't creative in the expected sense. It paid well, and they treated me well.

"The fact was that I was a master's degree holder whose main job was filing. I told the VP, 'I don't think I want to work here because I can contribute more somewhere else.'

"He talked me into staying. It was the end of the time when you advanced in Hollywood by starting in the mailroom, and he convinced me that better days would come.

"Several years into my stay, the department moved from its location off the studio lot. We moved to offices in Fox Plaza, which is connected to the main lot, and many people didn't want to accept the change. I was excited to be close to the action and the stages.

"There were near misses in finding other jobs at Fox over the years. I tried to move to Marketing, for one. They expressed interest. I didn't want to act too excited to leave my current job, so I played it cool.

"I didn't hear anything for a couple of weeks. Finally, I contacted them and found they thought I wasn't interested. I'd lost an opportunity that might have worked for me.

"My department and I got along well until a reorganization moved us into a new group called Enterprise Operations. New management seemed to sort of freeze me out. I had been there about twelve years by then. Everything changed and became competitive and intensely crazy. It didn't feel right for me anymore.

"My fate was sealed when, during the transition to the new organization, I suffered a disability that kept me out of the office for three to four months. When I came back, my job had been downsized. I should have known that something was up, but I didn't see it. I wasn't invited to meetings as before, and, when I talked to my boss, he acted like it was nothing—like I was being paranoid.

"I was laid off during another planned reorganization for the department, which never actually materialized. Of course, now I can say that it was the best thing that could have happened.

"Back in my San Francisco days, in 1997, while I was studying for my Master's in Social and Cultural Anthropology, I went to Shanghai for three months, completing a research project studying gay male culture. It was wonderful, but I always felt that I didn't have the chance to learn everything I needed in China."

When his Fox job ended, it was two decades after his original Chinese visit. He decided he wanted to know more about current China.

"After sixteen years at Fox, I was beginning to feel like I didn't fit in Hollywood. When I was laid off, I tried to find another job in entertainment and found I couldn't get an interview.

"I realized I could do something really different. My relationship ended, and I decided to cut ties with L.A. I sold my loft, rented movers and sent everything to my hometown in Michigan. I bought a house there in two weeks, paying cash. My sister became my house tenant."

Before moving back to Michigan, Mark received an online TEFL certificate so that he could teach abroad.

Suddenly, everyone wanted to interview him. "It felt so good. I found a job quickly. After everything was settled in Michigan, I left for China."

His feelings about his new job are beyond enthusiastic. "When I arrived in China, I taught sociology and a class called Study Skills at a university in Hunan Province. I also taught some required English classes in a business program. My lessons were designed to be entertaining and kept the students interested, which challenged my creativity."

Mark also co-founded the Wild English Garden, a small English language school for students age six to twelve, and it's still in operation today.

From Hunan Province, Mark moved to Shenzhen and taught grades seven and eight for one year at a middle school's international program. Two years ago, he moved to a different university.

"I'm now teaching at Guangzhou University, in the Foreign Language School. All students are learning a language, English, French, Japanese, or Farsi, for business, translation or teaching. All my classes are taught in English, which is not an issue for these students. The kids all learn to speak English beginning in kindergarten. The students really want to study, which motivates me more.

"I will most likely stay beyond my current two years. I teach freshmen and sophomores, and I'd like to see my students graduate. The university provides me with an apartment. I'm paid for the summer off, which I spend in Michigan.

"Pronunciation is a new class for me this year. My favorite class is called Survey of English-Speaking Countries. For that one, I'm teaching myself before I teach the students. We're currently learning about the history of the UK. I can now explain their judicial system like a pro. After the UK, we'll move on to the US and Australia.

"Writing is another favorite class. I teach writing just like I would teach American students. In today's class, we talked about pre-writing, brainstorming and clustering."

Mark has immersed himself in the China of today. He's gotten better at speaking Chinese. "I can't have a conversation, but I can order food. They notice all foreigners here, not as a bad thing, but as a characteristic. They like my neutral American accent, which is sought after. I keep wondering what it will be like if the tariff war gets going. Will they treat me differently then?"

He will tell you that he's found the perfect mix of life experiences for him. He's a teacher in a place that values his contributions, and he lives where he's comfortable.

Eager to tell everyone he knows, Mark says, "I love teaching in China. Maybe I'll return to the US one day and teach social studies and sociology at a community college. I feel my experience here will be an advantage for my future students.

"On a personal level, I'm disappointed with meals here—particularly breakfast! They seem the same, savory with noodles or rice, every morning. Sometimes I get my western breakfast fix by getting McDonald's delivered at the beginning of my day. In China, almost anything can be delivered.

"I'm a bit of a snow bird, living here in southern China. This area is surrounded by water—where Guangzhou, Shenzhen and Hong Kong are located. It's called the Bay Area, and is relatively warm all year. We have palm trees, and it gets hot in the summer. That's why I'm grateful I can go to Michigan for the warmest months. I think I'll keep this up for awhile."

--- Interview 11/2018

CHAPTER 26

MARK KANER: It's All About the People

Mark Kaner's vision finds its best expression in encouraging innovation and challenging his team to move forward with him. He is perhaps the best executive I worked with during my career.

As President of 20th Century Fox Television Distribution, he moved the business forward for the studio's customers—the international broadcasters that license Fox TV shows and movies for exhibition on their channels. In my case, he championed the TV Distribution website my team built and managed.

At that time, digital video was coming into its own as a viable technology on the Internet. To advance the new FoxFast brand, Mark encouraged us to design the first international network for customer viewing of television screeners, the full-length videos of TV shows and movies. He continued to support innovation on the site by challenging us to enhance it to enable online delivery of high-quality broadcast masters to customers around the world.

I'm grateful I was there at the right time to help define and implement digital delivery services for Fox. I learned the distribution business and felt the thrill of creating a product that broke new ground in supply chain technology. If it sounds boring, it wasn't. Not at all.

I am hugely grateful to Mark for including me on a team of such talented, creative and forward-thinking professionals.

Mark's Story
Mark Kaner learned early in his life that music was magic because he had the good fortune to see great entertainers, like

Sinatra, at the height of their talent. He was born in Brooklyn, but grew up in Las Vegas.

"Dad was in the gambling business. I was there from age two to seventeen and initially planned to get into the music business as a performer. What I realized very quickly is that an incredible number of very talented musicians were my competition. There was an intimidatingly high standard because so much talent was coming into the city. I was OK as a singer, but there were people all around me who were GREAT who couldn't get arrested.

"My mom left when I was two years old and my sister was six. When she moved back to Las Vegas seven years later, she was remarried and at that point my sister moved in with her. I stayed with Dad, and he and I became incredibly close."

Ever a pragmatist, Mark switched from performing to the business side of entertainment. He studied film and television, and then entertainment law.

"After high school, I traveled internationally, further developing my interests in global business, art and entertainment. After graduation from college, I decided I was ready to pursue the law partly because Dad wanted to go law school, but never could. He quit school to support his mother and two brothers.

"I got accepted to a couple of law schools, but didn't actually show up. I started thinking about what I might really want to do, which led me to move to Topanga Canyon and become a hippie, living in a one-room cabin.

"While I was there pursuing my thinking, my father came looking for me. He'd become concerned. I told him that law school wouldn't make me happy, and I wanted to work before getting any more education."

To help him make progress, Mark's father introduced him to a guy in the music business named Danny Davis. "Danny's boss was Lester Sill, who was the head of Screen Gems Columbia Music and previously partners with the legendary Phil Spector in Phillies Records.

"Lester was easily the coolest guy I ever met. We hit it off. His division at Columbia was being sold to another record company, EMI, at the time, and he couldn't give me a job himself. Instead, he got me interviews at all the major record companies—at Decca, Warner Elektra, Chrysalis, WEA. No one would hire me because they were sure I was overqualified and would quit even though I'd never held a job! Still, I couldn't get hired."

Mark was desperate when he met someone at Universal in the Television division. "When I told him about it, Lester heard the word 'television' and said, 'I thought you wanted music.'

"My reply was typically practical: I can't get a job, and I need to pay the rent. I have a degree in film and TV, so maybe I can get into music later."

Lester knew everyone, even in television. He introduced Mark to Norman Horowitz, "a fantastic larger-than-life guy who was head of TV Distribution at Columbia. He was gregarious and smart and innovative. I got in the door and told him I didn't know what I wanted, but I knew I could do anything."

His response was encouraging at first: He told Mark that he'd just taken over TV Domestic Syndication and Worldwide Distribution, and that there might be a job in Chicago.

Mark decided he wasn't thrilled. Both of his roommates were from Chicago and what he knew was that it is too hot in the summer and too cold in the winter. He'd rather stay in L.A. He leaned on his honesty and, even though he needed the job, he turned it down.

At some point in the conversation, Horowitz said, "Listen I am incredibly busy right now and I have too much shit I gotta take care of. I'm leaving for London tomorrow night, and we can talk when I get back to L.A."

Immediately, Mark replied: "I am great at doing shit!" And Horowitz laughed.

The next morning the phone rang in Topanga. "It was a call from Horowitz's assistant. 'Mr. Kaner,' she said. 'Mr. Horowitz would like you to start tomorrow.'

"'Excuse me?' I managed to reply.

"She continued, 'Can you start tomorrow? And, you forgot to leave us your résumé, or I must have lost it. Please bring one when you come. We'll be out to lunch when you arrive, so just slip it under the door.'"

Mark started to panic. "I didn't know how to type, but I carefully typed out a résumé. The next day, I raced to Burbank Studios and went in through the Olive Gate. I planned to deliver my résumé as instructed and go, but Norman's assistant was at her desk.

"She looked up and said, 'Mr. Kaner, what are you doing?'

"The first words out of my mouth were, 'You're not supposed to be here!'

"She responded, 'I know, but Mr. Horowitz wants to talk to you.'

"I was wearing an old pair of overalls from my hippie wardrobe, a Mickey Mouse T-shirt and a pair of moccasins. 'I can't,' I pleaded. But she sent me in.

"I apologized to Norman for not dressing more appropriately. His look clearly said 'this is a bit too casual for the office!' There was another great guy with him, Herb Lazarus, who was the head of International Distribution and his number two. They were dressed immaculately in shirts and ties from Savile Row. Lazarus looked me up and down twice.

"Norman introduced me and Lazarus said, 'Nice to meet you, I think.'

"That's how I began my first job in TV as Norman's gofer. I fixed coffee pots and worked on big deals—whatever he needed."

Mark's fond memories of that time are obvious. "Norman passed away, but Herb is still running Carsey-Werner Distribution, a top TV company in town. He's one of the nicest people I ever met. I'm in touch with him weekly. An amazing man.

"I was 22 when I started with Norman and stayed for three years. He gave me a choice of domestic vs. international projects. That was an easy decision! They sent me for a planned year to Australia, London, Brazil, Tokyo, Toronto, and I came back with all the right experience.

"What a great opportunity! I didn't go to Australia first because they hired a guy in London and wanted me to be with the new guy. Lester, who was still my friend, introduced me to EMI in England and his music contacts there.

"While I was in London, Norman was fired. When I moved back to the US after three years, I found I had a few opportunities. I could stay at Columbia, go to Metromedia, where Herb Lazarus was by then, or move to Lorimar where another great friend, Ken Page, was the head of Distribution. They were all good choices."

Mark's most intriguing opportunity was to follow Norman and start a TV company at Polygram Records, which was owned by two European companies. "I went with Norman and became the head of International Distribution at Polygram for another three tumultuous years.

"Now that I was back in the US, Lester decided to help me make a different connection. He was like a yenta, trying to find me a nice girl to settle down with!

"Lester suggested, 'You should take out my assistant Kim.'"

Mark didn't want to do that because he'd just come out of long-term relationship with a woman from London.

"Kim understood that I was uncomfortable, but said, 'I'd like you to meet my sister. Would you like to meet her?'

"Skeptical, I replied, 'Do you like your sister?'

"Kim said, 'What kind of a question is that? I love my sister. She's fantastic.'

"I told her the reason for my hesitation. 'Look, Kim, all I do is work, so I'm not a good guy to start a relationship with. If it fails, it'll be awkward between you and me, and that will cause a problem every time I want to see Lester. So let's not do this.'

"Kim was relentless. One day, she 'just happened' to be having lunch with her sister at the exact same time and place where I was having lunch with Lester. Her sister's name was Colleen, and we've been married for 35 years."

At Polygram, Mark worked on new TV shows as well as TV Distribution. "It was enormous fun. The people were the best. Polygram signed an agreement with Producer Robert Stigwood, who'd made huge money from *Saturday Night Fever* and movies like *Shampoo*. In the end, Polygram was running out of money, and I was going to be out of work.

"I found opportunities at different studios and at Westinghouse Electric, which owned the second largest broadcast station group in the US.

"Westinghouse wanted to start an International Division, and I almost signed on to that endeavor. It went well until their executive said, 'I want you to hire other people with degrees like yours.'

"When I told him I would hire the best person for a job, he told me, 'We have a certain pedigree.' Uh oh. I knew by then that everything learned at school was not applicable. At the last minute, I didn't take the job.

"Instead, I started my own company because I was sick of corporate bullshit. I thought I wouldn't have to deal with it in my own space. Surprise—that's not how it goes. Just because you work as a consultant, you're not immune to the politics."

Mark signed clients all over the world, including Canal Plus in France, TV New Zealand and Artists Services in Australia, which was co-owned by Steve Vizard and Andrew Knight, writer of *Hacksaw Ridge*. "My first client was Yorkshire Television in England. I acted as a behind-the-scenes executive producer and acquisitions guy. I also represented the Cecchi Gori Group in Italy and Southern Star in Australia, and consulted for MGM in the US. The consulting gigs lasted for over eleven years."

In the early 90's, an intriguing opportunity presented itself, tempting Mark back into corporate life.

"I could give up my company and work for 20th Century Fox. In 1992, I pursued an idea to merge NewsCorp [owner of Fox at the time] and my then client, Canal Plus, in France, which would have created the biggest pay TV company in the world. That's when I met Rupert Murdoch, founder and visionary for NewsCorp.

"Rupert began in the newspaper world in Australia and grew his holdings into one of the most powerful media companies in the world. I also spoke to Peter Chernin and Chase Carey, two of his senior executives. I already respected Peter from when he was the senior creative exec at Showtime. Back when I was working with Yorkshire Television, I put together a miniseries that we co-produced with Showtime, and we connected.

"When they came to ask me if I would work at Fox, I said, 'No.' They were in the market for someone because another executive, Jim Gianopolus, wanted out of TV Distribution and into Theatrical Distribution. Therefore, he needed to replace himself.

"I liked my little company and my independence. They persuaded me to discuss it with the president of the studio, Bill Mechanic. I hit it off with him, but I still turned them down. I just didn't think I would be a good corporate executive. Peter Chernin finally called me to close the deal.

"He seemed puzzled at my reluctance to sign on and said, 'What is the problem?'

"'I don't know that I would be a good corporate guy,' I replied.

"He laughed and told me, 'This whole place is entrepreneurs. We constantly talk about what we want to build.'"

Mark saw the truth in that statement. "I saw that Rupert was so far ahead of everyone else in the room. He viewed the big picture as a chessboard and knew how to build things from combinations of companies. His vision to change the business was extraordinary in my opinion. He was simple and clear about what he wanted to do.

"Before I officially accepted, I offered two conditions. 'One: you need to leave me alone. I'm not good at being micro-managed. If I make a mistake, you can fire me.'

"Peter said, 'OK. What else?'

"'Two: you have to allow me to build different things, new businesses. If you only want me to come here to make the world safe for reruns of *Doogie Howser* [one of Fox's popular shows currently succeeding in syndication], I'm not interested.'

"Peter gave me a look. 'Why do you think we're coming to you? We want to build new things.'

"I thought about it. My wife and I had two children by then and were thinking about more. I thought maybe I should take something that offers better health insurance.

"I called them and finally said, 'Yes.'"

That was 1994 and the beginning of Mark's twenty-five years at Fox. "During that time, Peter, Rupert and his sons, Lachlan and James, have allowed me to do all the things I wanted to do, particularly building new businesses. Rupert remains extraordinary. I would see him early in the morning or at the end of the day most days. Once, we had a conversation about Italy. He knew entertainment tycoon Silvio Berlusconi, who would become Prime Minister one day. Berlusconi was pressured to sell a network, and Rupert was going to buy it.

"He told me, 'I think we should build out the market in Italy.'

"I agreed with him and thought we needed a partner, but he didn't want a partner.

"I pushed back, telling Murdoch, 'In Italy, it's different. Plus, I don't trust Silvio. We should get someone who's not in the business, like Agnelli, to join us.' He replied, 'We'll talk more on Monday.'

"I told him I wouldn't be there because I was going to Latin America. I had been so busy over the past eight months doing deals with HBO and Sky Broadcasting in the UK that I'd ignored my office in Latin America, and I thought that was just plain wrong. I warned Rupert that I didn't think we'd done a good job building the business there.

"He came back with, 'We have a venture with Televisa SA [one of the primary networks in Mexico].'

"I replied, 'Rupert, they're just taking our money. They're the biggest telenovela producers in the world and don't need us. I want to build something diversified, like Sky.'

"Rupert asked when I'd be back, and then said we'd talk in two weeks. That was Friday night. I flew to Santiago on Saturday. When I arrived on a Sunday, there were five messages to call Rupert.

"I called, and Murdoch said, 'Well, what's happened?'

"I thought I had forgotten to do something, so I responded, 'I'm sorry Rupert, what's happened with what?'

"He said, 'What's happened on the Latin America thing?'

"'Rupert, I just arrived and it's Sunday in Santiago. I need to get to Brazil and Mexico before I can really evaluate our opportunities.'"

Next, Mark met with Roberto Marinho, the owner of Globo in Brazil; Emilio Azcarraga Sr., owner of the leading broadcaster in Mexico; and all the other major players in Latin America. He returned to L.A. and went immediately to Murdoch's office.

"'I think we should expand our business there,' I told him. 'In Latin America, it's all about family. Contrary to what everyone else is going to tell us, I think we start with the Marinhos. They're more like the Murdoch family. They started in newspapers and expanded into TV. Plus, I've learned that there's some problem between their organization and the Azacarraga family, and we could be the glue that puts them together.'

"Rupert's response was, 'How much?'

"I said, 'How much what?' Murdoch said, 'How much will it cost?'

"I told him that I didn't know yet.

"'Just approximately,' Rupert shot back.

"'I have no idea.'

"'Just think about it right now and tell me.'"

Clearly, Mark was being forced to give him a number. "I knew we needed new channels, satellites, people, product. I said I really didn't know, but maybe $500 million to start.

"Without blinking an eye, Rupert said, 'Great idea. Do it.'

"I took a year and a half to do it. With tremendous help from people like Alberto Pecegueiro from GloboSat and Elie Wahba from Fox in Brazil, we created Sky Latin America. We then had to give it up and sell it to John Malone when he made a run on NewsCorp years later."

Making new businesses that grow companies is the touchstone of Mark's career. He sat on the Board of Sky Italia for ten years, and on the Board at Sky Deutschland for eight. "James Murdoch deserves the credit for the German business. He was the only one who believed in that company and pushed it to his father.

"I am also on the Board of FOXTEL, the Australian pay TV company, which is being re-imagined by Lachlan Murdoch. Elizabeth Murdoch, Rupert's daughter, built Shine Entertainment Media, which was another brilliant idea. This is a brilliant family!"

Recently, Mark found a memo thread between himself, Rupert Murdoch and Peter, written in Sept, 1994.

"Rupert wrote: 'Warners is our biggest competitor, but we are going to produce more and better TV, and you need to monetize it through innovative distribution.' I had a plan; but, I wanted him to know that our biggest competitor was local programming, on a country-by-country basis. We needed to harness local talent and make programming for a global audience. The wisdom of that strategy is more evident today than ever before."

Mark makes sure to highlight the other segment of Fox that he's equally proud of.

"Most importantly, over the years, I enjoyed the great good fortune to work with the people in TV Distribution at Fox. My job was to find new businesses, but also to run distribution. It was my privilege to work with the best people in the business. And that has been my greatest accomplishment.

"We started the high-profile FoxFast website by going from tape and film to digital files. I initially announced the launch of the site at L.A. Screenings, the annual international broadcasters market. I gave customers a chance to collaborate with us, and two years to catch up. If they built a receiving end, we would build the sending network. If they didn't do it, they would have to pay for everything it takes to get their product to them and get it back to us when their license ended. Most have built excellent technology that blends with ours.

"We've taken the distribution business at Fox from $300 million to $3.2 billion annually today [as of 2018]. We have people who are among the best anywhere in the world. They built the automated distribution network before anyone else created a similar system.

"FoxFast was designed for international marketing; then it expanded to digital content delivery. The same services are being opened up as a library service for all of 21st Century Fox. It's an incredible asset.

"In the last several years, the sales force improved to meet the challenges of selling into markets revolutionized by new platforms and new companies. My colleagues, like Marion Edwards before, and now Gina Brogi, also believe it's all about the people. There is constant change, but we adapt and learn to like it."

--- Interview 8/2018

CHAPTER 27

JOHN KOSCHEKA: The Glamour of Cleaning Out George Carlin's Garage

John Koscheka's vision challenged my team to create a digital TV distribution method that didn't exist before we built it.

For me, that's the absolute best environment for fulfilling work. I'm grateful I was in the right place at the right time to lead the IT team that launched the FoxFast website. It was snazzy, ground-breaking and high-profile.

We were thrilled to see its acceptance by Fox International TV customers all over the world when FoxFast pioneered online episode screeners and broadcast-quality file access just as, or in some cases just before, the Internet became a viable service in previously unreliably-serviced countries. Today, this access is routine, but when we started, it was only a vision.

John has a proven ability to conceive innovation, both complex and simple, champion his ideas to approval and shepherd the teams that turn those ideas into reality.

His enthusiasm for bringing the TV International supply chain into the digital future was the catalyst for one of the most enjoyable, productive times of my career.

John's Story

John Koscheka begins talking about his career by sharing that "the ability to envision has always been part of my DNA. I was the ninth of nine kids—seven boys and two girls. As the baby of the family, I assumed the role of dreamer. In that mindset, I didn't necessarily benefit from the traditional parental focus on education and upbringing. My parents were just too tired!"

He grew up on Long Island and used his relative freedom from restrictions to become creative and artistic, with an attraction to experimentation. Between that and his early tendency to be sort of a ham, he expected to pursue arts or sports in one form or another.

"I wasn't a great student in high school because I lacked the proper discipline to learn traditional subjects. But working outside the norms was right for me. I developed a love for film after early experience with photography. A couple of my older brothers are photographers who taught me what they knew. Soon, they wandered into film and I, too, came to appreciate it. They made super-8 films or 8-millimeter shorts, often using stop motion animation. I bought a camera and started making films for myself."

After high school, John realized he needed to get serious and decide what to do with his life. He vowed to get his academic act together, which was difficult at first. He struggled even to write an essay.

"I took remedial writing and learned to love the creative process. I started reading books on writing. Strunk and White's *Elements of Style* is still a personal favorite.

"I guess I inherited my love for words from my mother, a literature major at Kent State in the 1940s. She worked for the State Department, spending time in Brazil, in Washington, DC, and the Belgian Congo, where she met my father. Five of my brothers were born there."

During his college years, John immersed himself in Jung, Freud and Maugham. He read about the theoretical aspects of filmmaking in books about the life and careers of Frank Capra, Harold Lloyd and Buster Keaton, among others. He took a liking to film musicals, especially the work of Gene Kelly.

Ultimately, he parlayed his expanding interest in the movie industry into an Associate Degree from SUNY Farmingdale, a local New York school. After that, he transferred to Hofstra and earned a Bachelor's Degree in Communications, with a focus in Film.

"I expected to be on the creative or production sides of the film business after school, where I entertained [pun intended] a simultaneous interest in stand-up comedy and performed at a variety of clubs in New York City. It was fun—my version of skydiving. I did that for at least a year, writing my own stuff for open-mic nights. I only performed for strangers. It was too nerve- wracking to let anyone I knew see me on stage."

It wasn't long before he heard the West Coast calling and began a rare period of time off when he relocated from New York to L.A. in 1991.

"I took my belongings in an old hand-me-down Mazda 626 with a bad oil-burning problem. I told my family and friends I was heading to Hollywood because I just knew I had to go. Always certain that things would be OK, I listened to my inner voice."

When he arrived, he called the one person he knew in L.A.—a distant cousin who allowed him to stay with her in Glendale for a month.

"I worked as a temp and film extra on movies such as Disney's *Rocketeer*, even on a couple of Fox films long before I knew I'd work there. My perfect intro to Hollywood was on *For the Boys*, starring Bette Midler. We shot a scene at the Van Nuys Airport with realistic WWII military paraphernalia around. Half of the extras were shipping out the next day to go to Iraq."

John has filled binders of writing that tell the stories from this time in his life. "I wrote short stories about the things I observed. One day I'll do something with them. I read them occasionally to my kids, and they get a kick out of it.

"For a while, I worked a dream job for a musical theater lover as an usher at the Schubert Theater, for shows like *Chorus Line*. I earned management's trust and was assigned to watch the stage door. I was extremely respectful and treated everyone like the professionals they were. The names were major A-list: Glenn Close, Michael Jackson, Whoopi Goldberg."

John soon fell back on what he knew and tried stand-up in L.A. The gigs were mostly open-mic nights in Santa Monica clubs. "One night, there was a guy with strange red hair who was very funny—he killed it. Of course, I'm talking about Carrot

Top. I realized I couldn't compete. Plus, I learned I didn't like being on stage or working as an extra all that much. I don't like to seek attention and prefer to not stand out.

"When I was sitting on a movie set during down time, I couldn't match the extraordinary behavior of people around me who were trying to get noticed.

"This trait is applicable to my style today when I'm presenting in my business career. I'm wiser now, and I don't feel pressure to be always 'on' in my communications. Maybe I would have loved performing eventually. But the magic break others talk about never happened for me."

Back in the real world, John continued to work temp jobs. He started a job at the CAA talent agency in the proverbial mail room. "The guy running the room was probably a Harvard grad, but he seemed like a punk to me.

"I next worked for producer Lawrence Kasdan, who at the time was producing L.*A. Story* with Steve Martin. Martin was my biggest hero, and I was hoping I'd meet him. One of my jobs was to make the copies for meetings, which was my task on the day Mr. Martin showed up. Lo and behold, the copy machine wouldn't work. I was deeply embarrassed. Eventually, things worked out. I survived."

On another random job, he delivered hams and turkeys for the holidays in a big white rented van. He loaded it up and delivered to producers and actors, including Arnold Schwarzenegger. This job took him all over town and enabled him to meet lots of personal assistants to famous people.

He worked for George Carlin's manager at his house in Brentwood. "Oh the glamour of cleaning out George Carlin's garage!

"On another day, I was called to Culver Studios. They sent me to *Candid Camera*, where someone screwed up and left me in the wrong place. A guy in a big wig appeared and told me that all I needed to do was answer the phone on a nearby table. The guy was clearly Allen Funt's son. I knew what was happening, so I played along and answered the big phone. I was on the show for a few seconds when it aired."

John appeared on *Wheel of Fortune* and won $9,000. "The guy next to me was figuring out the puzzles after only two letters were revealed. He was freaky good at that game!

"One morning, after a bit too much to drink the night before, I was sleeping in. At 9:30 the phone rang. I wasn't sure I wanted to answer, because I knew it was the temp agency. Sure enough, they proposed a job at the Sam Goldwyn Company in Century City.

"Once again, I was put in the mail room. This job had its moments. I impersonated one of the American Gladiators at one point to answer fan mail.

"Later, I started working as a marketing assistant with a team called International Servicing. They shipped films, scripts and video tapes to home entertainment and TV customers. When an assistant position opened up, I applied and got the job. No more temping!"

He worked for a hard-driving British woman who was a real perfectionist challenge. After six months, she left on a medical leave, and John took over. "I learned international distribution servicing by being thrown into the fire. A man named Tom Rothman ran Business Affairs at the time. He'd bring in promo reels we used to create supplemental marketing materials. I would run into him later at Fox."

During the next two years, John learned about film and video labs, shipping companies, contracts. He realized that distribution is a job in the middle of everything—production, legal, marketing, sales.

When his boss saw that he'd learned all he could learn in his position, she proposed a job at another company, and he moved to New World in 1993.

"When I'm coaching others today, I tell them to seriously consider offers like this. Chances are it can be a great, unexpected opportunity. Learn all you can where you are and don't expect everything immediately. You'll be able to take your knowledge anywhere when you're ready.

"At New World, I worked for another woman executive as her team's manager. She was the opposite of my previous boss—

expecting things to get done without her involvement with any of the details. She gave me carte blanche unless something went severely wrong. She designed a new servicing model using Lotus Notes, which I saw as something we could use to leverage the newly exploding Internet. Eventually, she left to commit to her vision full time and build a product to sell to the industry. The gap at New World was filled by me ... after a promotion to VP.

"I went to my first Mipcom international TV sales market in Cannes. That was thrilling. Little did I know it would eventually become torture on a yearly basis. I went to the similar MIP Asia, too. For each sales office, we created a library of tapes of shows we wanted to sell. We traveled with twenty sales people and a hundred VHS tapes, each with numerical labels—in alphabetical order—on tapes and cases. It was two weeks of sheer hell. We added a giant TV and sent it all on a plane. Half the labels would fall off in transit. That was my exposure to the inefficiency of product distribution. I didn't know yet that I'd be the one to change it in a big way.

"During my three years there, I developed more hands-on managerial experience. In 1996, Rupert Murdoch purchased New World. Not sure what that meant, I eventually heeded a suggestion to look outside for my next opportunity.

"Before I left, I experienced a vacuum where you can taste the toxic, fear-based culture. At one point, my wife's grandmother passed away and they wouldn't even let me get out of work early.

"I left and worked briefly for Saban Entertainment before my rescue call from Fox came the next January. Mark Kaner and Marion Edwards, who ran Fox International TV Distribution, wanted to bring my operation from New World to Fox.

"I prepped for the task of building a new group focused on distribution servicing. We planned to hire several people from one of New World's previous distribution suppliers. I met them and assessed who would come to Fox. Not an easy job. I had the power to affect people's livelihoods, an uncomfortable learning experience."

In spite of the challenges, John's Fox job was a great fit for him. He fell into it with no plan, but was good at it and recognized for it. "I'm one of the few people I know who never needed to ask for a raise. I've never been mistreated or ignored. My philosophy of management is that if you're good at it, passionate, consistent and capable, that will be enough.

"Managers should recognize talent. Talent should know that reward won't necessarily happen when you want, but it will be a part of a symbiotic relationship. Unfortunately, that philosophy is not necessarily commonplace in business. You can tell me you should be running the company, tell me why and I will assess you fairly. You may disagree with my decisions, but we can work together."

The Distribution Servicing office at Fox was set up in Ocean Park [near Santa Monica and off the studio lot] in an old New World location that was also the former offices of Stan Lee. John was, in effect, running his own business inside Fox.

"There was no bureaucracy to speak of in my world. Visionary room was plentiful. Writing and presenting were not my strengths, but I developed them as my two greatest assets. We pioneered a series of innovations that completely revolutionized television distribution and sold them inside Fox, which became known as an industry leader willing to break new ground for customers worldwide.

"One of the first things we did was go out to Xerox and get flatbed scanners and copiers we could use ourselves for efficient duplication in the distribution process. At the same time, the concept that would become the FoxFast project was starting to blossom in my mind.

"For example, even though the copiers were disconnected, every time we shipped a new show—eleven seasons of *M*A*S*H* for dubbing in Italian, perhaps—it took weeks to copy all the scripts and related documents and get everything to Italy, at great cost. I wanted to enable the copiers to send everything over the network. The vault stored a copy of all show scripts and served as our resource. When they found out what we were doing, they stopped providing script service and we got the requests from all company departments—now we had a whole new business to run. This wasn't the plan, but it worked out to everyone's advantage."

The same thing happened with script synopses and images, and eventually all marketing materials.

"9/11 was a catalyst. We were copying scripts. Marketing was digitizing images. Everything was loaded into the first versions of FoxFast. After 9/11, planes weren't flying for five days, which meant no content was being sent to the world's broadcasters, and we missed air dates. What if there was a prolonged shutdown? I started thinking about how to digitize videos and broadcast masters.

"At the time, I was also organizing distribution of the *America: Tribute to Heroes* telethon. Each studio was assigned one element of the telethon. Some had talent, some production. Fox was responsible for global distribution deals. TV Distribution President Mark Kaner and his team set up the deals, and we sent the contracts to get executed. My job was to reach out to satellite companies for free distribution and make sure that everyone who signed off got the feed coordinates. The eye-opening moment for me came when we distributed the show live to almost 200 countries simultaneously. Between that and 9/11, I felt an 'aha!' moment that helped me define a better way to distribute.

"I worked with our facilities and a company called SmartJog on the first phase. One of my guys went there to run their process to provide test delivery for preview screeners to customers. Eventually, they experimented with promo content and full-length video. We were bummed because it was so expensive. They were setting themselves up to be video FedEx. One show cost $1,500, which was not close to FedEx tape rates."

John and his team kept experimenting with the technology. They proposed using DVDs instead of tapes, but got vehement push back from tech people who just couldn't get used to the idea.

"They first said that customers would pirate content if we gave them a digital version. Current operations always fight change. I knew we were eventually going to do this, so I was as patient as I could be. I tend to see five years in the future, and some people won't keep up. It's a fight and you can get tired."

Of course, show screeners were soon converted to DVD. At first, they used SmartJog to send them, then the FoxFast website took over. For smaller jobs, they tested a product from a company in South Korea named Arcos that made a media player with a hard disk drive. John and team sent a few of those to the Mipcom and MipTV markets as an alternative to the DVD.

"Our genius Technical Services department head began experimenting with similar things on the Fox lot. We hooked up with him and figured it out together.

"He, too, had the vision. It was the beginning of the golden age of digital distribution, where people came together in an informal way to design a new digital path and make it work. It wasn't always smooth, but it was successful.

"After that, the rights to manage digital distribution became a land grab between Fox groups. That stage was not appealing to me. I'm ready for the fun of innovation, not the managing of a commodity. No one group was passionately driving it anymore and it wasn't as successful. Business, IT, Marketing all collided."

John was at Fox for twenty years. After the heyday of FoxFast, he moved to a new enterprise group designed to service and support all Fox business units. He found that his peers were not interested in continuing his success.

"I honestly don't need the recognition or glory. Credit should go to the team. These managers never embraced that mindset; they were out for themselves and unwilling to come together for the success of the group."

His personal philosophy is unwavering. "I think about things that are completely crazy. Luckily, there is an environment where that attitude totally works. To build my skills, I'm taking a twelve-month course in visionary thinking at Stanford, which is wonderful. In the wrong environment, people get resistant and discredit you before your vision can have time to gel. The people I've met at Stanford are mind-challenging and supportive. They want more and more ideas.

"My next thing must be in a culture that is open and collaborative and something more entrepreneurial, I think—an opportunity not based on ideas from one individual.

"Huge changes are coming from the purchase of Fox by Disney, and after the Weinstein revelations and the recognition that the male-dominated culture in entertainment must evolve. It's the start of an evolution that needs to happen in Hollywood, if not in every industry. The idea of strict hierarchies that can be abused must be over. People need to be respected in a more equal way."

--- Interview 4/2019

CHAPTER 28

MIKE BESSOLO: Where Creatives With Discipline Go in Business

Working with Mike Bessolo was a joy. His expertise is a major reason the FoxFast website was well received by its customers.

I had no idea about his impressive background when we began working together. We knew he wanted us to succeed at creating a first-of-its-kind site that no other studio could match and that he was qualified to lead because of his unique marketing skills, honed over years at Disney.

An SVP of Marketing for Fox International Television Distribution, he worked alongside John Koscheka in Servicing and President Mark Kaner to champion and design the technology, sales and customer service features of the site. Mike's first concern was how FoxFast would be perceived in the wider world, particularly by the customers it was designed to support. I loved brainstorming with him and with the other executives on the team.

He was my ally for the site's launch plan. Our teams collaborated on marketing messaging, graphics for the site itself and the roll-out strategy. Low key in style, Mike's passion was infectious, and his understanding of how to reach an audience masterful.

His enthusiasm and collaborative spirit helped make the IT team's work powerful and innovative. He trusted us to build it, and we trusted him to explain it to our audience. It's just plain fun to work with someone who traffics in making ideas a reality.

Mike's Story

Mike Bessolo has a career to envy. He achieved success in spite of what he says is a true lack of planning.

"I tell my children to think about what they'd like to do for forty years as they start their adult lives. When my son announced that he wanted to study criminology at UC Irvine, I suggested he get a summer job with law enforcement to test drive his idea. He found out that he did love it and is now a police officer. My daughter did the same thing with being a nurse. She hated it. She then test drove as a volunteer at an elementary school, and she's now a happy first grade teacher."

He's honest about the fact that "my choices were not well thought out. I didn't know what I wanted, so I went into business because I thought I could feed myself with it. I learned that I liked arts and advertising, which led to marketing, where creatives with discipline can go in business."

While in college, his first exposure to popular TV came from the inside. "I was a contestant on *The Gong Show*, which was the rage in 1977. We were college guys drinking beer one night when we decided to go on the show. To succeed, you had to be really talented or really stupid. We weren't the talented side, so I came up with the idea of wearing costumes made from trash cans and dancing the Can Can—more difficult that it might sound.

"We performed at three auditions before we performed for host Chuck Barris. I looked through my can as we were dancing, and he seemed not to be paying attention. Two weeks later, NBC sent me a letter with a date for the taping. Apparently, we would be on one of the Christmas shows. Our judges were Jaye P. Morgan and Allen Ludden. We won second most outrageous act of the week, and took home a toaster oven, pork products and Johnson Wax. For years, they continued to give us stuff. Johnson Wax came every year. I tried to get copies of our show from NBC and Chuck Barris Productions, but was never able to do that. Maybe it's better that we not be seen again!"

After college, Mike began his job search. "My father worked for Disney in the late 30's, so we grew up in Glendale. The obvious question for me as I looked around was, 'What more creative company could I work for?' I graduated from college in 1980 and went to Disney for a job.

"They hired me as three steps below a coordinator. I started as a grunt to the grunt and built a career at Disney that lasted for twenty-one years. In the early days, we marketed educational products, including Disney film strips for teachers, via Disney direct mail catalogs sent to K-12 schools."

To get ahead, Mike realized he ought to get a graduate degree. He went to school at night and completed a Masters of Science in Business Administration and Marketing in 1983. At the same time, he moved to a reorganized division called Walt Disney Telecommunications & Non-Theatrical [WDTNT], which pioneered Disney Home Video. While he was there, division management created a cable TV entity called The Disney Channel, and he was pulled over to be one of the first seven people there and part of the original launch crew.

"We worked twenty-four hours a day and launched in April 1983. Our first National Free Preview was hosted by Ernie Borgnine and Buddy Ebsen. Those were the days when HBO was the big kid on the block, and then there was everybody else. The industry was creating itself.

"At first, The Disney Channel was movie reruns and some original programming, including a children's exercise show and a show with Steve Allen. Our first trade ad spoke of fourteen hours a day of Disney magic. Now The Disney Channel is a complete network with lots of incredible original programming. Back then, there were lots of hours to fill.

"In 1985, I got a call because they needed a marketing guy in Disneyland Records and Tapes. I went over there and became the Head of Marketing. This was the music division started by Walt Disney himself in 1956 after the success of the hit song from the TV series *Davy Crockett*. At that time, we were still releasing LPs and 45 singles. I was there through 2001."

Mike's division later became Walt Disney Records. He was there for the growth of cassette tapes, the transition to compact disc and the beginnings of today's download and streaming technology.

"We produced and distributed a range of children's music and read-along products. I'm actually listed as a producer on two albums, *Minnie and Me* and *Children's Favorites Volume 3*.

"In 1989, The Little Mermaid began the rebirth of Disney soundtrack hits. Then came *Beauty and the Beast, Aladdin, Nightmare Before Christmas, The Lion King* and many, many more. I'm proud to have lots of gold and platinum records in my house as a result.

"*The Lion King* album even knocked the Rolling Stones out of the number one position on the Billboard charts. We also distributed the *Disney on Broadway* cast recordings for the theatrical productions of *Beauty and the Beast, Lion King on Broadway* and others. It was a fantastic time to be working there.

"There is a window that I lived through that included the renaissance of the motion picture soundtrack. At Disney, the talent was always the top of the top. Every day, I wondered how I got in the same room with people like Tim Rice and Alan Menken. Today, they don't have the prominence they once did, but then we sometimes shipped a Gold release on day one. Now if you ship 20,000 or 30,000 copies, it's called a hit.

"My job was wonderful because music is integral to the process for just about everything. I worked with all divisions to create true synergy marketing. When a Disney project launched, I got to work with all divisions of the Disney kingdom. I was a guy who got to play in everyone's ballpark. When the plans came together and the launch consumed the country, you were proud that you were shaping culture. You would see kids singing and dancing and wearing the clothes. You were a happy part of America. Sales went through the roof, but, beyond the business success, I was proud to say that I was part of all that.

"It was a moment in time, and I was lucky to have participated in it. Most of the people I worked with are retired now. It's a shame that sometimes when you live through something, you don't realize what it is."

He emphasizes that you say, "Wow" only after it's over.

Walt Disney Records was one of the first divisions to put a website together to support their business. Mike confirms that he didn't spearhead that.

"A graphic designer in my Creative Services group in 1995 came to me and said, 'You know, there's this thing called the Internet.' It was mostly all text at the time.

"He proposed, 'Let me create a site for you.'

"'Why?' I responded. 'There's no one out there to look at it.'"

Mike finally gave him $10,000 to go do it and leave him alone.

"Then, in 1996, Disney devised a vision of how they could dominate the internet. All the divisions wanted a site, and we already had one. We looked like marketing geniuses! I never told management how that came to be. We stumbled into the future."

Mike's career began a second act when he moved to Fox in 2002. He moved to help lead the team that created FoxFast for a target audience of one—the broadcast licensee.

"I moved after tragedy struck my management at Disney. My boss, whom I loved, was killed on 9/11 on the American Airlines flight that hit one of the buildings. The new boss from Europe was fine, but he wasn't her. I was going to sign for three more years anyway when, in October, I got a call from Mark Rosenbaum and Greg Yen at Fox, who knew me from their days in finance at Disney Records.

"They said Fox needed a marketing guy, and I agreed to the conversation. On Halloween night, I drove over and met TV Distribution President Mark Kaner. We had great chemistry. I became more interested and started at Fox on January 2, 2002.

"My style needed to change to build the project at Fox. For Disney, I did presentations in Arkansas for Walmart and for other mass merchandisers. We made huge displays for retailers. My thinking was focused on selling volume. To be successful for FoxFast, we tailored a custom mix of titles for a broadcast company. I learned a different way of looking at marketing.

"Mark wooed me by saying he ran a great department that needed great leadership. What he actually needed and wanted was a change agent. He envisioned an organization and strategy that gave me direction. I drew an organization chart on a piece of paper, and he brought me in as 'the heavy' to create a department that worked. If I'd understood what I was in for, I'm not sure I'd have taken the job.

"We built a new group from the ground up. Disney is an American company, and here I was heading international marketing at my new company. I learned what true international marketing was very quickly. I went to markets in Europe and met broadcasters from all over the world as we built a global organization.

"Today, Disney is forward-looking, and Bob Iger is a key part of the reason. Previous President Frank Wells was a beautiful, smart man who acted as a good balance to Michael Eisner. It was tragic that Frank died when there were so many great things yet to be done. Bob is moving the company forward in a wonderful direction. In fact, he's merging Disney and Fox."

Mike left Fox in March 2011 to focus on an accounting business he and his wife, a CPA, started in 1987, as well as to return to a faculty teaching position at California State University Northridge that he began in the 1980s and continued through the 1990s.

"Our company specializes in accounting for trusts and estates. The business grew while both of us worked twenty-four hours a day at our day jobs. After about thirty years, I knew I was done with corporate life. Conveniently, the business was in a place where we could focus on it, grow it and live off it."

Mike and his wife moved out of crowded Southern California to Northern Nevada, but his company and University job have him back in Los Angeles every month.

"When you run your own company, you're the boss. There's no one to blame but ourselves!"

--- Interview 9/2018

CHAPTER 29

JUSTIN PRIMO: My Creativity Was Required

If you licensed a Fox series to air on your network, what assistance could you expert from Fox to help you hook viewers for your new content?

The answer to that question comes from Justin Primo. He collaborates with your team to find the specific elements of the show that will most appeal to your audience. You know, the quick fifteen-second promo that gets people to say, "I'm going to watch that!"

Because you're working with Fox, you have access to a database of videos, web assets and social media materials on the FoxFast site. That's great, but maybe what's there isn't quite right somehow. You contact Justin and he becomes your partner in customizing the existing choices, or maybe creating something new just for you.

I met him in my capacity as IT Director for the FoxFast application, and he quickly became one of my favorite subject matter experts.

As the website evolved, we collaborated on the design and interface that licensees used to access FoxFast. During our regular meetings, he was always willing to demo the latest creations from one or more of his customers.

Because I was intrigued by his process, we continued regular meetings even when no specific FoxFast project was in the works. These sessions allowed me to keep up with the promotions, hear what customers were requesting, and incorporate all he told me into future plans for FoxFast content and technology.

Plus, he's just plain positive to be around. I never knew him to treat the job as 'just a job.'

Justin's passion for finding the best ways to promote Fox library titles and current shows draws others in. It often made my week because I could escape into his unique brand of fun and temporarily forget the stresses of my job.

Justin's Story
Justin Primo says he was an average college student who studied what interested him without necessarily focusing on a specific industry. "I didn't target a career in television, but I was always a fan. My high school offered TV production classes, which I took. My college major was Marketing and Management."

He loved his classes, but moved slowly in order to combine class work at Cal State Northridge with paying jobs.

"I eventually found myself in my fifth year, which made me what they called a 'super senior.' To make a living, I worked at a drugstore and a Blockbuster video store. At times, I didn't know how to keep it all going. One day, the head of internships at the CSUN Business School told me about a placement at Fox, which I thought sounded great. I was sure I'd have plenty of time for that!"

Justin's first assignment was in the Publicity Department within the TV Distribution Worldwide Marketing group.

"I realized I'd landed in a particularly exciting group. Assigned to assist with press junkets, I recorded interviews with the stars, then had the tapes transcoded. Every day I made photocopies and helped with filing, not the most exciting of tasks.

"More interesting was the assignment to process press clippings. I cut them out of the papers, copied them and made a package of Fox items and industry articles from the day's news, then delivered them to various executives. That's how I met Mark Kaner, International TV Distribution President. Today, the news summary is handled via email and walking about isn't required. I was lucky to have the opportunity to visit multiple offices and meet those in charge."

By the time his internship ended in December, Justin was hopeful that this didn't mean the end of his time at Fox. "I was graduating in May and I knew I wanted to stay at Fox if I could. I hoped they wouldn't forget me by then."

It wasn't likely he would be forgotten. First, they agreed to extend his internship. In the new cycle, he worked with Marketing SVP Mike Bessolo and with the Publicity Department.

"I guess it worked out because they extended the internship again for another 6 months. They told me they wanted to hire me, but there were no open positions. Not forgotten!

"One of the executives set me up with interviews at NBC and a few other places. When I didn't get the NBC job, someone mentioned the Fox temp agency, Ultimate Staffing, as a possibility for me in the short term. I applied there and they called me the next week to come in to take their tests. I passed the tests and entered the temp pool. More luck—a week later, a temp position opened in TV Distribution Servicing, and I was back at Fox."

His new position was available because TV Distribution needed immediate staffing to replace four people who were let go. The job Justin filled was as assistant to TV Servicing EVP John Koscheka.

"I knew him from my internship work at the annual industry event called L.A. Screenings, the event at which the studios host international broadcast buyers and showcase their new Fall Season shows. Marketing, my previous department, created the materials used in the promos. One of the roles of John's unit was to make sure all the promos played flawlessly in the theaters during the event. After three weeks, John offered me a full-time assistant position, which I did not pass up."

Justin was now responsible for delivering promo videos to international broadcasters. For example, if *24* was to premiere in the next week, a copy of a tape containing the US network promo was ordered and then shipped to the licensees, who would localize it for their territory. The Servicing staff repeated the same process for any title in the immense Fox library that a broadcaster planned to air.

"There was plenty to do. Over time, we moved all the tapes to the Fox vault and created an ordering system. I submitted orders and the vault would ship to various dubbing houses via a new, more efficient process that we helped design."

He stayed in that job for three years. "One day, my internship supervisor in Publicity let me know he was leaving. The executives there, who hadn't forgotten me yet, asked me to interview for the position. I enjoyed my current job and had just been promoted to Coordinator. John went out of his way to make me feel wanted, but he knew I was interested in Marketing and urged me to go for it.

"Of course, I ended up accepting the position. In my challenging new job, I became part of the team that produced the promo videos, rather than just shipping the finished products. I also got assignments to handle international publicity for a group of series. At first, I oversaw *Family Guy, My Name Is Earl, Futurama* and later *The Simpsons*.

"Creativity was required more than in any of my previous jobs. This was the time when digital delivery grew in importance and began to replace our tape-based system with easier access to options for publicity and advertising. Customers wanted more and more content and our objective was to help them get it. Sometimes, broadcasters created their own content to supplement ours. We carefully watched that to be sure the custom content followed brand guidelines and did not contain red flags for legal ad restrictions.

"Within the next few years, Fox was seen as a pioneer in the digital transition because of a new application called FoxFast. Marketing became a powerhouse, and Fox was one of the first studios to convert to international digital delivery."

Justin helped drive this evolution as FoxFast first focused on delivery of episodic screeners and marketing materials, and then on transmission of digital broadcast masters made available for each current series or library title. "I helped create videos to explain our transition—to compare the journey of tapes with digital files—a lot of fun to do and hopefully a successful explanation of the benefits of going to a digital delivery system."

His career continued to expand in parallel directions. "In addition to the Publicity role, I produced video-based presentations for the Marketing VP. My videos were featured at industry screenings like the international television sales market, Mipcom, and used by our sales team when meeting with clients to help close potential deals.

"Today, I run a team called Video & Digital Marketing within the Worldwide Marketing group. We're responsible for the production, acquisition and distribution of all video-based marketing materials used for sales publicity in all international markets, across on-air, online and social media.

"Deal structures are forced to evolve along with the technology. We're moving from volume/output deals, where a broadcaster licenses large numbers of titles, to custom deals for broadcasters who want to license different US TV series under different terms. In other words, many contracts provide for individual sales of a custom list of titles. FoxFast allows us to define processes, and provides tools to support those deals."

Justin's core responsibilities include helping the sales team license content in the pre-sales phase and working with broadcasters to promote the content they have licensed. "In terms of time spent on a daily basis, pre-sales is about 30% of the job, while the other 70% is post-sales. To support each sale, we give customers everything they need to market their licensed content.

"Digital delivery brought huge changes. The most influential one is that many shows now air in what's called a 'day and date' pattern. That means that a single episode will air in the US on the same day it premiers in countries around the world. There is no longer any delay, which means marketing materials must be international-ready by being dubbed and delivered on the US air date or shortly thereafter.

"Some materials we create; others we get from the networks. I have a team of three, and we work with outside agencies.

"The series *This Is Us* is simulcast in Canada, for example. For this show, we can't wait for NBC promos, so we produce our own. We work with show production to get cuts from an episode as early as we can and then we cut the promo— without giving away too much of the story!

"We don't have the budget of the network, but I hope that our promos are as good and easily localized for every territory airing the show around the globe."

With all these demands, Justin's team is crazy busy as Fox produces diverse current TV shows. In the era of Peak TV, with players like Hulu and Netflix, there can be more. Plus, they must represent the entire library, not just new programming. It's often hard for them to prioritize.

The job is never static. Requirements constantly evolve. "Pre-sales is becoming more demanding. To provide required automated support, we recently helped redesign the online FoxFast Screening Room. There's now a mobile app and it's easier than ever to watch whatever video you choose.

"From a tech point of view, the software must work, and we have to have the content in time. We're working next on what's called a 'push' model for marketing materials. What that means is that customers don't have to submit orders for specific video. If they have the proper contract options, the materials will be 'pushed' to their servers as soon as it's ready. Everybody wins, and the job is easier all around."

He's been at Fox for his entire career now, and the job still energizes him. "You can think of MipTV and Mipcom like car conventions, but we're selling TV shows instead of cars. We have a booth, but it's a huge space—three stories tall for some markets. I've been to Cannes for the markets maybe six or seven times now, but I've never seen Paris. That's like going to L.A. and only seeing the Convention Center. I don't know restaurants or anything outside the venue. Of course, the conference in Cannes is on the most beautiful beach I've ever seen!

"My role now touches every business at Fox. I talk with TV, Consumer Products, Feature Film. The type and volume of marketing materials customers require has significantly expanded. Five years ago, all they wanted was on-air videos. Now, they want social content and other extensions of the brand. There are 360-degree videos and VR on YouTube that must be produced.

"We're constantly trying to figure out the best ways to improve viewership. How much will it cost vs. the benefit? I like being immersed in figuring out synergies with other groups in the company and with the networks."

"The blending of entertainment and technology is one of the things I'm fascinated by. I like working with IT to define and solve problems and find a tech solution. I've been to Golden Globe parties—but it's not always as exciting as watching FoxFast get better and better.

"Some of the things that people perceive as the most glamorous part of the industry are a lot cooler on paper than in reality. I don't want to miss any of it, though."

--- Interview 4/2019

CHAPTER 30

LIGAYA LANGE:
Leading Our Digital Minglers

Every once in a while, you meet someone like Ligaya Lange who immediately impresses. She was 24 when we first worked together, inexperienced in business, but smart, ambitious and great with people from the beginning.

Assigned to the team responsible for introducing FoxFast to customers during its initial launch, she designed and led webinars for a worldwide audience, excelling at helping others manage change during a pressurized time when the reputation of Fox International TV Distribution was on the line.

Yes, she was inexperienced, but she seemed to intuitively understand what was needed. Her attitude and results were a hit with my team, our management and, most importantly, the customers. Once the launch was in the record books, Ligaya moved to the Customer Service team full time. It was a perfect place for her and she thrived. When enhancements were made to the site, she led the team that introduced the changes to customers and helped when they encountered problems.

Needless to say, I found Ligaya to be someone with a great future ahead of her. For the remainder of my time at Fox, Ligaya and I worked together frequently. By the time I left, she was indispensable to the ongoing success of FoxFast.

I counted on her to tell me straight out when things weren't working and what she thought would fix them. I listened. She earned multiple promotions and now reports to the Disney organization after the merger. Recently married and due to have her first child soon, she's figuring out how to balance the challenges many women face as they orchestrate a career and growing family. I know she'll be just fine.

Ligaya's Story:
Ligaya Lange loved TV when she was a little girl. "I think I know every episode of I Love Lucy. She was my hero. My parents were strict and wouldn't let me watch much, but I could see old things like The Dick Van Dyke Show, I Dream of Jeannie and Bewitched. I was transfixed as I studied the details of each episode.

"My Dad noticed my interest and said, 'You have a great memory for this. Maybe you should work in entertainment.' I knew early on that I wanted to take him up on the idea."

Her mom had a slightly different perspective when she named her Reyna Ligaya, which means Queen of Happiness in Tagalog (Filipino), hoping her daughter would become a newscaster like her idol Connie Chung, the first successful news anchor of Asian descent.

"She even wrote a letter asking Connie to be one of my honorary godmothers. When she replied, 'Yes,' Mom was beyond thrilled. My parents figured that if I ever wanted an on-air career Reyna Lange would be perfect. I decided to go with Ligaya, though, which wasn't the plan! To be absolutely sure I didn't want to be on camera, I interned for newscaster Hal Fishman in college. I found the internship interesting, but sifting through tapes for stock footage felt archaic, and other than the 10 pm news anchors, everyone else seemed more like talking heads. So I targeted Hollywood where I could feed my fascination with how movies and TV are made."

In high school, Ligaya was asked where she wanted to be in ten years and gave a rather specific answer: "I'll go to USC, get a masters, graduate and work for a major studio." That's exactly what she did.

"I entered USC on a running scholarship, didn't like it, and transferred to community college and then to Berkeley as a Mass Communications major. I loved my time at Berkeley but kept my plan to go to USC's Annenberg School for Communication for my MA.

"I was bored in grad school, so I decided to use my free time to get practical Hollywood experience. My first job was working as a temp for a production company in Century City, assisting the CFO/COO.

"One of the executives at the time would be considered a #MeToo nightmare today. He didn't like me because I was one of several who inadvertently found out too much about things he wanted kept private. In an attempt to bully me, he embarrassed me one day in front of everyone, which made me realize I needed to work somewhere with an effective HR department. He eventually tried to fire several of us, but my immediate boss by then protected me and I didn't lose my job.

"After a year, the atmosphere hadn't improved and I knew I had to leave. I saw an ad in Variety for a position at Fox, which seemed the perfect place for me because many of the episodes I loved as a child had aired on the local Fox station. Plus, the studio store stocked plenty of *I Love Lucy* stuff!

"I scheduled interviews with John Koscheka and Scott Gregg, both of whom I liked instantly. They liked me, too, and I got hired for my second job out of college after my only real interview ever.

"I was honest with John and told him that I didn't know too much about Servicing, but did know that it doesn't matter how great your content is if you can't distribute it efficiently. I'd learned that while working for my first production company. The interview with Scott was more formal. I went to the 19th floor of Fox Plaza and sat in his office with that fabulous view as backdrop. At the end of our talk, he told me he was impressed I went to Berkeley and that I had interviewed well. It seemed to him that I could fit into his department easily."

Ligaya became an official Executive Assistant for both of them in 2007. Her role was strictly admin, answering phones, scheduling meetings and keeping them on target.

"I was serious about doing a good job no matter the task and felt lucky to have settled somewhere so quickly.

"A year or so later, John began writing a document he called the Digital Initiative White Paper, which introduced the vision that became FoxFast. When it was ready to be distributed to our business partners, I helped organize that communication and assisted in prepping him to present it at the annual International Broadcasting Conference (IBC) in Amsterdam. As the project developed, he gave me more to do and I asked a lot of questions. The need to onboard more customers for digital delivery from FoxFast grew, and they partnered me with one temp who couldn't do it all himself and didn't enjoy the sales portion of the job as much as I did. It was also clear I couldn't be both an admin assistant and work on the digital initiative, so digital onboarding became my one and only job.

"In 2009, I was promoted to Digital Coordinator, a role with no job description when I started. I helped with everything: onboarding clients to FoxFast, scheduling digital conferences on the lot and assisting John with reaching out to sales people, clients and business partners.

"The goal was to convert everyone to the new system by 6/1/2011. After that date, customers could choose between free download of titles from FoxFast or physical shipment of tapes, for which they paid the cost.

"We contacted about 800 Pay and Free TV broadcast clients in total, adding others over time to include businesses like EST (Electronic Sell-Through). TV Distribution President Mark Kaner was a great sponsor, and John had endless and infectious energy. We were joined by folks from Marketing, FMS (Fox Media Services) and IT, who were all drafted to play their parts.

"The annual spring LA Screenings sales event was a great venue for introducing FoxFast to new customers and upcoming enhancements to existing customers. John commissioned an in-house team of 'Digital Minglers,' which I led. We were evangelists who interacted directly with the visiting international sales team and clients, showcasing FoxFast on iPads, devices new to the market at that time. We worked from a script, and everyone was so well educated they could handle anyone! We did this over the course of two LA Screenings, which gave me experience presenting and speaking publicly to the sales teams.

By the June, 2011, target date, 80% of the customer base had been converted to digital. For her next challenge, Ligaya was deputized to various projects whenever they needed someone who could speak to both engineers and customers. It was the perfect way to develop additional expertise for the entire business and a crash course in how to create a comprehensive strategy with a cohesive message.

She planned and executed multiple traveling road shows and liked going all over the world, visiting both vendor and client offices. For her efforts, she was immersed in how clients worked to receive Fox content, localize it for their audience and get shows on the air. "I saw the process end to end, a total whirlwind and unmatched training in marketing to the industry.

"By the time I turned 30, in addition to customer service success, I had ample experience training our international employees and product preparation partners in the new digital supply chain. As the tech evangelist, I taught them how to use the Fox Media Cloud to access titles, create properly formatted files modified for local markets and upload them back to the platform. It was also part of my job to test system enhancements during UAT (user acceptance testing). I lived in the two worlds of tech and sales and interacted with both groups in broadcaster offices everywhere.

"My mentors were invaluable. Mark Kaner, Scott Gregg, John Koscheka and IT VP Tom Tralongo each believed in and trusted me. It helped that we had a great product and a great supply chain team that I believed in as well. That leadership team was not afraid to let the younger generation shine.

"John was the catalyst. He put me in that position and said, 'Go for it.' I learned the organization and confirmed that the best people to ask for help are those behind the scenes. The IT team helped so much, and I saw myself as a member of the team. When there was a big hurdle to clear, I involved an executive, but always sparingly. The truth is they knew I could make things happen, and they liked the results. You learn who does the best work and how to make things happen because you know who can deliver."

Ligaya is aware that she was part of a unique moment. "It ended in 2013-ish when there was a new group created called Enterprise Operations and new management with new priorities took over customer service.

"Beginning in 2014, I ran a meeting called COPS, the cross-operational project status meeting. Its purpose was to synchronize IT and the business with enhanced communication. The group still exists today. Disney is evaluating who should own it and how to transition it to their environment. The challenge is that there can be as many as 50 different stakeholders, depending on the active project list.

"As the leader I had to learn how to maneuver through the politics. You must manage up and down and all around. It's hard, but to me it was fun to learn what people care about and what makes them tick. It helps that I like people and finding ways to ensure smooth communications.

"The meeting is bi-weekly now. I think it works by connecting people who might not talk otherwise, as we tend to work in silos and not recognize how much we do it. One challenge has been that, because I run the meeting, people tend to think that I know the answer and I don't always. I'm the facilitator and have had to learn how and when to use authority. Even if I do know the answer, I need to respect the chain of command.

"I was also put in charge of implementing a database called the Enterprise Customer Profile, which linked to order management and FoxFast. We mapped it all and ensured that everything meshed together.

"Unfortunately, all of it was less energizing than launching a major change like FoxFast.

"Outside the office, I revived my success as a high school and college runner, eventually co-founding the Fox Triathlon Team. The team grew from five people to hundreds. In 2019, there were both assistants and C-suite executives involved. It's a great way to get exposure to diverse people and roles.

"In 2015, I was thrilled to learn I'd been nominated for the Fox High Potential program, run by the studio's CFO and designed to groom future leaders. The timing was perfect to help me devise strategies for accepting change in my world and adjusting to the upheaval of becoming part of Disney.

Ligaya's personal life has recently become her priority. "You have to calculate that about two years of your life will be totally focused on a new baby, and you can't really be a powerhouse executive at the same time. I'm aware that I want stability and a balanced life because I'm a bit burned out on demanding situations where I'm not the expert even though people want me to be. In other words, politics is exhausting. I've worked on the Disney transition for three years now and will admit to more than a little change fatigue.

"Unfortunately, I can see that the successes in my personal life have slowed down my career. The limiting effect isn't right, but I'm comfortable prioritizing my family right now. Later, I can refocus on my career.

"I believe you can do whatever you want in the world. I can stay at Disney, or maybe start my own company. I intend to do good, exciting things, but I'm not one to jump around, even though I'm a Millennial, and I guess that should appeal to me.

It seems a risk to move from a place where you have a good reputation. More money is inviting, but so is stability as long as the opportunities are there."

The pandemic has given Ligaya the option to work from home and that means more time for life in general. She believes that if this forced upheaval teaches businesses how to reduce or eliminate the commute, parents will be more present and still able to sustain successful careers. Companies in turn will be more successful if employees have a more balanced life. She will be happy to be available for her daughter without being any less productive at the office.

"Disney is asking employees how they feel about working from home. Once all the dust settles with this acquisition and pandemic, I do plan to work where I'm happy and fight for the title and salary I deserve if it comes to that.

"You have to ask for what you want or the powers that be will assume you'll take less. I don't give less, so I won't take less. My mentors at Fox encouraged and empowered me, never making me feel as if I deserved less as a woman. That gives me confidence to think big and be whatever I choose to be.

"That's not always the case in entertainment. I'm fortunate."

--- Interview 5/2020

THE FOXFAST TEAM

The remaining stories in this memoir spotlight people from the FoxFast team, which was initially staffed by Tom Tralongo, using his remarkable intuition about how to build a top-functioning team. As I've said, the team and its partners created a unique, never-before-available website for Fox International Television Distribution. It was a privilege to work with them, but an even bigger honor to know them. To those here and other members of the team over the years, thank you.

CHAPTER 31

ASHISH BHATT: I
Believe I Was One of the
First Binge Watchers

When you find a team member you can rely on, it's a glorious thing. I quickly learned that Ashish Bhatt is smart, congenial, organized and committed, with an appropriate dose of common sense.

He joined the FoxFast team as a Business Analyst and handled any assignment with excellent results. I knew he grew up in India, of course, but he seemed to have our American work style comfortably down when we started creating together. By that I mean he understood IT and how to talk to the Fox user community and was at ease as a member of a closely collaborating high-tech team.

Unfortunately for us, family concerns required him to relocate back to India after a time in L.A. He continued to work for Fox remotely and could be counted on for prompt deliveries, detail-focused accuracy and unwavering FoxFast team spirit.

We've remained long distance friends. I'm glad I met him and glad that he enjoyed working with us. I know we benefit from knowing him.

Ashish's Story
Ashish Bhatt started his career as a computer teacher. He decided to study computers because the father of one of his friends started a new computer institute, and he wanted to work there.

He remembers it this way: "I first studied computers in the seventh grade. My friend's father tempted me with this thought: 'You should come here. You might like it.' I took his advice and I did like it."

He also began teaching because he needed cash. It was the late '90s and computers were new in India. Businesses were emphasizing computerization, which meant his timing was perfect. His first students were transportation employees, like those who work for the DMV in the US.

In 2000, he got his break with Sandvik, a Swedish company whose focus is mining tools; they specialize in stainless steel.

"My first job was as a developer. At that time, there was no formal structure for IT groups. There weren't titles like BA [business analyst], QA [quality assurance] or developer. Developers did everything. We met with the business to define requirements, collect existing workflow data, design screens and then develop the code. I did my own testing, including full QA. The final step was to work with the business on UAT [user acceptance testing] and publish the application. I wasn't even part of a team. There were three developers on staff and each of us completed our own modules."

After five years, Ashish decided he wanted to move to the next level. He liked developing front-end modules best because the job included lots of talking with the users, but that meant he needed more business savvy. He focused on an MBA, applying to schools in both India and the US, and eventually left India for the US with a full scholarship to study at the Jesuit Scranton University in Pennsylvania.

"At that time, lots of people in India went to the UK to study, but those degrees were not qualifying for getting good jobs in India, and I really wanted to learn something with a future. I taught students and assisted professors as part of the agreement. The scholarship included a stipend, so my time there was well funded."

A year later, Ashish received an honorary directorship at a nearby Jesuit school, Our Lady of Peace. "I did all the computer work for them even though, according to the rules, they couldn't pay me while I was studying. I installed hardware and did repairs, as well as providing computer support."

After graduation, he began an internship at the Sandvik office in Scranton. Following that, he moved to New Jersey, where he was hired by PB Systems, a successful outsource consulting company. "The founder's brother is a computer technology professor at the Scranton school. He knew about my computer experience and suggested the job at PB. It was an excellent choice for me."

He was employed by PB for many years, most of which was spent as a consultant for the Fox studio in Century City, California.

"At first, I was scared to move to California because I knew no one on the West Coast. I finally agreed to try it after completing my first project in New Jersey, for Clifford Paper."

He moved to Irvine in April 2008, and began his first assignment at Fox. "I didn't know about the company, except that the contract allowed me to work remotely in Irvine and not commute up the 405 Freeway to the studio. My first project was a new website called FoxKona. I did the research for the design but was never identified with the resulting application because of a reorganization that shifted me to a new team. A person from the Home Entertainment group took over FoxKona in IT, and I was given his position with a TV distribution system called Avalon.

"I hit it off with Elaine, the team leader. I was nervous, but the interview worked out. Accepting the new assignment meant I would, reluctantly, start the commuting grind. It was two hours in the morning and the same or longer at the end of the day. I ended up doing that until 2011, when I returned to India and worked remotely for the PB offsite team contracted to Fox.

"During the interview, Elaine asked if I liked movies. I responded that I liked *Die Hard*. When she revealed that I was sitting in the building where they shot it, I was hooked. The environment at Fox, at least on that team, was more laid back than I was used to, but still very professional. Other than that awful commute, everything at Fox was wonderful."

Ashish's job was perfect for a TV lover. "I watched all of several Fox series, including How I Met Your Mother and Bones. I watched White Collar, too. My team wrote the system that put the shows online, and I devoured them on the weekends. I believe I was one of the first binge watchers."

When family priorities dictated, Ashish made the difficult decision to move back to India. For one thing, it could be tricky to interact with L.A. because of the time difference. "We are 12.5 hours different from L.A. At first, I found it hard to adopt, in essence, a 24/7 schedule in order to work during L.A. days and India nights. But I thought it was important to be available and became the exception on the team. It was fun most of the time.

"For the first eighteen months, I did the same job as in the US, but I missed the innovation part of the projects—being in a meeting and providing input as things developed real time.

"I became less sure I was doing important work. It was hard to participate in screen design, for example. Most of my communication was with IT, not the business people, which meant that I lost contact with the idea people in the business. That's the part of the job I most enjoyed. I didn't want to focus on the technical challenges, but that seemed to be where I could contribute most often."

Ashish felt forced to slow his expectations to reduce frustration. He still gave one hundred percent to the executives who drove the business, but he worked fewer hours. "Fox reorganized into something called the Enterprise structure. Things became increasingly difficult. My challenge became more that I was just a voice on the phone, working with people who didn't know me in person. It's hard for them to learn who you are and what you can deliver only over the phone."

The offshore team moved away from the business analysis role to QA or technical support tasks, which required less interaction with L.A. staff.

In spite of the difficulties of working remotely, Ashish was again recognized as someone who could help sort out ongoing issues. "I took the initiative to help rectify problems that arose. Users started to know me again. We became visible as part of the team and recognized as pros that were contributing."

As the website became more stable, support became routine. The India operation assumed responsibility for automated QA and testing, as well as support.

After staying in his remote role for nine years, Ashish decided it was time to leave Fox. "I earned a total of fourteen years of experience, and my job became monotonous. I realized that someone with less experience could do my job just fine.

"Then PB Systems was sold to Ebix, a most unsettling upheaval. Local management issues were ignored. The new parent company didn't believe in taking care of employees in the same way.

"They are work-focused and told us we must make profit the goal. We worked under a totally different management mindset."

He fought it for two years, and then realized he couldn't change it. "I was unhappy every day. I saw starting my own company as perhaps my best option because I also understood that I had nothing to sell to another company that would get me the job I wanted because people saw me as a support person.

"There was not much available in my area of India with the studios like Star India or Sony. Most have apps developed in the US. One possibility was to take over what Ebix was doing for Fox. But they were reluctant to switch to a brand new vendor, even one run by a familiar person."

Ashish found a customer who wanted to move with him. "I finally did it. My initial customer is one I worked for at times at PB when I wasn't full time with Fox. They've worked with me for ten years and wanted a company who could handle a larger portion of their IT work. We are both happy with the new arrangement.

"It took almost a year to get things established and leave Fox. I was open with them about what I was doing when the time came. It's been much better since I made the break.

"My new company's first client is one of the biggest firms in the paper industry. They buy paper from the mill and sell it to their customers, acting as bulk buyers for the end customer. We support them with a team of ten on a yearly retainer.

"I'm happy now. My customer is happy and aware that the situation is better for us. I work from home, but I have an office where my employees work. I commute there once a week, a total of 200 miles on Monday, my only long day."

Ashish doesn't plan to come to the US any time soon. When he's ready for new customers, all of that could change.

He sums up his history like this: "Working in entertainment is amazing. It's fun. It's an industry going through lots of changes, and I was there for some of them. "For example, in 2011, after the Japanese tsunami, Fox was the first to ship disk drives to customers when tapes could no longer be used because the vendor that manufactured them was destroyed. We kept digital copies of files and could send hard drives quickly.

"It's not just the industry you choose to work in, it's the group you work with that makes it fun and challenging. When I did the same work for different management, suddenly the job wasn't fun. I've seen what happens when the business emphasis takes over a focus on the people. I would work at Fox or anywhere if I could find a good group. Still, entertainment is the business I've liked the best. The people are the most fascinating. I love what they're doing. And I like being part of it."

--- Interview 6/2018

CHAPTER 32

KOUNDINYA GADAMSETTY: They Listened And Wanted Our Feedback

The ability to accurately test a computer application is critical to the success of any project team. To be good at it, a quality assurance [QA] professional must be willing to live in the details, to exercise each and every path through complex code. Before certifying that something works, the tester must prove it by using the app in ways most users will never experience. And, do this not just once, but every time the app is changed, enhanced or upgraded.

A good tester is worth everything to the business that publishes an app.

Koundinya Gadamsetty sealed our ability to succeed with the launch of FoxFast when he came on board as a QA analyst in 2008 and assumed the role of gatekeeper, reliably testing everything the team built.

He worked remotely from the office in India maintained by the third-party company we hired to be the technical team for the project. On his first visit to our L.A. office, I found him to have one of the quickest minds I'd met in some time. It was a pleasure to get to know him in person.

His personality is quiet, yet gregarious, and he's always smiling. Humble and collaborative, he calmly went about his job and proved to me that I could trust his results. If he said the code was tested and ready to launch, I knew we were safe. The fact that he apparently was honest when he told me he "loved to test" was the only thing that gave me pause. I think testing is a bit tedious, especially when we were required to test the same functions across all the possible machines and software versions we supported for FoxFast.

I was really glad Koundinya was on my team. He's still on the FoxFast QA team today, and I'm glad about that, too.

Koundinya's Story

Koundinya Gadamsetty left home after 10th grade to attend high school in a different state in India. He'd expected to move far away for school and live in housing provided by the school. Interested in studying engineering and communications in college, he did that next.

After graduation, he found he couldn't get a job that he liked. To expand his options, he completed a few computer courses, which showed him that there were more opportunities in IT.

"After one course, I participated in a placement effort by the course provider. They interviewed us and selected a few people to hire as software testers. After two years at that job, I accepted a position with a new company, PB Systems, also as a QA person. They were looking for testers to assign to a new project at Twentieth Century Fox."

He didn't know anything the job required and nothing about the entertainment business. However, he learned a great deal quickly because "you have to know the business better than most professionals to thoroughly test the computer systems that support that business.

"I started on FoxFast in 2008 as the first person on the QA team, and began by testing the site's database, called DAPR. After we added two more people, I was named the team leader. At first, we worked remotely from India with instructions from the team in California. As part of my new role, I made my initial trip to the US at the end of September in 2008. It was time to learn how the business worked by talking with the people who did the job."

After a few weeks, he returned to India to start detail work with his team. They were responsible for reviewing business documents for processes to be automated, understanding how they would be translated to software requirements and screen layouts, then creating a test plan and test cases.

"The development team was also in India, which gave me easy access to their work as the site was being built. I participated in daily calls with the team in L.A., which enabled us to stay in touch with any changes in the design or objectives of the site.

"The business analysts didn't use today's method of writing user stories to define a path through a site. Instead, the development schedule was more traditionally defined based on features that needed to be finished. The QA Team tested changes for existing screens on sites called FoxScreening and FoxNow, and then verified test screens for new features to add businesses like EST/VOD [Electronic Sell-through and Video On Demand]. We also helped plan new features that were to be part of the full FoxFast environment.

"I liked the job once I understood what we were trying to build and what we wanted to achieve. It was a new thing for the company and for the industry.

"I was genuinely interested in movies, which made it exciting to try to understand the problems the new system was meant to solve. The team leader encouraged me to be part of business meetings so I could best hear first hand what the users wanted. We were helped by the fact that the business community was tightly integrated. After we heard the requirements, I was involved in drawing the mockups and creating screen wire frames that illustrated the basic look and feel of the interface. I was a part of all of it."

The FoxFast process was different from Koundinya's past projects. "In previous jobs, QA people were separate from the development effort. There was less feedback as we worked. At Fox, they listened to what we said and wanted our feedback."

Koundinya continues to work at Fox today. "Mostly, the job became more formal as the scope of the site grew. From an initial tight-knit team of five developers and two to three QA staffers, we grew rapidly as FoxFast expanded to incorporate the online Screening Room and new features like broadcast-quality downloads. Having a bigger team meant we had to evolve to a more formalized process to record activities as we completed them. We developed a workflow applied consistently to each iteration of the site as it was finished.

"Now we have a streamlined process that documents everything. That's possible because we learned lessons from our mistakes and incorporated changes as we needed them.

"There are multiple teams responsible for QA these days. I lead the team in India. There are also teams in L.A. and the Philippines."

Koundinya's group is responsible for both automated and manual QA tools to combine the benefits of both testing perspectives. They used the QTP automated tool at first because team members were experienced with it. "We abandoned it when the site was rewritten for the launch of FoxFast 2.0 in a way that wasn't working for the automation services we used." Now they prefer Selenium, an open-source tool.

"Today's team in India is nine people who are responsible for testing new functions via test cases to exercise the software and the hardware. The entire site now includes four different portals for different Fox groups. There are about 20,000 test cases, only about 1,700 of which are automated. Each portal [screen that provides access to the site, which varies by business group] includes about fifty core test cases. For each development sprint or build, we add new automated cases and new cases for new features. Since all aspects of the site are rarely updated with each release, we choose the relevant cases for verifying each deployment.

"After a deployment, the final step is to run a regression test to confirm that the site is whole and operational, which means we run another 1,500 cases to verify the build."

Koundinya loves his work. "In the past ten years, the most interesting thing was the opportunity to visit Fox, meet the people who work for International Distribution and collaborate with them. I was in L.A. once every year to maintain visibility to the businesses we support.

"Our team works because many members have been around for so long. The team's motivation is high because the pay is good and we are recognized for what we contribute. In India, it's exciting to work for Fox. I've enjoyed job security, and the money is good.

"My current goal is to spend more time working with new QA tools for apps. We're testing on different browsers, including, of course, Android and Apple operating systems. It's a challenge just staying apace with the rapid evolution of software capabilities. I always feel like maybe I can't keep up. The constant change motivates us to learn new things, that's for sure!"

Over the years, during periods when the team organization was changed, there was sometimes an opportunity for Koundinya to work on other aspects of the FoxFast project.

"I was on the customer support team for about nine months. We combined that with a reduced QA workload for a while. TV Distribution Servicing and Marketing teams would send us their issues, and we sent them recommended solutions. And, the best thing: as part of customer support, I spoke directly to FoxFast customers I would not otherwise know, in places such as Australia."

Koundinya recently relocated to L.A. with his family. He sees the future as promising and ripe with enticing possibilities. "Opportunities are expanding beyond IT to other well-paying jobs. Who knows where I'm destined to be. The latest big thing on the agenda is the Disney purchase and how our roles evolve under new management."

--- Interview 1/2019

CHAPTER 33

UMESH MANDADAPU:
They Hired 15 Out of 400 Applicants and I Was One of Them

Technical expertise of the highest caliber was integral to the success of the FoxFast launch. In addition to the QA test team led by Koundinya Gadamsetty, we hired a coding expert named Umesh Mandadapu, who fit supremely well into a team that was a joy for me to lead.

He signed on as another of the talented experts we found when we hired PB Systems to be the tech lead for FoxFast. Yes, we were planning online services that didn't yet exist. And, yes, we stretched the known limits of digital video, particularly when we sent it over unreliable networks to customers in far-off places. Because of pros like Umesh, the FoxFast team was populated with people willing to try the untested and to pursue excellence every time.

I began working with him when I joined the team in 2007. The group had a great reputation and I soon learned why. We employed more than one enthusiastic, skilled and committed techie in our midst. It was wonderful that I never worried about whether Umesh's work would be delivered according to specs.

At first, he programmed for the remote team in India, but eventually decided to move to the United States. He joined the team live and in person in L.A. and continued to contribute with humor, competence and a powerful work ethic. I can confirm that there was lots of fun along with the hard work.

One day, he looked at me with a straight face and continued a conversation about the average age of the team's members. "Well, Elaine, I'm newly 35 and you're what, maybe 45?" Well, I was over 55 at the time, so I assumed he was trying to be funny. He insisted that he couldn't believe I was much older since I fit right in. I will say that working with that team did help to keep me young in heart and mind.

I've not met a nicer, more giving person than Umesh. His smile could be counted on to make my day better. He's continuing to be indispensable to FoxFast, and can take a chunk of the credit for its reputation as the best online customer-service site in the international television business.

Umesh's Story
Umesh Mandadapu did not choose IT at the start of his career, in spite of his formal education. He grew up in a small town and headed for college in a larger city when it was time. "I completed my college degree in computer engineering because I loved math. I remember that there was one computer for the whole classroom. The teacher did the work and the class watched. It was a very precious machine!"

His interests also included finance, which he thought he might pursue later.

"The engineering courses in college included a focus on Signals & Systems. After college, I saw ads for an Indian naval base that was looking for just that expertise. There was a rigorous process to join the team, but it was a great opportunity. I applied and was one of seven accepted for the program.

"When I suffered an injury soon after I started, I changed my mind about pursuing that career. I didn't want to chance another accident with more physical training coming soon.

"I returned home, where everyone suggested that I should go back. Sure that I wasn't cut out for such a physical job, I started looking for something else to do. From a listing in the newspaper, I saw that PB Systems was looking for programmers to train.

"It was an opportunity close to home, so I went in for the interview. The process took two days, and they hired fifteen out of four hundred applicants; I was one of them. After three months of training, I earned the best scores, which led to an assignment for a project at 20th Century Fox in 2003. Until recently, my boss was the same as when I started there. Team members stayed for a long time because it was and is a great job."

His first assignment for Fox was as an application and database developer, working remotely from India.

"The assignment was for new systems that would streamline international TV distribution. I worked on projects called DAPR, FoxNow, FoxPress and FoxFast. DAPR was a content management application for the new FoxFast system. FoxNow and FoxPress provided the user interface for online access to marketing and press materials for Fox shows. Both these sites were eventually folded into FoxFast.

"I stayed in India through 2006, when the DAPR system went live. With PB's financial support, I was able to continue my education via online classes and get a Master's degree in Software Engineering from one of India's top ten universities, also in 2006. The school, BITS Pilani, is equivalent to a similar school in the US. Its program is limited to people who have full-time jobs with good academics and proper mentor support."

During the final months of the DAPR project, Umesh made his first visit to the US to meet the home team and stayed for two and a half months. Two years later, in 2008, he returned during the FoxFast upgrade that would launch digital delivery of video screeners. He enjoyed being in the US even more the second time around.

It became clear to him that his best way forward was to move to a new country, which he did on New Year's Eve, 2009. He started work at Fox in L.A. as a PB Systems contractor on January 4, 2010.

The FoxFast project continued to provide unique challenges for his programming skills. "Next, we set up digital delivery of broadcast quality [BQ] episodes and films via FoxFast. The studio video people collaborated with us to define coding standards for video in different formats. The videos were uploaded to the site, ready for distribution based on contract rules. Security and protection for each file and control of authorized access had to be unbreakable.

"The rules were defined in a new set of logic we built called the Access Control List [ACL]. The power of FoxFast is to automatically figure out who can view or download a video based on contract authorizations. To do that, we needed to automate rules for who gets deliveries of licensed shows and when, and implement layers of security to ensure the content was only provided to users with proper credentials."

Umesh may have initially seen finance as a career alternative if he soured on computers, but he immersed himself in entertainment and is very happy at Fox.

"I like learning and applying the technology and the challenge of seeing it all work together," he says. "It sometimes takes long hours and frustrating code redesigns, but I love it.

"In 2016, I went through a hard time after what became negative management changes. Luckily, things went back to being supportive and challenging again. Sometimes you can't control the changes, and sometimes you need a great boss to make the challenges worthwhile. I'm happy to say that we went from feeling demoralized to a much better place."

He now spends sixty percent of his time as the architect for solutions to improve FoxFast. "It's still the online storefront for B2B [business to business] digital delivery for the Fox library. I'm the core enterprise architect for the UHD [Ultra-High Def] component-based delivery called IMF [Interoperable Master Format]. New technologies keep arriving and I keep learning how to make them work in our environment."

For the remainder of his time, he acts as the liaison to other Fox IT teams, which brings him visibility throughout the larger Fox tech community. When other groups design automated interfaces to FoxFast, Umesh guides those teams on how to get the job done.

"The site is becoming central to distribution for all Fox divisions, which means the number of integrated systems keeps growing. And so does the effort required to keep everything in sync as the central and satellite systems change and improve. I do enjoy being in the center of the activity, driving greater adoption of our toolset."

For a number of years, he commuted for more than sixty miles each way to work and back, a mind-numbing drive from his home in Orange County to Century City. He recently moved his family closer to L.A. and the Studio and is much happier. He made that commitment because he loves his job and plans to stay with Fox and FoxFast for as long as they'll have him.

"If you're smart at Fox, you can make real contributions. FoxFast is one of the best systems in the marketplace today, and I'm proud to help keep it running."

Now that Disney purchased Fox, there will likely be further changes. Should something happen and he must move on, he has ideas about how he could change his career path.

"I may want to try real estate; it interests me. My dad and I have a real estate office back in India, and we can expand on that."

Or maybe it would be time for his finance passion to play a larger role at last.

--- Interview 6/2019

CHAPTER 34

RAMESH GURRAM:
Anyone With a Problem
Is Made to Feel Heard

Ramesh Gurram, now in charge of FoxFast worldwide site operations, guides his team and site visitors through upgrade transitions beautifully, as only he can.

In addition to being a wonderful database and software technician, Ramesh has a positive attitude that he brings to work every day, plus the unexpected ability [for a tech guy] to interact with people at all levels of the businesses supported by the site. He's happiest when he can deliver exactly as promised. His mission is to help where needed and, in every case, to make sure that anyone with a problem is made to feel important.

He's been with the site for more than a dozen years, which means his knowledge of all corners of the application is comprehensive. He can answer most questions without looking anything up. Well liked not only by the team and the business people he supports, his role as licensee support team lead has given him a positive reputation with Fox customers all over the world.

When I visited Fox recently after my retirement, I stopped by to say hello to Ramesh and the rest of the team. He looked up at me, grinned and said, "We're about ready to launch an update to the site. The process has been pretty much automated now and it's a one-button operation to make the changes happen." Back when I was there, launching a deployment took multiple people multiple hours to complete, so I was impressed.

He continued, "Would you like to have the honor? If so, come back in a few minutes and we'll be ready."

I showed up behind him as he stared at his screen shortly thereafter. He rolled his chair back and said, "Just click that button right there."

I did and the launch was done! Just that easy. Amazing. Ramesh was grinning even wider, if that's possible.

"Thank you," he laughed. "I knew you could do it!"

As I listened to his story, I realized that it's uncannily similar to Umesh's. They've followed basically the same path through PB Systems, working first in the offshore FoxFast team, and then moving to L.A. and staying with the project because it feeds their passion for innovation and productive collaboration.

They're obviously two different people and both are key to the success of FoxFast. As you read Ramesh's story, don't blame them for having similar trajectories. It's apparently a successful approach to finding and maintaining a career!

Ramesh's Story
Ramesh Gurram is from a small village in India with around 400 residents. He completed 5th grade in his hometown, and then moved to a small city for additional education.

"My whole family moved with me," he explains. "I finished middle school and high school in 1996, then went to college for a Bachelor's degree in engineering. I moved to the bigger city of Chennai for the degree program, and my family did not follow this time."

He knew he was good at math and science, so engineering made the most sense as his major. He earned above 98% in these subjects.

"I'm not at my best in chemistry or medicine, so I followed what I was good at. After four years in Chennai, studying electronics and communication, I studied microprocessors and semiconductors, as well as programming on larger computers. I liked programming microprocessors the best. Then I learned more programming languages as well."

After completing the degree, he had three options: working for a semiconductor company, which wasn't a big industry then; continuing for a masters degree—which usually meant studying abroad; or finding a job.

"My family had supported my education so far, but now it was time for me to help them. My brother was ready to go to school, and I wanted to no longer be dependent on them while they supported him. Because I knew computing concepts and languages like C and C++, I found a position with PB Systems. The job came because PB was looking for people and posted an ad, which, luckily, I read. One of my cousins also worked there, which helped.

"I was fortunate to first start on a project at Twentieth Century Fox, working from PB's India offices. The project was FoxPress, a website that broadcast licensees used to access press materials for shows and features under license."

Ramesh enjoyed the work. "An existing team member told us how the system needed to work. He'd worked for Fox for a while already and knew exactly what we should do. If he could describe it, we could code it!"

In 2003, the team began the DAPR [digital asset product repository] project, which was designed as the data repository for TV Distribution marketing and digital video assets. Ramesh led the offshore team responsible for building the technology. The project team was trained to utilize the Microsoft .net syntax, which was very new.

The first version of DAPR launched in 2004. There were a few problems, but they were ironed out and the sites ran smoothly. The customers in TV Distribution were most pleased.

For his next project, Ramesh met a new IT Director named Alison Jessup [now Lyons], who worked with him to launch the Client Presentation website in 2005. This new team also created two other sites focused on relatively new but similar lines of business. FoxEST and FoxVOD were portals that catered to the specific requirements of electronic sell-through and video-on-demand customers.

"For the first time, I was given an opportunity to visit with the business to gather requirements for these new sites. To meet them in person, I traveled to L.A. on my initial trip outside of India—also my first plane ride. Except for short trips back home, I've been here ever since."

Ramesh loved meeting the people he'd been working with remotely from India. "Early in my stay, I had a studio tour, which was wonderful. And, then, Tom Tralongo took over as the VP for our area. I am very thankful to him because he gave me the opportunity to continue on fascinating projects at Fox.

"For a time, I was officially based in India, but traveled back and forth quite regularly. Each time I returned to India, I became more convinced that I wanted to live in the US.

"Once again, a team tour guide helped convince me by showing me around L.A. I liked what I saw. I felt comfortable with the culture and became certain that a full-time move was what I wanted. I approached the guys at PB Systems, who agreed to move me to the California office in Irvine. My dream had come true. I started a fresh life in a new country with a job I loved."

On September 1, 2007, he got married. His new wife joined him when he arrived in the US on April 20, 2008, and they started their family in their new location.

Ramesh feels grateful for the visibility of working on FoxFast. His role expanded until he was the Technical Project Manager for the site.

"The project was one of the most prominent in television. The team was challenged to build innovative features that didn't exist at the time we created them. We worked on FoxPilots and FoxScreening, which became the first online video screener sites in the industry, before they were folded into FoxFast. With them, Fox licensees could log in and watch full-length episodes and movies from the Fox library. No other studio could match the performance and capabilities of our site.

"I was the technical architect for the initial FoxFast project. I designed the database. I also built the architecture for the front-end portals. That was the piece I liked the best. It was innovative, and it allowed me to learn new technology. I liked making it work.

"I've never regretted my decision to move here. I'm still on the FoxFast project, which became known as FoxFast 2.0 after we enhanced it.

"The team is amazing to collaborate with. We work as a family. We also have a great relationship with our business and even get together after work. Our families are included. We have wonderful team lunches. We'd go to restaurants like Gladstones, which is closed now, but which once was a fabulous place for lunch by the Pacific. I have many fond memories.

"In 2013, we started the project to design and build FoxFast 3.0. Unfortunately, soon after that, there were changes in management that affected the tone and style of our work. Our smooth ship went a bit off course. The company realized what was wrong and took care of it eventually."

As part of this management changed at Fox, all development was moved onsite. That meant that, as a PB Systems consultant, Ramesh could no longer build the site. His role evolved, and he became responsible for a group called Dev Ops, which managed operation of the production website and user support. His group kept the servers running, launched production deployments and responded to troubleshooting requests from users.

"The management change that came along with the organizational restructure resulted in a more unstable website, and the business was not happy," Ramesh says reluctantly.

"Nag Mantena took over in 2016. I'm grateful he was there and that management shifted back to being the way it was. Things are going great now. In 2017, I left PB Systems and went to Fox as an employee.

"Today, I am a Director, managing the FoxFast operations team. I have staff in the UK, Australia and India. We train these teams for each site upgrade. They can provide better support in a time zone closer to the international users."

Like most people at Fox, Ramesh is unsure of his future as a result of 'the Disney thing' happening in 2019.

"I'm content where I am, but I'm looking for more tech challenges. I'd be thrilled to be able to learn how to automate the site with AI, perhaps installing chat bots. We have the beginnings of this now, but other priorities have slowed implementation a bit. We're also looking at preset tasks that are automated in multiple languages, using Alexa and Google."

He sums up his obvious admiration for his company and his team as follows: "Once you joined the FoxFast team, you stayed. It's a great place to work."

--- Interview 4/2019

CHAPTER 35

LARRY OWENS: Never Think of What You Do As Unimportant

A successful development team mixes a pool of diverse skills. It must include big-picture types and people with the crucial ability to translate the big picture to the tiniest details of user experience and code requirements.

Larry Owens is one of the best detail guys I know. He's able to contribute to overall design and also cover the details that must be perfect for a website to be well received by its user community.

He's the FoxFast team's go-to guy to make sure nothing important is missed. Since I retired, he's become the project's text editor for onscreen and off-screen documents—the one to count on to find spelling, grammar, and content errors, and inconsistencies in words and images created for the site and its management. His proofing skills are officially legendary!

Larry and I met many years before we began working together. We worked in IT for Universal at the same time, but for different areas of the company. We also have mutual friends.

One of those mutual friends, Tom Tralongo, my boss during my second stint at Fox, asked me one day if I remembered Larry. "Of course," I said. "Well," Tom replied, "he's looking for a job and I think he'd work well on the FoxFast team."

Since I had a favorable impression of him, I agreed to bring him on board. Good decision. It worked out, and he's still a part of the team today.

Larry's Story

Larry Owens says he "just stumbled" into his first job in entertainment after years in technology. "What I really wanted to do in junior high was advertising art. I liked art production and was on the team for the school yearbook. In one of my classes, we were asked to sort out our career ambitions, but I couldn't find jobs in art. Since I was also good at math, after conversations with the school guidance counselor, and at the prompting of my parents, I shifted gears to focus on that. I figured if art happened, it happened."

He started college as a math major, but switched to a computer science major when the new degrees became available. This was way before PCs, and he eventually completed a double major in math and computer science.

"In those days, a computer expert was considered like a rocket scientist—people said 'Wow' when they heard what I studied. Now you would be compared to a sixth grader who is already an expert."

His first part-time job in college was with an oil and gas engineering company. They were working on programming and analysis to create simulation models designed to help refineries improve operations. His company was the only one doing simulations that yielded good results. They offered him a full-time job after graduation, and he took it.

"After three years, they wanted me to collaborate more with clients, all of whom were out of state in places like Texas and Louisiana. I traveled for a time, but I was newly married and wanted to travel less."

He accepted a position at Great Western Savings as a business analyst, working on a new savings and loan application. "At first, the job was in Beverly Hills, then they moved to a campus in Northridge. At about the same time, we bought a house in Valencia, and I settled into a much easier commute.

"After a while, I wanted to broaden my horizons and took a job with Saab as a regional software manager for their software and hardware division, called DataSaab. We programmed bank terminal systems. My small team and I worked with Sales, so I learned about that. We were responsible for their pivotal product, an expensive proprietary banking terminal that eventually couldn't compete with other companies, who were creating PC-based systems at half the cost. They closed the office I was in, which meant my last job there was to lay off my team. I turned off the lights when I left."

For his next position, Larry decided to look into something from his art roots—how computers could assist in animation.

"I cold-called Disney and showed them my white paper on the subject. They hooked me up with one of their producers, John Lassiter, the eventual creator of Pixar. This was in 1983, when John was saying he wanted to use computers, but he wanted them to do all the animation.

"Nothing came of my new connection because I knew what computers were capable of, and I knew they weren't quite where he wanted them to be. Too bad in hindsight. Obviously, John got there, but after a long road.

"My next job came from a Great Western friend who was now at MCA Universal. The job sounded interesting, so I accepted a position on their new PC team in corporate IT.

"The inventory for the entire company consisted of six PCs, each of which was highly justified before purchase. We went through the transition to standardization of the equipment, setting up a system for ordering PCs and standardizing the software, using Lotus 1-2-3, and also Word rather than other word processors. Soon I was involved with production companies to help them get *Scriptor,* an early tool for formatting scripts. Politically, the film and TV divisions wanted their own PC staffs, which meant our niche became non-production functions."

Larry had arrived in the entertainment industry. That first entertainment job lasted four and a half years. Then he left to chase other dreams.

"When I was first at Universal, I wanted to improve the quality of life for my family. We moved to Oakhurst, in the Sierras in Northern California, for three years in 1988. I joined a company called Sierra Online, which makes computer games. I worked there for only a year because of issues with nepotism, and I left after a mutual parting of the ways.

"Before completely giving up on my dream to live in the mountains, I struggled to find other work in Oakhurst. I worked odd jobs, including at a print shop doing graphic design and other print-related tasks. The work was great, but the pay was awful. Eventually, we acknowledged that we weren't making it, and we moved back to Southern California, where I returned to working for Universal for another five and a half years."

That was followed by five years at DreamWorks. While there, Larry moved into an IT Director role that reported to the CIO. Again, he was forced to leave his job when business went sour.

"Because Jeffrey Katzenberg was over-exuberant about upcoming movie performance, good results didn't meet the unrealistic expectations. The company cut back and laid off 20% of the staff in IT. I was in that group, and was really sad because I liked DreamWorks, my role, the campus in Glendale and the people.

"I left entertainment to work for my old boss from DreamWorks, who was now at XCare.net, a health care tech company planning an expansion.

"XCare had a name problem as a .net site. They wanted to be a .com site, but couldn't get the URL. So, XCare become Quovadx and planned to rebrand after the .com bust.

"For some reason, they also wanted to be in entertainment. In health care, you have thousands of potential clients, but there are fewer than a dozen studios. That didn't deter them. I was useful to them because I knew connections at the studios, and we soon landed a project at Sony Home Entertainment that lasted four years. When Sony called and said they wanted to make me Project Manager on their next project, I left Quovadx to become an independent contractor on that job, which also ran for almost four years. When it wrapped up, I went back to DreamWorks for three months."

Contracts became harder to find after the .com breakdown, and, by the end of 2006, Larry had been out of work for a year.

"I tried working with different consulting companies. I linked up with Tatum—a financial consulting company with an IT arm. My one project, in downtown L.A., was canceled early due to economic uncertainty in the marketplace. In total, I would only have three months of paid work over two difficult years. That rocks your world. I got interviews, but none of the jobs met my financial needs. I exhausted all my savings, and we arranged to sell our house.

"I received an email from the guy who ran the print shop where I worked in Oakhurst.

"He said, 'I don't know if you'd be interested, but my daughter is doing all my graphic design and she's leaving. Would you consider taking over?'

"I would, of course, as that was the only option that presented itself.

"We moved back to Oakhurst, and I worked for the print shop for two years. Customers loved my work, and I loved the job, even though I didn't make much money. It seems impossible that we supported our growing family on my earnings up there, but we made it somehow. Looking back, I realize I spend more on my current travel expenses than I made back then.

"From time to time, I would touch base with friends and coworkers from past jobs, like Tom Tralongo, who was now working for 20th Century Fox. One day, Tom called me back and asked if I would help finish up a five-week project, because the current business analyst was moving away."

Larry decided to accept Tom's offer. The extra money would certainly help with expenses. To get started, he took a five-week leave of absence from the print shop and stayed in L.A. during the week, doing Fox work during the day and some graphic-design work in the evenings.

"The five-week project at Fox was extended, and extended again. I finally just stopped working for the print shop after I'd finished up my projects because I knew I couldn't do both. I've been working for Fox ever since, still living in Oakhurst, but driving to L.A. most weeks."

He's a bit surprised about his long entertainment career in a place he never planned to be. "I still like it. Our project, called FoxFast, is built and maintained by a great team. Management changed a few times, but we've survived quite nicely. Nag, our leader for the past couple of years, is great in managing both the app design and the technology. He's also good with people."

Larry's job has now been absorbed into Disney. His son worked at Disneyland, and he and others have told Larry that Disney can be a tough place to work.

"They can seem unfeeling because the attitude of the company is that there are plenty of people who will take your spot if you don't want it.

"I'm thinking about retirement, but it will be awhile before I'm ready. My gap in the working world forced me to cash in my assets way too early. I should have bailed on my house much sooner, and, as a result, was forced to sell when it was under water. I'm a contractor with Fox, so I receive no benefits from the company. I've bought a new house in Northern California with the idea of retiring up there once it's paid off."

There is one thing about the Disney transition that may change his plan. "I believe Disney's policy is a maximum contract term of twelve to eighteen months for freelancers. If that affects me, then I'll need options. Right now, I travel to L.A. to work on the Fox Century City lot between Monday and Thursday, when I return up North. It's a long drive. It helps that I can work at home every few weeks.

"If the Fox work came to an end, I would approach my contacts for other freelance opportunities. Where my family lives now, jobs are mainly in the travel/hospitality industry. If my pay was reduced as a result of working outside of L.A., at least I wouldn't have to travel as much, and that would be nice.

"All the time I was in entertainment, even though I was in IT doing somewhat boring stuff, I could learn fascinating things. After all, a studio job IS different from working for a bank or a health care company. At Universal, I could wander around the back lot. If a tour bus drove by my golf cart, the tourists wondered if I was somebody important. I guess I was, because I was an insider there!

"I saw a lot of things that you don't ever see in insurance or pharmaceutical IT jobs. You can walk onto a sound stage before and after filming, see what the illusion is all about and know you play a little part in it all."

Because of his work at Universal, he met Steven Spielberg, Kathleen Kennedy and Frank Marshall, Bob Zemeckis, and Bob Gale, and worked with them.

"At Steven's company, Amblin, we installed the first production local area network. I trained Steven on his computer, and set up his computers in the office, in his homes, and on the Warner jet, which he used as needed.

"He expects people to be intimidated when they first meet him, so he does what he can to lessen the tension. My first training session with him took place in the era of floppy drives. One of the first things I did was hand him the floppy disk in an envelope. He tossed the disk across the room and tried to install the envelope, effectively breaking the ice and giving us both a laugh!

"I went to New York to set up equipment at MCA/Universal and also in Steven's apartment in Trump Tower. He had a big piano bar—literally. It was an over-sized piano with a built-in bar along the back.

"He called me once when he was in New York for Thanksgiving, very apologetic, with a question, which I answered. I was somewhat distracted, because I was babysitting my two-year-old at the time. He said he understood—he was alone with his one-year-old. Whenever I would see Steven in the office or on the Universal lot, he recognized me and acknowledged me, but, of course, I was a provider of a service and that's all. He probably doesn't remember me now, but I will never forget working with him.

"In my current job on FoxFast, I have access to all the shows in the Fox catalog on demand. We're supporting the business in making profits and enhancing the bottom line because we make distribution flow more smoothly. Disney has expressed an interest in using FoxFast as the foundation system for all TV Distribution needs, so things are looking up.

"The art stuff comes out in my work—even when I'm color-coding spreadsheets. It's a way of communicating and improving communication by applying artistic principles.

Working for a print shop, I developed many documents for print and publication, and I learned how to hone in on typos. I'm now the FoxFast content typo king. It all matters, and it all becomes part of the contribution you can make. My advice is to never think of what you do as unimportant."

Larry also dabbles more directly in the artistic side of his personality, but only for fun.

"I'm currently working on an art piece that I started in high school, a watercolor rectangular stained glass image. The design is on paper, and I like it. I scanned it at high res and will produce it digitally and hang it in my house. It's primarily blues and purples with black dividers like the lead in stained glass windows. I looked at it not too long ago, and it still resonates."

--- Interview 5/2019

CHAPTER 36

KEN MIHARA: Do You Want to Join Tech in Entertainment?

When we considered him for an analyst position on the FoxFast team, Ken Mihara interviewed extremely well.

I've been around long enough to know that a good interview does not necessarily a good employee make, however. In his case, the good interview preceded a wonderful experience for the team.

Since he was moving to my team from another team at Fox, he already knew a bit about our business and adapted to international distribution quickly. Most importantly, his work standards are admirably high, which matches how the others on my team viewed their work. I don't remember exactly, but I would say that he proved our feelings about him were right from day one or very soon thereafter.

Ken fascinated me with his ability to fit in. He knows how to join a team as though he's been there all along. He becomes a member of the family who can challenge ideas with better solutions, a wonderful trait in the best team members.

I enjoy talking with him about a host of subjects. Toward the end of my stay at Fox, and a few times since I left, we've booked dinner at our favorite barbecue restaurant, ordered ribs and spent the meal in conversation that is just plain fun.

The members of the team are glad he joined the group in time to be there when the leadership role opened up during the transition to Disney. He's now Director for the FoxFast project and proving to be the kind of leader the team needs to continue its enviable track record of innovation and technical excellence.

Ken's Story
Ken Mihara graduated from high school in Japan in 1975 and went to the University of Hawaii for a year as a Chemistry major. His dad was in the Air Force, and they were stationed in Germany, Japan and Korea during his childhood, but he'd never been to the US before.

His initial grades at college were not good. "I spent most of the year smoking pot. 'Hmm,' I thought to myself. This is not the way to get a college education. I stopped and went back to Japan to teach English to Japanese students for a bit."

Eventually, he enrolled at UCLA—a real university in his mind—this time majoring in physics. "When they got to the theory of relativity, they lost me. I switched to computer science, where I figured I could make money after graduation. I also got an MBA from UCLA's Anderson School along the way."

In 1995, Ken joined Symantic as Development Manager for the popular Norton Utilities. He stayed for thirteen years and rose to become a VP, with almost 290 employees on his team.

"My dad got very ill, so I took a sabbatical and went to take care of him in Dorset County in England. When I returned in 2008, the company had reorganized and moved to Cupertino, which meant my job didn't exist anymore. They offered me a different job, but I said, 'No,' instead accepting a generous severance package and moving on to be a consultant for a variety of companies."

After a time, he formed a consulting group with a few friends. They worked for social media companies and distribution companies like infomercial giant Guthy-Renker. Other clients were defense contractors and software developers. One of his best clients was a Facebook gaming company. They were funded by Disney, but eventually flopped.

"My preferred consulting experiences were the smaller ones at startups. We helped them apply for venture capital and created business plans."

Ken likes consulting for reasons similar to those of many other professionals. "Working as a consultant is good because of the freedom. You're doing new things all the time. The next project can always be the best one ever."

His next steps were dictated by a priority outside his career. "Finding the best options for treating my son's medical condition was most important to me. His treatment was based in L.A., so I needed to find jobs there. On the other hand, I realized that if I wanted to improve my consulting business, I needed to move to San Francisco."

Determined to succeed in L.A. rather than uproot his family, he decided to get involved in a business that was prevalent there, and that meant entertainment.

"In 2011, I was trying to sell patio furniture on Craigslist one day when I saw an intriguing job listing. The ad asked, 'Do you want to join tech in entertainment?' I answered the ad and met Greg Rinsler from an outsourcing company called Zaszou. That conversation eventually got me a contract at Fox. I didn't get the first two jobs they sent me to interview for. Then one of the Fox IT groups hired me in May 2012.

"I worked with my new team until their project money ran out. The director recommended me for an opening on another Fox team, and I joined the FoxFast project.

"I transferred because it was the only open job. In fact, I was close to accepting another contract at Guthy-Renker. I chose to stay at Fox because I liked the people. It's years later, and I'm now a full-time employee as IT Director, with a staff of developers, QA analysts, business analysts, and the team's graphic artist in L.A. There are additional team members in remote locations. We handle design for new features on the site, which often requires us to explore new digital technologies. I love that.

"We started a really cool project that took me to Europe to pitch it and get it funded. The idea was to create a big new theatrical portal for delivery of international marketing materials. Current methods are haphazard and outsourced to different companies in different countries.

"The vision is to unify how the businesses work and allow them all to do business in FoxFast. We're planning to combine portals, platforms, processes and information metadata, which will be a massive, but productive, effort. Our progress has been killed for now by the Disney offer to purchase Fox. Boo."

"The whole Disney thing is a big unknown," Ken says. His and the team's fate is evolving, but it looks like the site and the team will stay as part of Disney, at least for now.

In spite of that uncertainty, Ken's world is quite OK at the moment. "I'm still in entertainment. My team is great and I like the people. I have subject matter experience now, and I'm in a position where I'm not struggling to learn and get to the next level.

"My management philosophy was honed at Symantec. I was promoted to a few management jobs before that, but the large company atmosphere forced me into more of an extroverted role.

"Their training program included a personality development workshop at Cal Tech. One of the exercises is to sit across from another student and see who blinks first. I did not blink first. I don't know what that proves!

"I like to think that I have skills that many engineers don't have. I don't see myself as on the inside of the fence looking out, but rather as someone who finds the door, goes outside and looks back in. I put myself into the business user's shoes every time. I find it interesting that a lot of developers have no clue how to do that. You can lead them to the door and tell them to open the door and go outside, but they won't know how to do it.

"I'm a good judge of character and I know whether I'm going to hire someone after thirty seconds of talking with them . Their tech skills are measurable, but the interview is about whether I can work with the person. I've only been wrong once, when I completely misread the applicant, who was a sales guy. He lied, and I didn't see it. I found out the truth in about four months, when he was put on probation and then fired after six months."

Ken does struggle with what his future should be. "I don't know how much longer I will do this. My dream has always been around my personal life. I've been forced to be single for much of my life, and that's not what I want. I'm approaching retirement age, so it's becoming about transitioning into the next phase."

He's looking for a house in Calabasas with his fiancé as the vehicle to get himself closer to his dream. "I'm trying to save as much as possible so that the life I see is a real possibility for me."

Meanwhile, he's not quite ready to move in a different direction for the career side of his life. "The entertainment industry does grab me. I'm watching more TV. I was never a series junkie, but I'm now immersed in several shows. The people around me do it, and now I'm hooked, too. We sat and watched Season 2 of *American Crime Story.* I like *The Orville.* I look forward to discovering new shows that entertain and enlighten me.

"My business card says 'IT Director, 20th Century Fox,' and that conjures up the wrong image in my mind because my focus is shifting from tech to TV. I'm clear that I'd like to grow in TV for the rest of my career."

--- Interview 3/2019

CHAPTER 37

NAG MANTENA: We Didn't Expect to Study Computers

When Nag Mantena told me something could be done, I knew it would happen.

I met him when I was assigned to the Fox IT team with the job of creating what became known as FoxFast. One of the most talented and personable technical experts I've ever worked with, he's blessed with that rare combination of technical inventiveness and interpersonal skills.

We enjoyed our work. He took over for me as the FoxFast team Director when I retired from Fox and handled his new role as well as I expected he would. He was promoted to Executive Director at the pre-Disney Fox and then VP of Technology for the new Fox Corp that remained after Disney's absorption of the rest of the company.

Whenever Nag came to my office, I knew he would tell me the truth, and I could pass that truth on to the business. He made me look good every single time.

Occasionally, my phone rang in the middle of the night. Nag never called unless it was an emergency, so I always took his call. He also never called with a problem without offering a potential solution, even if said solution was only that "the whole team is awake and working on it as we speak."

At least part of the reason we worked so in sync could be that we share the same birthday. Every year, we were forced to share a celebration, which actually just doubled the fun.

Lucky to have been at Fox at the time FoxFast was launched, we shared its initial success with our team. Over the years, as the site evolved to be even more integral to the business, Fox customers appreciated our work, as did management. I'm glad the 'right place, right time' maxim brought us together in that time and that place, for that project.

I'm also happy that the current powers that be recognize his potential. Whenever I talk with him, he reminds me how much I respect and like him. It follows that they do, too.

Nag's Story
Nagaraju Mantena grew up in southern India. His parents are farmers in the countryside where crops grow in rice paddies and fish farming is prevalent.

He knew that his father wanted more. "My father wishes he had gone to school, but his situation didn't allow for that. He is the seventh child in his family and always had to help out. My grandfather was a farmer and my father eventually took over for him."

Nag attended the local schools—not yet learning English. He exhibited an interest in math and made sure he got good grades. His brother, who is three years older, went to work with industrial tools at a manufacturing company, and Nag could easily have followed him there. However, a different fate intervened.

"When I went to school, we didn't expect to study computers. After my dad changed his focus to fish farming, one of his new partners suggested that if I was good at math, maybe I should study technology.

"Dad and I researched options with a nearby college professor, who supported the idea. In due time, I started a computer science bachelor's program."

He excelled in his new classes and considered getting a master's degree, but it was too expensive. Instead, he moved to Hyderabad, where his brother lived. He arrived at a propitious time and qualified for jobs with free computer training designed to make engineers ready to become developers.

"Many were selected to travel to the US and help with Y2K problems. There was widespread panic in the computer industry because of the change from the year 1999 to 2000. Systems often weren't programmed to handle the change in a 2-digit year from 99 to 00, and companies scrambled to make updates in time.

"I didn't get a US assignment right away. Instead, I took small jobs in India and soon realized that what I just learned was outdated compared to what businesses were actually using. I hadn't learned Java or Oracle, for example."

The disconnect between Nag's training and current employer needs eventually made it difficult for him to get jobs. He decided to teach, which could enable him to earn money for the master's that would bring him up to date.

"After three months as a teacher, I was given the opportunity to run the whole training company. I would be responsible for training students in DOS, Windows and Word. I did that for six months, but it wasn't designed to meet my main objective of earning enough money for higher education. It was time to get creative."

Nag built up his professional connections and found his way into institutions, teaching advanced technology. After a year, he joined a corporation called Pentasoft.

"I even taught Java and Oracle. I used to read a whole book at night and teach it in the morning. Finally, I was making more money."

It was enough to allow him to start graduate work in an institute with a weekend program. The teaching job and weekend classes kept him very busy for about three years, when he moved to a new company. The job at PB Systems came after an introduction by a connection at the institute, a move that would serve as the launching pad for the rest of his stellar career.

"PB hired me as a programmer in a new office that functioned as an offshore outsource company providing services to businesses in the US. I moved to a new city and began working. On the weekends, I went back to Hyderabad to continue the master's program."

Persistence and diligence would pay off and establish him in a brand-new life. He finished the master's program, even though he began to question why he needed it after he was promoted to a better job with PB. They wisely recognized him as a leader.

"In my first assignments for PB, we developed software to assist with filing and cataloging corporate annual and financial reports. We built large financial databases and wrote software to manipulate them. I also developed custom software to manage finances, invoicing and other admin functions. Similar to what PeopleSoft does. It was relevant experience for what came next."

In 2002, he was assigned to a 20th Century Fox project—the first of many jobs he successfully completed for the studio. PB Systems maintained a strong connection with a Fox IT executive, who hired the company to create multiple new systems, and Nag collaborated on each one.

Their first launch was for a system called FoxPress, the beginnings of what would become the innovative FoxFast services for international marketing and distribution of licensed Fox titles. Next came FoxNow, the digitized catalog of those titles. "The idea to manage media online was communicated from the business, and we learned how to program a computer to do it as we went.

"Our successes led to additional, expanded applications. We were asked to build a system to support the PPV [Pay Per View], VOD [Video on Demand] and cable businesses. Today, there are multiple analytical data systems for similar processes, but at the time they didn't exist. We invented them."

Nag was named to lead a project called Hoboken. "We defined what the business needed and planned how to create the system, designed screens, tested our code and implemented a well-received application. As a result, I was asked to come to the US for the first time in 2004."

He didn't immediately bring his family to join him for a new life in L.A. "My wife stayed in India while I came here for three months to gain an understanding of the business. It turned into a six-month stay, and I never looked back. We've been here ever since. My children are being raised here."

Nag's career at Fox illustrates how technology pros become experts in the businesses they support. After the successful Hoboken launch, he was responsible for updating its original design to meet the more complex requirements of the changing business. Hoboken morphed into a system called Suisse.

"At Fox application names could be anything for a time. I was there during a phase when some were named after places. There was a system called Tuscany. The first iteration of FoxFast was named Bordeaux!"

He explains the evolution of his business knowledge like this: "I learned a great deal about how data flowed to support international distribution. The concepts of exhibition windowing, licensing contracts and multiple delivery platforms became familiar to everyone on my team. After that, we began working on Client Presentation, which was an early customer-focused app for international sales. Thus, my scope broadened into how the product was marketed and sold."

In 2007, his growing knowledge made him an ideal candidate for the team creating the FoxFast vision innovated by International Television Distribution.

"We expanded the display of product info, talent and marketing messages. The site became a front-end with a content management back-end called DAPR, or Digital Asset Product Repository. We consolidated FoxPress, FoxNow and a third system that maintained talent data, and added industry-first features we pioneered.

"While we were building DAPR, for the last month or six weeks, we only slept five or six hours per day. We didn't always get to go home every day either.

"It was ultimately quite satisfying when it worked so well. DAPR gave my team knowledge about all aspects of the detailed data and how to maintain and mine the associated metadata. We visualized how to leverage it for a unique international customer experience and for integration with other Fox systems."

After DAPR, Nag was assigned as a tech lead on the FoxFast customer service front-end application until his boss retired in 2016, when he took over for her.

He summarizes the success of FoxFast like this: "We were the first studio to create an online-accessible Screening Room for current and library videos. The biggest challenge was to figure out how to replace the costly shipment of physical broadcast media, in the form of tapes shipped to a customer, with digital files that could be downloaded and used in the broadcast licensee's program preparation workflows.

"In my opinion, Fox was and continues to be the best in the business at providing digital customer self-service for large, high-quality files in multiple formats, files that grow bigger with each technology upgrade to higher resolution viewing."

Most recently, Nag and the team created the latest version of FoxFast, called FoxFast 3.0. "Its main purpose is to automate more services and improve ease of use with ever-evolving technology.

"As of last year, we pioneered auto download and auto push of digital content. This means that a customer doesn't even need to log into the site to request new content. Based on the terms of a contract, the content is identified when it becomes available and automatically sent to the licensee. For example, when a new episode of This Is Us is delivered to the Fox vault, the correct technical version can be immediately delivered with no effort by humans. All the customer needs to do is specify digital format type, delivery time requirements and receiving location. It's a fantastic step forward for them, which was confirmed for me when I attended a conference in Amsterdam and heard directly from many satisfied Fox customers."

The FoxFast team continues to design new features, including a more automated customer screening service. Screenings are a crucial part of the front-end sales process, and they must work on demand. Once the sale is made, customers also don't want to come to FoxFast to acquire marketing assets or screener files for their staff to view.

"We'll likely be the first again to take the next step in providing improvements for this service," Nag predicts.

His other main responsibility is the result of a business decision to use the FoxFast concepts and platform as a consistent delivery experience across all business units at Fox.

"We're working cross-platform and cross-media because multiple divisions are selling to the same customers to meet the demands of the fragmented viewing audience. We expect this initiative to be successful, because even though business rules in each division or product line are different, the process for working with customers is the same. We incorporate new formats and media as we go."

Today, Nag is the VP Technology West Coast for Fox Corp, the entity that encompasses the businesses not purchased by Disney: including FoxSports, FoxNews and Fox Entertainment. His new team is responsible for designing and launching a business application platform for the re-imagined company from the ground up. He's more than ready for the challenge.

--- Interview 4/2019

PART VI: Name-Dropping Essay—Hi, I'm Carol [Burnett]

While writing this book, I conducted interviews with people who said approximately the same thing about their careers. At some point, they each thought, "I can't believe I'm in this room." Or, "How did I get so lucky as to be here?"

They were expressing a sentiment I often felt. Whenever I was invited into the room where entertainment leaders and talented innovators created, it was such a high. I wanted to be a part of it, and I was for almost forty years. Everyone in Hollywood, rich or struggling, famous or waiting tables while waiting to be famous, powerful or asking for a seat at the table, is a person pursuing a dream. I was privileged to know some of them as coworkers.

I started writing this chapter to create a place to keep my name dropping. Sometimes, I admit to being star-struck by the company I kept. But mostly I loved the fact that I was in the room while entertainment history was being made. For those who wonder what it's like to be a part of daily Hollywood from that perspective, this is how it was for me.

Living in the center of television production in L.A. was invigorating. Non-work sightings, just around town, included people like Michael J. Fox and Jonathan Winters. Mr. Fox was a customer in a restaurant I visited. One weekend, Carol and I went for brunch at the famous Toluca Lake landmark Paty's. As we were enjoying our meal, in walked Jonathan Winters. He proceeded to entertain each table with a running commentary that had everyone in the place laughing so hard they ignored their food. Our waitress told us he often showed up for impromptu comedy.

Elaine Spooner

Mom found the unpredictability of these encounters fascinating, as did we. She always asked, "So, who did you see at work today?" I told her and she loved it.

When she and my dad came to visit L.A., the first person they saw after walking off the plane was Jack Lemmon, apparently also meeting new arrivals on another flight nearby. OK, they were impressed! I took them to a taping of the series *Newhart* while they were in town. My brother visited and wanted to see *The Arsenio Hall Show*, so I got tickets.

But... the business I lived every day isn't about seeing someone famous, because, in most cases, I don't know famous people directly. More often, I knew the people around them as the collaborators who make TV shows work week in and week out, an impossibly difficult task to do well. At times, I spent my days helping promotion people manage press junkets. Or, I made a trip to the home of a producer, writer or actor who reported a computer problem and helped fix it.

When I left home to go to college in Boston, I was excited not just because I was leaving small-town New Hampshire, but also because the big city would give me a chance to get closer to some of my idols. In due course, I saw *That Girl* star Marlo Thomas in a Broadway-bound play. I loved her TV show and was thrilled to see her perform in person. I also saw Hair and a play starring Katherine Hepburn and Christopher Reeve of Superman fame.

One birthday in my early twenties, my then-husband took me to my first Neil Diamond concert. It was back in the days of *Hot August Night*. The closer I was to professional entertainment, the more I knew my passion for moving to L.A. and working for the studios was the right path for me.

Over the years, I've seen live performances from many people I consider the best in the business. I saw *A Chorus Line, Phantom of the Opera* with Michael Crawford, *Cats* [in London with my sister], *Fiddler on the Roof* with Zero Mostel, *Les Miserables, The Wiz* and *Pirates of Penzance*. I attended multiple Neil Diamond concerts, as well as performances by Paul McCartney, Barbra Streisand, Joan Baez, Willie Nelson, Billy Joel, Bernadette Peters, Robin Williams, Cher, Liza Minelli, Bette Midler and Rod Stewart.

296

My first studio job was at Burbank Studios, a lot shared by
Warner Bros. and Columbia. It was a very different time in
that we were able to wander the studio at will and visit sets to
watch whatever happened to be shooting. I saw Michael
Landon and the Little House on the Prairie cast work, as well
as the stars of *The Waltons*. We watched many scenes of
Fantasy Island, where I saw stars such as Gene Barry and Eva
Gabor. I was a major fan of Gene Barry from his work in
Burke's Law, which I watched while doing my high school
homework.

For a time, we were housed in a trailer across from the stage
where George Burns was shooting *Oh, God!*. On one of our
regular calls, I told Mom that he was right outside my window.
She was thrilled to think she was 'close' to such a famous man.
He looked SO old.

On the same lot, I was almost run over by the General Lee as it
sped between two buildings while filming a scene from *Dukes
of Hazzard*. I would see star John Schneider sunning himself
on the lot during breaks. I admit I had a bit of a crush on him.
He was gorgeous!

Today, sets are closed and no one who isn't supposed to be
there can get in. I was lucky to have that experience while it
was still possible.

I ate in the Fox Commissary regularly when I worked there.
On occasion, there would be a famous face or two or three in
the crowd. One day, I happened to be looking at the entrance
when what seemed to be a nondescript woman entered and
went to the Hostess Desk. I didn't really take notice until she
smiled. What a smile. Suddenly, she was the most beautiful
woman in that or any room.

Meryl Streep can definitely light up the place when she smiles.

I adored being on the Fox lot in that era. M*A*S*H was
shooting on Stage 9. I attended an event honoring Shirley
Temple Black, who, of course, was a major Fox star in her
youth. Queen Elizabeth visited once. Fox was a public
company and President Gerald Ford was on the Board. We
knew when a meeting was scheduled because the Secret
Service arrived en masse. Then, Marvin Davis bought the
company and took it private. The atmosphere changed as

quickly as images fade when the end of a filmstrip flaps on a reel. I was soon to leave, and I saw the beginnings of a different place.

After I moved to Universal for my next job, I was assigned a position that required direct contact with TV shows and their staff. My department, Television Information Services [TVIS], provided installation, training and support for all the personal computers on sets and in the production offices.

It was the time I was happiest at a studio. I was involved in production at last. At the start of each TV season, I met with the producers of all of the current shows to define PC hardware and software needs for their series. I came to know the people behind *Knight Rider, Airwolf, Quantum Leap, Miami Vice, Magnum P.I., Charles In Charge*, Amblin's *Amazing Stories* and *Blacke's Magic*, starring Hal Lyndon.

Miami Vice creator Michael Mann met me in his all-black office. I mean everything was black: walls, ceiling, floor and all the furniture.

I became friends with a gregarious writer named Tom Sawyer, who was on staff for *Blacke's Magic*. We are still in touch on occasion.

Magnum creator Don Bellisario collaborated with me on automation for multiple shows. He encouraged the use of computers for his projects and challenged us to try out new things first with him. Don also hired me as an independent contractor for some of his shows after we both left Universal. He was sometimes considered difficult by studio management, but not by me. We were in sync about innovating with PCs on sets and worked together very well.

One of the best parts of the job was the travel to locations to help set up equipment and train local staff. When I visited Honolulu for *Magnum P.I.* I met Tom Selleck, one of my favorite stars, for the first time.

The show's stages were tucked in behind Diamond Head Crater in what felt like a summer camp environment. The day I arrived the crew was shooting an episode on the Big Island. When I went into the office that evening to set up PCs, I was all alone. That is, until I heard someone come into the office behind me. I was on the floor under a desk hooking up cables when I heard, "Hello." There was no mistaking that voice. I slowly retreated and glanced up to see Mr. Selleck in cowboy hat and chaps, fresh from the set. He looked wonderful!

We chatted for a few minutes, and I tried to forget that his first impression of me was from behind as I backed out from under a desk. I didn't see him again on that trip, but my work allowed me to meet the core of the crew on the show. I loved Hawaii, of course, but the optimistic atmosphere on that set was unmatched. It was near the end of the series run and everyone knew each other very well by then.

My friendship with one of the Magnum producers gave me perhaps the best star-struck experience ever. We were at lunch one day when a very recognizable woman walked up to our table. She held out her hand to me and said, "Hi, I'm Carol." That's how I met Carol Burnett. The three of us chatted for a few minutes and she left. I will never forget that lunch.

The same producer would later work on the series, *Dr. Quinn, Medicine Woman*. I visited her there one day and saw the show's star, Jane Seymour, a very beautiful woman.

Sent to Miami to install computers at the start of the second season of *Miami Vice*, I was assigned a hotel room on gorgeous Miami Beach for ten days in July. It was hot, but it didn't really matter. We worked from early to very late. I had one day off— the 4th of July. I used it to drive as far south as I could just to see more of the state.

I visited the set, so did see stars Don Johnson and Philip Michael Thomas. The atmosphere at the time was pressured almost beyond belief, and people didn't smile much, although they were all nice to me. I stayed in the production office most of the time and helped get scripts out.

While I was at Universal, I experienced my first sighting of Steven Spielberg. For a reason I can't remember, I was in Steven's office when he wasn't there, but I saw the man himself in the commissary one day. His pink, southwestern-style Amblin Productions building on the Universal lot was unique and architecturally renowned; it was unlike anything else there at the time. Steven occupied a corner office on the top floor and it was gorgeous.

I saw Robert Redford and Debra Winger one afternoon as they were heading across the lot to the set of *Legal Eagles*. Mr. Redford was someone whose movies I adored. He looked great in person, too! I visited the office of his production company one day to install a PC, but he wasn't there. Darn!

Another day I was working on something or other in the office of Sydney Pollack, director of some of my favorite films, including *Tootsie, Out of Africa* and *Electric Horseman*. I stepped out of the office and there was Reba McIntyre in the lobby, waiting to see Mr. Pollack. Her massive red hairdo was like nothing I'd ever seen, especially on such a tiny person.

If you worked at Universal at that time, you were keenly aware of Lew Wasserman, the legendary founder of MCA/Universal. One day, I was called to his office to help his assistant with a computer issue. It was impossible not to be nervous as I got off the elevator in the Black Tower executive office building. Soon, I relaxed—Mr. Wasserman was not in residence at the time. He was quite visible around the lot, though. Every day, he and a few others would go to the commissary and sit in the same corner for lunch. I often saw him hurrying across the lot, perhaps to make the next lunch on time.

One year [I believe it was 1989] I attended the Emmys. I remember being thrilled at belonging in the room and feeling a part of such a fabulous industry. Candace Bergen won Best Actress in a Comedy for *Murphy Brown*, one of my favorite shows. I saw the four stars of *Designing Women* standing together in the lobby. Annie Potts, who I thought of as more casual than stylish, stunned me with how beautiful she looked that night—the most gorgeous woman there in a sea of gorgeous women.

In spite of the glitz and glamour of being there in person, I never ached to attend the event again. It's fun, but it's really much easier and better to watch it on TV at home!

I was involved in one other project during those years that directly exposed me to Hollywood talent and became one of the best experiences of my life. The original musical *Shades of Grey* was produced by two friends of mine. They created a team of many of their friends to mount the show at a waiver theater in Hollywood in 1989, and I was lucky to work in multiple roles throughout the project.

I loved casting, where I learned firsthand how many talented people there are in L.A. We could pick and choose the best of the people we saw in a private showcase of up-and-coming actor/singers. Bebe Neuwirth auditioned for us, and we offered her the female lead. This was a bit before her breakout role in *Cheers*. She accepted at first, but then backed out because she'd gotten a paying gig. We understood and cast Sharon Mahoney, who turned out to be an excellent choice.

Casting the male lead—the role of Dorian Grey—was our biggest challenge. According to the script, Dorian was the "most charismatic performer in the world." No pressure on the actor! Our first production was a backers' audition to raise money to mount the show, which meant we put together a concert-style staging of some of the music for potential investors. We cast a wonderful singer who moved us every time he sang the show's songs as Dorian. He made the audition performance memorable enough that we got commitments for the money we needed. My parents invested, for which I am eternally grateful.

Unfortunately, we couldn't keep our first Dorian. The producers determined that, while he had a marvelous voice and impressive presence, he wasn't "the most charismatic performer in the world." We kept looking and, one day, in walked a Tony-nominated actor from the Broadway show *Starlight Express*. I was seated on the sofa next to the producer when we first saw him. My jaw dropped and the producer grabbed my arm, saying something like, "Please let him be able to sing." Bob Torti was a few bars into his audition number— an Elvis song—when we knew we'd found our Dorian. He, too, was a terrific person as well as the proper star for our show.

The show had its flaws and was not a success. The experience, however, was priceless. Each performance was unique and I learned how unpredictable live theater can be. One night, the crucial gunshot did not sound on cue. That was fun!

During our multi-week run, we were thrilled to have a famous face in the audience one evening—a very young Robert Downey, Jr.

Our director was responsible for my invitation to a party at Luci Arnaz's home during the run of the show. At some point, the icon herself, Lucille Ball, showed up with her then-husband, Gary Morton. We didn't speak to them, but it was certainly memorable to be at the same event with Hollywood royalty.

After Universal, I felt burned out on L.A. and Hollywood. A group of my friends were moving to Portland, Oregon, and I decided to follow them in 1990. I started my own company and worked as a consultant for the next ten years. For most of that time, I served on the Board for an event called the Portland Creative Conference. It is what it sounds like—a celebration of all forms of creativity.

Because of the conference, I learned from speakers in all disciplines in film and TV, including acting, producing, writing, effects and directing. We hosted Martin Sheen, Steve Buscemi, Gus Van Sant and Dennis Muren from Lucasfilm. *Northern Exposure* actor Barry Corbin stunned the audience with the best monologue we'd ever heard. He said it was a perfect vehicle to demonstrate the actor's craft. From him, it was astonishing. The audience sat in total silence, and then gave him a lengthy standing ovation.

I worked with writer/director Brad Silberling [*Casper, NYPD Blue, L.A. Law*] during my time at Universal. I knew him well enough to invite him to speak at the conference one year. He was married to actress Amy Brenneman [*Judging Amy*], who came with him and took the stage as well. Both were captivating speakers who were enthusiastically received by the audience.

Much of my professional time in Oregon was spent working on producing teams for interactive CD-ROMS. I worked on two titles that were never completed. One with composer and singer Mason Williams that was to be titled *Time and Rivers Flowing*. Mason wanted to showcase his music [he's best known for *Classical Gas*] and the history of the rivers of his childhood. It was lovely getting to know him.

The other project was a CD-ROM about the symbolism and meaning of mandalas in the Buddhist religion. Our subject matter expert was renowned Professor of Indo-Tibetan Studies, Robert Thurman, father of actress Uma Thurman.

Named one of the 25 most influential Americans by Time Magazine, Professor Thurman wanted to create the definitive information title about Buddhism, and a friend of mine asked me to join the team.

One independent contract took me to New York City to work on the launch of the eDrive website. Being in New York was heady. At Christmas, I visited the skating rink at Rockefeller Center and attended a free concert in St. Patrick's Cathedral. The performance of one of my favorite songs, *O Holy Night*, brought me to tears.

While at eDrive I was assigned to assist the team with the online broadcast of the *Hercules* premier at the Disney theater in Times Square. I'd never participated in a premier before, so I looked forward to it. The idea is to grab a few minutes with the stars as they enter the theater and record the best interview you can. I found it awkward and highly staged, which of course it is.

I moved back to L.A. in 2004 to get away from the months-long dreary weather in Portland and back to the Southern California sunshine. When I began working at Fox for the second time, my office was on the 20th Century Fox lot in Century City in what is affectionately called the *Die Hard* Building because during its construction it was the setting for the movie.

When *Modern Family* debuted, I saw its first episode in a meeting and thought it was the best pilot I'd ever seen. The show went on to be an award-winning hit. Initially, the cast could often be seen around the lot. As time went by and they became more and more famous, they disappeared from casual view.

In 2009, a friend from Fox who worked with local figure skating clubs signed me up to volunteer at that year's World Championships, which were held in downtown L.A. I am a rabid fan, so the job was a dream come true. I helped with backstage support, which put me in direct contact with skaters like soon-to-be Olympic Gold Medalist Evan Lysacek, US Ice Dance Champions Tanith Belbin and Ben Agosto and Ladies legend Yu Na Kim from South Korea. I worked very briefly with one of my idols, Kurt Browning. As I walked past an elevator on another day, the door opened and out stepped legend Dorothy Hamill.

Each year, the major studios host an event called L.A. Screenings. Broadcasters from all over the world come to L.A. to screen the pilots for the new fall season. At the end of the week, the studios throw a wrap party, to which everyone comes, including the employees of the TV Group and the stars of all the new and returning shows like *Bones* and *Glee*. It's a star-watchers' dream event.

I attended several of these, which are too much like a press junket or a red carpet for me, which means I wasn't really comfortable there. It seems awkward to be caught in a place where everyone fawns over the stars with no real objective except to be seen with them.

The most memorable sighting of those years came in the studio commissary. I was having lunch when Kiefer Sutherland entered and sat with his companion at the table next to mine. By this time, *24* was ending, but I was thrilled. *24* is maybe my favorite TV drama of all time, and I'd heard through the Hollywood grapevine that he was a good guy to work with. I think it's nice when the good guys succeed.

EPILOGUE

It must be obvious by now that I loved my job—almost always. I was lucky to be working in technology in Hollywood when personal computers were introduced. I participated in defining how PCs were used on sets, in production offices and in studio corporate departments. I was there during the digital evolution of television processes and businesses.

For a time, I managed my own company and branched out onto projects for game developers, internet startups and interactive media. Because of my experience, I was invited to be in the room when digital change agents were envisioned, designed and built. I met and worked alongside some of the most innovative, accomplished and admirable people.

A manager from early in my career told me, "You have to just know that you love change and accept that you'll change jobs every few years. Staying in one place won't work for you."

She was right. Change can be scary and unwelcome, but it can also be invigorating and wondrous. Change is continuing in television, and its pace is accelerating. I'm fascinated by what's possible with Virtual and Augmented Reality, for example. Storytelling is the basis for all of it, and technology gives storytellers more ways to enthrall viewers.

I left Fox in May of 2016 to begin the next phase of my life. To be closer to family, I sold my L.A. home and moved to a coastal community in Florida. I still have warm winters, but I now live in a small town far from the entertainment spotlight. I won't lie—the small-town thing has been an adjustment. But not as big as I thought.

I've been asked what constitutes a courageous career and whether mine qualifies. I can't speak for others, but courage for me came from my determination to follow my instincts and go where they took me. The choice to not be afraid to play in the big leagues or be intimidated by people more 'successful' than me has been a philosophy I've lived and worked by. Most careers aren't linear, and mine wasn't either. What I can say is that my path worked for me. I pursued my ideal job and eventually got it. The decisions I made didn't always make perfect sense, even to me. But, they were the right ones. I guess that means a courageous career is one you build for yourself by following the path that makes you want to get up in the morning.

I will want to stay connected to the entertainment world, partially by maintaining my memberships in Hollywood organizations like the TV Academy and Producers Guild. I'll continue to read *Variety* and vote for the Emmys and the Producers Guild Awards. I can volunteer for the local theater guild and get to know its respected, passionate people at all levels.

I could even write a book that highlights the unsung success stories of the awesome people who made me better every day. Without them, my career would not have been the joy it was.

As Robert Frost, who spent time in my New Hampshire hometown, wrote, "Two roads diverged in a wood, and I—I took the road less traveled by. And that has made all the difference."

END

GLOSSARY

The Glossary includes terms the reader will encounter in this memoir that are specific to my career or that may not be widely known to people outside the entertainment and technology businesses. Each entry references the part of the book where the term is used.

IT Terms

MIS – Management Information Systems. Appears in the intros to Parts 1 & 2 and in the chapter about Omer Simeon. MIS was the name used by many corporations for the IT department in the early years of my career. Today, it's just called IT.

TVIS – Appears throughout Part 3, which covers my years at Universal. TVIS is the name of the new department I led at Universal Studios between 1985 and 1990. Television Information Services was part of the Universal Television Group, not Corporate IT. It's role was to define, manage and lead the transition to personal computers in all areas of the Television business. Universal created similar groups for other divisions: MPIS was the name given to Motion Picture Information Services, for example.

Entertainment Industry Terms

Above or below the line – Appears in the stories for Omer Simeon, Cheryl Birch and James Korris. The designation is used to classify the jobs on a production. Above-the-line jobs include the roles of producer, director, writer, actor and casting. Below-the-line jobs are part of the production crew and include camera operator, visual effects, grips, craft services, electricians, lighting designers, production designers, carpenters, transportation, hair, costumes and sound.

Call sheet – Appears in Jim Michaels' story. The call sheet is created by the assistant director as the daily schedule during production. It lists the scenes to be shot, specifies the actors and their call times for those scenes and provides the details of locations, props, stunts, etc.

Foley – Appears in James Korris' story. Foley is a function used to create sound effects in post-production. The Foley stage is the space used to add sounds to sound recorded during shooting. Foley artists know how to enhance or complete a scene by adding footsteps, squeaky doors or breaking glass, for example.

Moviola – Appears in Jim Michaels' story. A machine that allows an editor to view film while editing. Moviolas are not used for digital editing.

Video On Demand [VOD] – Appears throughout Part 5, which covers the years I worked for Fox the second time. VOD is a customer product that allows viewing of features or television on request, rather than relying on broadcast on network or cable TV. Distributors monetize VOD in multiple ways. PPV is Pay Per View; SVOD is Subscription Video On Demand via services like HBO and Netflix; AVOD is Advertiser-Supported Video On Demand like YouTube Premium that is a hybrid of traditional ad-supported television and an on-demand service.

Procedurals – Appears in Charles Floyd Johnson's story. It's the name given to a genre of TV series that focuses on the process of solving a crime in each episode. Examples include all the *Law and Order* series.

Rating vs. Share – Appears throughout Part 3, which covers my years at Universal when I worked for TV productions. The terms represent different ways of calculating the audience watching a TV show. The rating is the percentage of the entire possible TV audience that's watching; i.e. a rating of 1.0 means that 1% of the total possible audience is watching. Share represents the percentage of the people actually watching all shows at a specific time that are tuned to a specific show. If 10% of the population is watching all shows at 8 pm, the share of an individual show is a percentage of that. Even if your rating is low, the fact that you have a large share of those watching means your show is the most popular at that time.

Fragmentation of the TV audience has reduced both numbers significantly in recent years. Networks are also interested in the ratings after three, seven and 30 days, which will include viewers who record episodes to watch later and can sometimes increase ratings by more than double the initial rating. Live events generally garner the largest ratings. Ratings are also measured for different demographics because advertisers are focused on reaching the 18-34 age group, which represents the prime buying public.

Scriptor – Appears in Part 3, which covers my years at Universal. *Scriptor* is a software tool and one of the first developed to assist writers using PCs for scripts. The program could automatically format dialogue differently from descriptions and scene headers, for example. It also handled the formatting differences between film style and multi-camera comedy-style scripts.

Showrunner – Appears in Hilton Smith's story. Showrunner is the title given to the lead producer on a TV series. The showrunner is generally a producer who is responsible for overall management of the production, including writing, casting, shooting and post-production.

Steven Spielberg Method For Sneaking Onto a Studio Lot – Appears in Charles Floyd Johnson's story. Before he worked in the studios, legend has it that Spielberg was able to sneak onto the Universal lot multiple times and stay there undiscovered as though he belonged.

TBS – The Burbank Studio. Appears in the intro to Part 2. TBS was the name given to the current Warner Bros. lot in Burbank when it was jointly occupied by Columbia Pictures and Warner Bros. in the 1970s.

ACKNOWLEDGEMENTS

This project began because I wanted to spotlight the incredible people I met and worked with during my years in the entertainment industry. I thought maybe the result would be published in a blog, but the amazing people who agreed to participate began encouraging me to compile a book. It became clear to me that their accomplishments reveal how successful careers are forged and the amazing variety of ways you can contribute to entertainment if that's your passion.

Special thanks to the individuals profiled here, without whom the book would not have been possible. They agreed to be interviewed by me and then to review and finalize their resulting chapter in what became my memoir. I respect and enjoy them all and am honored to know them.

Thank you to my editor, Franny French. Thank you, Franny, for the insightful suggestions and the work you did to improve the book.

Thank you to Janina Paragele, whose cover design is perfect.

Thank you to my beta readers, who agreed to read my manuscript and provided valuable insights and suggestions about the style and content of the memoir. I appreciate the contribution each of you made to the finished product.

I am humbly grateful that I knew Karen Siegmund, who left us much too soon. While here, she encouraged me to follow my dreams and taught me that things that seem to be impediments can always be surmounted.

My sincere thank you to friends and colleagues who gave me much-appreciated and invaluable inspiration during my life in Hollywood. Three who have passed away since I knew them are included in this book.

Lastly, my heartfelt gratitude and love to my family. My parents and grandparents were the best. My sisters and brother and their families are terrific people. Thank you all for your constant encouragement. I couldn't—and wouldn't want to—do it without you.

ABOUT THE AUTHOR

Elaine Spooner worked in the entertainment industry for almost forty years, building a career she enjoyed while helping to define how technology would change the business.

"The stories of how entertainment pros build careers are fascinating to me. Many of us are attracted to the spotlight, yes, but don't want that spotlight to shine directly on us."

Fortunate to be hired by major studios Fox, Warner Bros., Disney and Universal), Hollywood Entertainment which owned the Hollywood Video store chain and new media startups, Elaine's timing drove her career when her arrival in the industry coincided with the introduction of the personal computer.

"The important thing wasn't only the camera or the set, but also the people who worked in every department on the lot and in every office anywhere in the world."